READING ASSESSMENT

Solving Problems in the Teaching of Literacy
Cathy Collins Block, Series Editor

Engaging Young Readers:
Promoting Achievement and Motivation
Edited by Linda Baker, Mariam Jean Dreher, and John T. Guthrie

Word Journeys:
Assessment-Guided Phonics, Spelling, and Vocabulary Instruction
Kathy Ganske

Learning to Read:
Lessons from Exemplary First-Grade Classrooms
*Michael Pressley, Richard L. Allington,
Ruth Wharton-McDonald, Cathy Collins Block, and Lesley Mandel Morrow*

Directing the Writing Workshop:
An Elementary Teacher's Handbook
Jean Wallace Gillet and Lynn Beverly

Comprehension Instruction:
Research-Based Best Practices
Edited by Cathy Collins Block and Michael Pressley

Reading Assessment:
A Primer for Teachers and Tutors
JoAnne Schudt Caldwell

Reading Assessment

A Primer
for Teachers
and Tutors

JoAnne Schudt Caldwell

The Guilford Press
New York / London

KH

© 2002 The Guilford Press
A Division of Guilford Publications, Inc.
72 Spring Street, New York, NY 10012
www.guilford.com

Printed in the United States of America

This book is printed on acid-free paper.

Last digit is print number: 9 8 7 6 5 4 3 2

Library of Congress Cataloging-in-Publication Data is available from
the Publisher.

ISBN 1-57230-727-7

10/25/04

For Linda and Darcy,
who were with me from the beginning.
And for Mops and Little Lady,
who insisted on joining the process.

About the Author

JoAnne Schudt Caldwell, PhD, is a Professor at Cardinal Stritch University in Milwaukee, Wisconsin. She was formerly the Chair of the Reading Language Arts Department and is presently the Director of Teacher Education for the College of Education. Dr. Caldwell is coauthor, with Lauren Leslie, of *The Qualitative Reading Inventory 3*, an informal reading inventory, and of *Reading Problems: Assessment and Teaching Strategies*, with Margaret Ann Richek, Joyce Holt Jennings, and Janet W. Lerner. She is a member of several professional organizations and has actively participated in a number of state task forces involving teacher certification and standards implementation.

Acknowledgments

Completing a book is never a solitary endeavor. However, it is impossible to name all of the individuals who contributed to this work. I must first thank those many teachers and graduate students whose continual efforts at assessing the reading strengths of their students and at offering appropriate and effective instruction provided me with the impetus to write this book. Without their insights, successes, and occasional failures, I would have had very little to say.

My colleagues at Cardinal Stritch University not only encouraged me but offered specific feedback that I truly appreciated. As busy as they were, Gloria Wiener, Suzanne Terry, and Donna Recht all took the time to read, comment, and make detailed suggestions. During the composition process, my wonderful secretary, Nancy Foti, made my life considerably easier in many ways. I am grateful to my reviewers, whose comments were taken very seriously and whose suggestions were incorporated. And finally, my thanks to Chris Jennison, my editor at The Guilford Press, who is always patient, always perceptive, and always positive.

Preface

Do you remember Beaver Cleaver in the old television series *Leave It to Beaver*? Occasionally the series visited Beaver's elementary school. Do you remember the name of his teacher? It was Miss Landers, and she presided over a classroom where children sat quietly at their desks, politely raised their hands when they wanted to say something, and stood neatly beside their desks when they said it. Miss Landers's students were remarkably alike. They all came from homes where the mothers wore dresses and pearls to prepare breakfast, and stayed home to wash clothes, vacuum, and bake cookies. All the fathers wore three-piece suits, carried briefcases, and sat alone to read the newspaper before dinner. Miss Landers never met children who did not have enough to eat, or children from neighborhoods riddled with crime, gangs, and drug dealing. Miss Landers did not have to worry about children who could not or would not learn. Her charges were all at a third-grade level for reading, writing, and math. Miss Landers did not have to concern herself about meeting the needs of struggling students or challenging those who could perform well above grade level. She did not have to address cultural differences or handle various learning styles. Miss Landers's students were all motivated to learn, and if one was not, a call to the student's parents or a conference with the principal quickly righted the matter. As a teacher, Miss Landers enjoyed the respect and admiration of the community. Of course, Beaver's classroom was fictional—a distorted figment of a television writer's imagination. However, that imaginary classroom provides a provocative contrast to the realities of today's classrooms.

Today's classrooms do not resemble Beaver's classroom in any way. Today's teachers face more challenges than Miss Landers ever envisioned. Children come to school from a variety of home environments and family structures. They enter our classrooms with a multitude of diverse needs. Some can read at grade level; others cannot. English is the first language for some; others come to school speaking a different language. Some children are motivated to learn; others are not. Some have supportive family structures; others do not. Miss Landers never had to deal with terminology such as *learning disabled*, *emotionally disturbed*, *ADHD*, *cognitively disabled*, *ESL*, or the like. Today's teachers are all too familiar with such terms.

There is a teacher shortage, especially in large urban areas. To address the need for teachers, various alternative certification routes have been designed. No longer does the prospective teacher prepare for a teaching career in a four-year college or university. More and more teachers walk into their first classrooms after a short summer experience. More and more teachers begin their teaching careers with provisional certificates. Many tutors are drafted to support teachers in dealing with the diverse needs of their students. These tutors often are eager and dedicated, but lack specific knowledge of teaching principles. In Beaver's television environment, if difficulties arose, Miss Landers could always count on the wisdom of the principal or the advice of an older teacher to set things right within a 30-minute time frame. Today's teachers often lack effective support within their school buildings and are left to fend for themselves. In addition, many problems are of long duration and cannot possibly be settled in a short time. Today's teachers lack the respect that Miss Landers enjoyed. The media and policy makers are all too quick to question their skills and effectiveness, talking glibly about teacher accountability and mandatory testing to ensure that teachers teach and students learn. It is no wonder that many teachers leave the profession after a few short years.

What does all this have to do with *Reading Assessment: A Primer for Teachers and Tutors*? Why did I write this book, and how do I hope it will support today's teachers? I have worked directly with teachers for almost 20 years. I have interacted with them in my graduate classes, visited their classrooms to plan strategies for improving reading instruction, and been an active part of district efforts to support their professional development. The teachers I know are incredibly busy! They are hard-working and dedicated, often overwhelmed by the sheer enormity of their task, and constantly seeking ways to improve their instruction: "Give me something I can use in my classroom,"

"Help me to help my kids," "Show me a new way of doing things." Today's teachers want simplicity and directness; they want hands-on practical classroom strategies. They are not initially captivated by research and theory. If a strategy works well and if their students learn, today's teachers are then willing to discuss the theory and examine the research. Similarly, school districts, faced with the need to support tutors and large numbers of alternatively trained teachers, need manageable guidelines for doing so. "Keep it simple and keep it practical" is what I hear from districts asking for workshops to provide professional development for their staff members. This book is an effort to do just that—to provide simplicity and practicality for teachers, tutors, and staff developers, but within a framework of basic theory and research. I have made every effort to provide references from journals that would appeal to busy teachers, and that would either provide pragmatic suggestions for change or affirm a teacher's present practices.

There is another reason for writing this book. Reading assessment often takes on secondary importance for teachers who are struggling to establish their classroom expertise. New teachers tend to focus on instruction—on filling the hours and days with meaningful and motivating experiences for their students. This emphasis is reflected in the large number of newly published books on instructional strategies. Classroom management is another huge concern. How should one deal with a disruptive student? What discipline policies should be in place? How can instruction fit effectively around special scheduling needs such as pull-out programs for needy students, times for gym class, and agendas for library visits? If assessment is addressed by teachers, it tends to be in rather vague and general terms. Teachers often evaluate instructional effectiveness in terms of student involvement as opposed to student learning: "The kids were involved," "The class paid attention," "They completed the work," "They listened to what I said." While all of these are certainly important, they do not address the crucial and central component of reading assessment: Are the students learning to read?

This book is an attempt to address that issue. How does a busy teacher assess whether or not students are learning to read? In our standards-driven environment, this is a crucial question. How does that busy teacher document the progress of individuals? If an anxious and involved parent asks, "Is my child learning to read?", can the teacher answer this question and offer supportive evidence for the answer? I hope that this book will offer practical strategies for what to assess, how to assess it, how to analyze the information that is collected, and how to use this information to make instructional decisions.

Learning a new skill (and, for many teachers and tutors, reading assessment is a new skill) demands a starting point. Effective starting points are simple in nature, but they provide the basis for later complexity. As I discuss further in Chapter One, when we learn a new skill, we first take "baby steps." As we become more skilled and confident, we take larger steps and move into more difficult territory. As a primer, this book is designed to help the teacher or tutor take those first baby steps in reading assessment. Some suggestions can be implemented immediately; others will demand more planning. A new teacher or tutor will start by implementing those suggestions with which he or she is comfortable. Later, with evidence of growing ability and success in assessment, the teacher or tutor will move on to more complex strategies. One suspects that Miss Landers's repertoire of assessment strategies was limited to paper-and-pencil tests. I hope that this book will challenge teachers and tutors to expand their list of assessment strategies far beyond those Miss Landers knew, at a pace that is comfortable for them.

Contents

ONE

Overview
of the Reading Process

What Do Good Readers Do and How Do
Teachers and Tutors Assess This?

CHAPTER TOPICS

PURPOSE AND SCOPE OF THE BOOK

The first months and years of teaching can be incredibly overwhelming. Teachers and tutors face a multitude of different tasks each day. They must cope with a complex array of issues—curriculum, classroom organization, classroom management, and the needs of individual students, to name only a few. They have to make decisions about what to teach and how to teach it. They must evaluate what their students have learned, and must assess their own effectiveness as teachers. When a carefully constructed lesson plan fails in the first moments of its presentation, a teacher or tutor has to make immediate adjustments and move on. When a "teachable moment" occurs, the teacher or tutor must recognize it and modify planned activities to take advantage of an unexpected opportunity for student learning. Every day in the classroom is different. Every day presents new challenges. It is not surprising that many teachers or tutors feel besieged by the incredible complexity of teaching.

This book represents a first step in reducing some of the complexity that surrounds teaching and assessing reading. It is a primer, and as such, it offers an introduction to the subject of reading assessment. This book is only a beginning. It offers the teacher or tutor some simple guidelines for effectively assessing the reading process. Reading is an extremely complex and multifaceted process, and assessing this process is also complex and multifaceted. However, a teacher or tutor must start somewhere, and this primer represents a starting point.

Think about other complex processes, such as knitting, woodworking, or developing computer expertise. The first steps in learning any process are small. However, confidence grows with each "baby step" that is successfully mastered. With confidence comes the willingness to move to more complexity and greater depth. The learner eventually takes giant steps. A beginning knitter does not attempt a complex pattern involving a variety of different stitches, but instead chooses a simple model. Later, after success with simple patterns, the knitter will competently handle complex designs. First computer efforts involving simple word-processing strategies may gradually extend to advanced formatting techniques, the use of clip art, and perhaps the construction of spreadsheets. Learning to assess a student's growth as a reader is no different. The teacher or tutor begins with small steps—with relatively simple strategies. These become the basis for developing increasing skill and competence in assessing reading.

This book describes a variety of beginning steps that a teacher or tutor can take to develop expertise in the complex process of reading assessment. Some assessment strategies are described in detail, with instructions for implementing them in the reading classroom. Others are mentioned for the purpose of expanding the teacher or tutor's knowledge base, but with no expectation that they will be put into practice at this stage of his or her career. They represent giant steps, and the premise of this book is that teachers and tutors must begin with the simple and move gradually to the complex. The primary purpose of this book is to guide the teacher or tutor through first steps in developing an effective system for assessing reading.

DESCRIPTION OF THE ASSESSMENT PROCESSES

This is a book about reading assessment, so it makes sense to describe first what we mean by *assessment*. Assessment is so much a part of our daily lives that we seldom think about it. We tend to take it for granted, and we just do it! When we assess, we collect evidence. Then we analyze this evidence so that we can make a judgment about something. This judgment generally leads to a decision or to some form of action. For example, we assess the weather in the morning. Our evidence may be what we see as we look out the window, the local weather report, or a combination of the two. Based upon this, we decide to wear certain clothes or take an umbrella. We assess our appearance by looking in the mirror, and as a result of the evidence, we may change a tie or add a scarf. We use the gas gauge in the car to assess the state of the gas tank, and decide either to stop for gas now or wait until after work. We assess the amount and flow of traffic on the freeway, and perhaps turn off at the next exit. We assess the mood of our coworkers by listening to what they say, considering their tone of voice as they say it, and noting their body language. As a result, we either attempt to meet their needs, or we decide to avoid them for the rest of the day.

Assessment involves four steps. First, we identify what we want to assess. We usually do this in the form of a question. For example, as we move out of the driveway, we might ask, "Do I need to stop for gas before driving to work?" Second, we collect information or evidence. We check the gas gauge. If it is very low, we may estimate how many miles we can drive before it hits empty. Will stopping for gas make us late for work? If we are late, will this cause any problems? Third, we analyze the evidence. The gas gauge is low, but not low enough to prevent us from getting to work. We would be late if we stopped for gas, and we have a conference with a very concerned parent. Fourth, as a consequence of our analysis, we make a decision. We decide to stop for gas after work, not before.

The Four Steps
of the Assessment Process

Identify what to assess.
Collect evidence.
Analyze the evidence.
Make a decision.

Most of the time, the assessment process runs so smoothly that we tend to take it for granted. However, when the process fails us, we become very aware that something has gone wrong. We can run into problems with any of the four steps. Sometimes we are not specific enough about what we are assessing. "What is the weather going to be like today?" may be less effective than a more specific question: "Will it rain today?" Of course, the effectiveness of any assessment is heavily dependent upon the quality of the evidence we select. A glance out the window may provide less sensitive evidence about the weather than a weather report may. Sometimes our analysis of the evidence is faulty. Does the presence of gray clouds always indicate rain? Should we place more weight on a glance out of the window or the meteorologist's predictions? Finally, we can make a wrong decision. Anyone who has ever decided not to take an umbrella on a day that became very rainy understands what that means!

Assessing a student's reading performance is no different. We ask a question about a student's reading. We select and analyze evidence, and use this evidence to make judgments about the student's strengths and needs. Then we take instructional action. At any point in the process, we can encounter the same problems we meet while assessing the weather or the state of the gas tank. However, reading assessment poses several additional problems.

First, we may not know as much about the processes of reading as we do about weather and gas gauges. Reading is an incredibly complex act! Good readers engage in a variety of different activities as they comprehend a selection. These activities are very different if the reader is a first grader who is just beginning to make sense of print, a fourth grader dealing with a social studies textbook or project, or an adult struggling with directions for filling out income tax forms. It is not enough to ask, "How well is the student reading?" That question is much too general. Instead, we need to know what specific student behaviors indicate good reading and at what level of development.

Another important issue is the type of evidence we choose to document good reader behaviors. There are only so many options for assessing the weather or the state of the gas tank. However, there are many published instruments available for reading assessment. In addition, we can construct our own measures. It is difficult to sort through all the possible instruments and judge their quality. And often, when we collect evidence, we do not know what to do with it. If we note that the gas gauge is almost on empty, we know exactly what to do. It is quite another thing to deal with a variety of scores or observations, some of which may conflict with each other, and none of which suggest a clearly defined direction for instruction. We need guidelines for selecting evidence of good reader behaviors and for using this evidence to design instruction. This book provides such guidelines.

Another issue is that the stakes for reading assessment are very high. If we make a wrong assessment about the weather or gas, we may just get wet or spend an annoying hour walking to and from a gas station. But a wrong or incomplete reading assessment can have serious consequences for a student.

PURPOSES OF READING ASSESSMENT

There are three basic purposes of reading assessment. First, a teacher or tutor uses the assessment process to identify the good reader behaviors a student displays, as well as to note those that are missing. Readers are not passive. They engage in a variety of activities as they construct meaning. Teachers and tutors must have an understanding of these processes, so they are equipped to select valid evidence that documents good reading or suggests behaviors that are missing.

Second, teachers and tutors need to know how to determine whether a specific book is too difficult for a student. They also need to know how to determine a student's *reading level*—that is, the grade level at which a student can read in an acceptable fashion. Knowing a student's reading level allows us to choose appropriate reading material for the student to read on his or her own, as well as appropriate material for instruction. In addition, comparing a student's reading level with his or her chronological grade level can suggest the existence of a reading problem and how serious it may be. For example, a fifth grader who can only read second-grade material is probably experiencing quite a bit of difficulty in school.

Last, teachers and tutors need to document evidence of progress on the part of the student. Unfortunately, much assessment compares the student to his or her peers. Often, for a student who is reading below the level of peers, this obscures any progress that the student may have made. A teacher or tutor needs to compare a student to him- or herself. Let us examine each of these components in turn.

Purposes of Reading Assessment

Identify good reader behaviors.
Determine student reading level.
Document student progress.

IDENTIFYING GOOD READER BEHAVIORS

What is this process called *reading*? What are readers doing as they read, and what do they have to learn? As teachers and tutors, what should we look for as we assess the developing literacy of our students? We have all been successful readers for many years. As a result, we seldom think about the act of reading; in fact, we tend to take it for granted. Let's engage in a short exercise to help us realize what we do so effortlessly every day of our lives as we read newspapers, magazines, grocery lists, road signs, novels, memos from the principal, and notes from a parent, to name only a few things.

I am going to ask you to read a short selection sentence by sentence and examine what went on in your mind as you read. Ready?

Peter led Bridget into the waiting room.

What did you do as you read this sentence? I am certain that you are primarily conscious of a mental picture of Peter and Bridget. But before you could form this picture, you performed a variety of other actions. You recognized the individual words, and you assigned some form of meaning to each one. You did this accurately and very quickly. In addition to constructing an image of Peter and Bridget, you probably made some inferences, predicting perhaps that the waiting room is in a doctor's office or maybe a bus station. How could you do this? You have some prior knowledge of waiting rooms, and you used this to make this prediction. You may have also predicted that you are reading a story. If the first sentence had been "There are a variety of ways in which viruses differ from cells," you would have predicted a nonfiction passage. You can do this because you have a sense of text structure and of how narratives differ from expository selections. You no doubt have questions. How old are Peter and Bridget? Why is he leading her? What is going to happen next? These questions lead you to read on to find answers.

He realized that she was extremely nervous,
so he gently suggested that she sit down.

You did the same things with this sentence, but in addition, you connected it to the first sentence. Good readers synthesize information as they read. Perhaps the fact that Bridget was nervous confirmed your prediction that they were in a doctor's office. If you had originally thought that they were in the waiting room of a bus station, perhaps the word *nervous* led you to think of another possibility such as a dentist's office. You have added to your visual image, and I suspect you are feeling quite positive toward Peter and his gentle ways. Developing emotions toward a character or situation is an important component of the reading process.

Bridget ignored him and began to pace frantically.

You have more questions than you did before, and you are using your prior knowledge and the clues in the text to predict possible answers. You are monitoring your comprehension. You are aware of your questions. You know what you are unsure of. Why did Bridget ignore Peter? Could they have had an argument? She is nervous, and nervous people might pace, but why is her pacing so frantic? You are probably considering several possible reasons—and, I might add, enjoying the suspense. Why do we stay up way past bedtime reading a book? It is because we have many questions about what will happen, and we want to find the answers. Otherwise, we know that sleep will elude us!

The other patients watched her warily,
and several also began pacing.

Perhaps one of your inferences was confirmed. It is a doctor's or dentist's office. As a good reader, you matched your knowledge of waiting rooms to the clue *patients* and arrived at an answer. Perhaps you are unsure of the exact meaning of *warily*. What did you do? I doubt that you reached for a dictionary. Caught up with the story action, you probably used the context of the story to assign a temporary meaning, such as *carefully* or *suspiciously*. You then read on, eager to find out what will happen next.

As a scream rang out from the inner office,
Peter angrily forced Bridget to sit down.

The plot thickens! Do you like the angry Peter quite as much as the gentle Peter? Who is screaming and why? What does this scream have to do with Bridget? You are not conscious of identifying words and assigning meanings. You are caught up with what is happening! You are very aware of what you understand and of the questions you have. You want answers! You are probably even impatient with my comments, which are interrupting the account of Peter and Bridget. So let's move on.

Bridget moved closer to Peter,
who leaned down and tenderly scratched her ears.

Were you surprised? And if you were, wasn't it fun? Had you considered the possibility that Bridget was a dog? Had a vet's office even entered your list of waiting room possibilities? If you are a dog owner, I'll bet the facts that Peter led Bridget into the room and that the other patients copied her pacing were powerful clues.

Let's summarize. What did you do as you read these few short sentences? First, you identified individual words. Most (if not all) were familiar to you, and you did not need to match letters and sounds. The words were what we call *sight words*—words that are recognized immediately without analysis. *Warily* may have been unfamiliar, but as a good reader, you were able to sound it out and pronounce it even though you had never seen it in print before. You assigned appropriate meanings to the words you identified. You connected the things you knew about waiting rooms, patients, and ear scratching with the information in the text. You made inferences and predictions based on your knowledge and the clues in the text. You asked questions and located their answers. You constructed visual images. You monitored

---

Good Reader Behaviors

Before, during, and after reading, good readers . . .

Pronounce unfamiliar words accurately.
Pronounce words automatically.
Read fluently—that is, accurately, quickly, and expressively.
Learn new words and refine the meanings of known ones.
Connect what they know with the information in the text.
Determine what is important in the text.
Recognize the structure of the text.
Summarize and reorganize ideas in the text.
Make inferences and predictions.
Construct visual images.
Ask questions of themselves and the author, and read to find
    answers.
Synthesize information from different sources.
Form and support opinions on ideas in the text.
Recognize the author's purpose/point of view/style.
Monitor comprehension and repair comprehension breakdowns.
Choose to read for enjoyment and enrichment.

your own comprehension or lack of it. In short, you were extremely active, and your sole focus was upon constructing meaning and finding out what was going on.

These key reading behaviors are the basis for reading assessment. We need to find out whether readers are able to do what you did so effortlessly. If they cannot, we need to teach them strategies for doing so. And it is not enough to identify which good reader behaviors to assess. We need to assess these in different forms of text. You were extremely successful with the Peter and Bridget scenario, but would you have been as capable reading an insurance form, a mortgage agreement, or a statistics textbook? Students may employ good reader behaviors when reading stories, but become hopelessly confused in a social studies or science textbook. We must help them to employ effective strategies in a wide variety of reading situations. We will return to the good reader behaviors in each chapter of this book. The box on the facing page provides a list of good reader behaviors that should be a focus for both instruction and assessment. We will return to this list again and again throughout the book.

DETERMINING READING LEVEL

Determining reading level involves two tasks. One is to determine whether a student can successfully read a specific selection. Texts that are used in a classroom, or those that are available to students for independent reading, can vary widely in difficulty level. The topic of the text, the presence or absence of pictures, the length of the text, and the vocabulary that is used are just some of the factors that can make one selection more difficult than another. The teacher or tutor needs to know which texts the student can handle independently. Which ones can the student read and understand if given support? Which ones represent a frustrating experience for the student?

The teacher or tutor also needs to have an estimate of the student's general reading level. Can the student handle most of the selections that are used at his or her grade level? What is the first indication of a reading problem? It is generally that a student cannot read as well as his or her classmates. If a third grader can read and comprehend selections that are appropriate for third grade, we say that this student is reading *at grade level*. A third grader who can read and comprehend selections appropriate for fifth grade is reading *above grade level*. One who is only comfortable with a first-grade selection is reading *below grade level*. An important category of reading assessment is determining what general level of text the student can read successfully.

The seriousness of a reading problem often depends on the gap between a student's reading level and his or her chronological grade level. A third grader reading at a second-grade level may have a less severe reading problem than a fifth grader reading at that same level. How big a discrepancy signals the possibility of a problem? Spache (1981) has offered the following guidelines. For first through third graders, a difference of one year or more between grade placement and reading level is cause for concern. For fourth through sixth graders, a difference of two years or more warrants concern. For students in seventh grade and above, a difference of three years or more is a signal that a reading problem exists. The younger the student, the less difference is needed to indicate a severe problem. Why is it important to consider severity? Students with severe reading problems often need more concentrated intervention in the form of daily and/or individual classes.

What makes a selection appropriate for one grade and not for another? In other words, how do we decide that a selection is at a specific grade level? One way to identify the grade level of a selection is to use a *readability formula*. Readability formulas are based upon the premise that longer sentences and longer words make text more difficult. These formulas count such things as the number of words in a sentence, the number of syllables in the words, and the number of words that are not considered common or frequent. There is software that will help you do this and you can also do it by hand. However, it is very time-consuming, and busy teachers and tutors generally leave it to others to fix grade levels through readability formulas.

Readability formulas have serious limitations (Zakaluk & Samuels, 1988). Various factors beyond sentence and word length interact to make a selection easy or difficult, or appropriate for one grade level and not for another. Readability formulas do not take account of these factors. The presence or absence of pictures can make a text easy or difficult. Predictable text with often-repeated refrains or rhyme is generally easier and more appropriate for the lower grades. Text organization is another factor. Narratives are easier to understand than expository text. Page layout and the presence or absence of headings and other graphic aids are other considerations. In addition, a reader's prior knowledge is a powerful determinant of text difficulty. A student who knows quite a bit about the topic of the text will find it easier to read and understand than an unfamiliar text at the same readability level.

Given all of these determinants of text difficulty, how do teachers or tutors choose appropriate text for instruction? Often they have little choice with regard to the texts used for instruction. Many schools and districts employ reading anthologies, often referred to as *basal readers*. Publishers of such anthologies generally do an acceptable job of matching selections to appropriate grade levels. Even if a teacher or tutor can choose instructional texts, he or she is probably too busy to use readability formulas or extended analyses of text features in order to determine whether a text is appropriate for a group of students. Sometimes the difficulty level of a book is indicated. If it is not stated, the teacher or tutor may be able to locate other sources for estimating difficulty level, such as publisher catalogues. However, this takes time, and time is a precious commodity!

A simple but effective way to choose an appropriate selection is to examine it in relation to other selections that your students have read and enjoyed. Would your students be interested in the topic? Is it a relatively familiar topic? Does the new text look like past selections (as far as length, number of pictures, size of print, etc., are concerned)? Ask one or two students to read a few pages out loud, to determine whether they can handle most of the words. You can use the same process to choose texts for individual students. If the text seems suitable to you, go for it. Trust your instincts! With more and more experience, you will become very adept at choosing selections that are appropriate for all of your students.

NOTING STUDENT PROGRESS

All too often, we assess students by comparing them to their peers. For example, we compare one basketball player to the team's star and say that he or she is an "average" or "poor" player. We compare a third grader to other readers in his or her class and say that this student is the "poorest" reader. In doing this, we miss a very important point—individual progress. The poor basketball player may have started the year with a free-throw percentage of 20%, but now maintains a 56% average. Wouldn't you call that progress? The third-grade child may be reading at a second-grade level, but may have started the year at a first-grade level. Again, wouldn't you call that progress? The most important comparison is that of a student to him- or herself. The effectiveness of our instruction must always be examined in relation to the individual student's progress. "What we should be interested in is whether each child is growing, not whether he is better than the child across the district or the country. We should compare a child's work to his own work earlier in the year: our reference point should be the child's work" (Johnston, 1992b, p. 250).

Gregg was a fourth grader who was having much difficulty keeping up with his peers. When this became apparent to his classroom teacher, she notified the school reading specialist, who agreed to work with Gregg. She gathered evidence in order to assess Gregg's level of reading and the good reading behaviors he employed. Gregg recognized most words accurately, but read very slowly and obviously needed to develop a greater measure of fluency. He was most comfortable reading selections appropriate for second grade. In his fourth-grade class, Gregg had much difficulty reading the social studies and science textbooks, and he became easily discouraged. The reading specialist decided to focus on activities to improve Gregg's reading fluency and on strategies for understanding and remembering nonfiction selections. After four months of instruction, she again collected evidence. Gregg was reading much more fluently, which led to more comprehension on his part. He was comfortable in third-grade material and more confident in his reading ability. In comparison to his fourth-grade classmates, Gregg was still the poorest reader in his class—but wouldn't you agree that, in comparison to himself, Gregg had made a lot of progress?

CHOOSING EVIDENCE
FOR ASSESSING READING PERFORMANCE

Many different measures can provide evidence of a student's reading performance. A teacher or tutor can use published instruments, or can construct his or her own instruments. Whatever the form, assessment measures should possess two characteristics: *authenticity* and *trustworthiness* (Valencia, 1990a). Authentic assessment assesses "what we have defined and valued as real reading" (Valencia, 1990a, p. 60). Trustworthy assessment uses clearly established procedures for gathering evidence. Generally, we divide assessment measures into two categories: *formal* and *informal*.

Formal measures are usually commercial instruments prepared by publishers. Many are *norm-referenced* or *standardized* tests, which are designed and often scored by individuals outside the classroom (Wolf, 1993). When we use a norm-referenced test, we compare the student's score with the score of the norm sample—that is, the sample of students who were used to standardize the test. What does that mean? To put it simply, suppose a student correctly answered 43 items. If the average third-grade score of the norm sample was also 43, the student would be assigned a third-grade reading level. Other formal tests are *criterion-referenced*: We compare the student's score to a cutoff score (or criterion) set by the test authors. Formal tests require us as teachers or tutors to follow all directions for administering and scoring, without adapting or changing any of the procedures. Although standardized tests describe a student's performance in terms of a number, they often do not tell us what we really need to know in order to design effective instruction. Chapter Nine discusses the advantages and disadvantages of formal measures in more detail.

Informal measures are assessments developed, administered, and/or scored by classroom teachers. They can take the form of conferences, observations, and reviews of student work (Wolf, 1993). Informal measures allow a teacher or tutor to design or modify an instrument in order to collect the type of evidence that is needed. Informal tests are extremely flexible, and a teacher or tutor can personalize assessment to the needs of the student. Although some informal measures are published, teachers or tutors construct the majority of them.

Informal instruments are more authentic than formal measures. They are similar to the actual task of reading. Reading a passage and retelling its contents are more authentic than reading a short paragraph and answering multiple-choice questions by filling in little bubbles on a scan sheet. Unfortunately, to some individuals, the term *informal* suggests assessments that are subjective or casual (Wolf, 1993). Nothing could be farther from the truth! Assessments designed and carried out by knowledgeable teachers "provide the most accurate and useful information about student achievement" (Wolf, 1993, p. 519). This book focuses primarily on the use of informal measures to gain maximum information about how a student reads different selections for the purposes of gaining both information and enjoyment.

SUMMARY

- Assessment is a four-step process: identifying what to assess, collecting evidence, analyzing the evidence, and making a decision based on the analysis.
- There are three purposes for reading assessment: identifying good reader behaviors, determining reading level, and noting student progress.
- A teacher or tutor identifies good reader behaviors as a specific focus for assessment.
- A teacher or tutor needs to find out whether a student can successfully read a specific selection. A teacher or tutor also needs to estimate the student's general reading level.
- A teacher or tutor determines reading level in order to choose appropriate reading material for a student and to estimate the seriousness of a reading problem.
- A teacher or tutor notes a student's progress and compares the student to him- or herself as opposed to classmates.

- Choosing evidence for assessing reading performance involves formal and informal measures.
- Informal tests provide the most sensitive and useful information to the teacher or tutor.

ACTIVITIES FOR DEVELOPING UNDERSTANDING

- Select something in your life that you assess frequently (grocery supplies, the organization of your desk, the state of your checkbook, etc.). Show how your actions fit into the four steps of assessment.
- Select a short piece of text. Read it sentence by sentence. Stop after each sentence. What were you thinking of as you read the sentence? Which good reader behaviors did you employ? Share this exercise with a friend. Compare your thoughts and your good reader behaviors.
- Choose two selections written at the same grade level. How are they alike? How are they different? Which one seems easiest and why?
- Identify something that you have just learned to do (knitting, playing golf, target shooting, etc.). What progress have you made? Do you feel that comparison to a master or pro is a fair description of your progress? Why or why not?

TWO

Assessment as Part
of Instruction

How Can We Assess as We Teach?

CHAPTER TOPICS

THE FOUR-STEP ASSESSMENT PROCESS
IN THE CLASSROOM OR TUTORING SESSION

Which comes first, assessment or instruction? Does instruction drive assessment, or does assessment drive instruction? There is a tendency to think of assessment as something that happens after instruction, something apart from instruction—such as asking students to answer questions after they have read a textbook chapter or a story. There is also a tendency to think of all assessment measures as paper-and-pencil tests. These represent very limited views of the assessment process. Good assessment is actually embedded in the pro-

---

**The Four Steps of the Assessment Process
in Reading Instruction**

Identify the good reader behaviors that you are teaching and assessing.
Collect evidence that is related to the good reader behaviors.
Analyze the evidence on the good reader behaviors.
Make an instructional decision about the good reader behaviors.

---

cess of instruction (Winograd, 1994). Assessment and instruction can happen at the same time. "The most powerful assessment for students' learning occurs in the classroom, moment-to-moment among teachers and students" (Johnston, 1992a, p. 60).

Instruction and assessment cannot be separated; they are two sides of the same coin! The goal of any literacy lesson is the development of good reader behaviors. A teacher or tutor who has identified a good reader behavior as the focus of a lesson knows what to assess. However, if the teacher or tutor is unsure about the lesson goal, assessment will probably be unfocused and ineffective. Teachers and tutors need to develop their own assessment system based upon their instructional goals. In this way, assessment emerges from the classroom; it is not imposed upon it (Tierney, 1998).

Assessment can happen at any point in a lesson. It can be a planned and carefully thought-out procedure. It can also be unplanned. Sometimes the unexpected occurs. A teacher or tutor who knows the goal of the lesson can use the unexpected as an added assessment tool.

Many sensitive and effective assessments do not look anything like a typical test. They do not necessarily involve a question-and-answer procedure or a paper-and-pencil format. For example, teacher observation of what students do and say in the reading classroom is a powerful assessment measure.

In Chapter One, we have identified four steps in the assessment process. Let us reexamine these in terms of reading instruction.

Step 1: Identify the Good Reader Behaviors That You Are Teaching and Assessing

The first step is to identify what you are teaching and assessing. In other words, you must decide which good reader behaviors you want to develop in your students. The focus of all literacy lessons should be on the good reader behaviors. These behaviors drive both the instruction and the assessment process. If you do not know what good reader behaviors you are developing in your students, it will be difficult to select appropriate evidence for determining whether your students have learned them.

I remember teaching a novel to eighth graders. I really did not have any specific goals for my lessons. I didn't know anything about good reader behaviors and the importance of developing these in my students. I just wanted my students to understand the novel and (I hoped) enjoy it. Class discussion focused on literal understanding of what happened to the characters. I simply did not think about teaching my students to summarize, to self-question as they read (I did all the questioning!), or to draw inferences about the characters and the time in which they lived.

After we finished reading and discussing the book, I constructed a long and involved multiple-choice test. I corrected the test, turned my students' scores into letter grades, and entered them into my grade book. If you had asked me what I was assessing, I would have said, "Reading." But what did that mean? Some questions revolved around unimportant details. Others required that the students make inferences in order to arrive at correct answers. Others focused on vocabulary. I never attempted to separate these. I never even considered whether a multiple-choice test was the best way to assess my students' comprehension. And because I did not allow them to look back in the novel to find the answers (I would have called that "cheating"), I actually didn't know whether I was assessing reading comprehension or student memory. Perhaps I was not even assessing anything at all related to reading! Perhaps I was simply assessing my students' motivation or persistence in completing such a lengthy task.

If I had focused my instruction on specific good reader behaviors, I would have known what and how to assess. For example, if I had attempted to develop my students' ability to synthesize information from different sources, a multiple-choice test would have been a sorry assessment instrument. Wouldn't it have made more sense to ask them to compare a character or situation in the novel to their own lives, to a movie or television series, or to the contents of another novel? What if I had focused upon teaching my students to summarize? I could have asked them to write a short summary of a specific episode in the novel from the perspective of one of the characters. Knowing what good reader behaviors you are teaching and assessing is the first step in the instruction–assessment process.

Tying the Good Reader Behaviors to Standards and Expectations

We have tended to break the reading process into many little pieces, assuming that if students know the pieces, they will know the whole (DeLain,

1995). Nothing could be farther from the truth! Have you ever attempted to put together a jigsaw puzzle without referring to the picture? It is extremely difficult to know where to begin or how to group the pieces. Do pieces of a similar color belong together, or do they form two separate areas in the puzzle? And the more pieces you have, the more difficult it is to see the whole. Reading is a very complex act, and we have attempted to understand it by dividing it into parts. But perhaps we have constructed too many parts and—as in the case of the pictureless jigsaw puzzle—have lost a sense of the whole.

When I taught from a basal reading anthology, I had a long list of reading skills to develop. It was called a *scope and sequence chart*. At the end of a grading period, I was required to check the skills that each individual student had mastered. Quite frankly, I had no idea. There were so many skills that it was impossible to assess each one adequately. All were regarded as being of equal importance. And many of them seemed to be the same thing! For example, how was drawing an inference different from making a judgment or reaching a conclusion? And because dealing with the scope and sequence chart was such an overwhelming task for me, I resorted to assessing "reading," whatever that meant.

The scope and sequence chart is still with us. However, we now talk about student performance expectations as opposed to student skills. In addition, we have overarching standards or outcomes that stipulate what students should be able to know and do at a particular grade level. States and districts have constructed these standards, and teachers and tutors are expected to use them. They are expected to connect classroom activities to "clearly stated instructional outcomes and evaluate student success on these activities against clearly stated criteria" (DeLain, 1995, p. 441).

Although the standards are well intentioned, they can pose problems. First, they tend to be very general, all-inclusive, or a combination of both. In some cases, standards are nothing more than the old scope and sequence chart served up in a different format. Consider the following fourth-grade standard from the state of Wisconsin (Benson, Fortier, Grady, Karbon, & Last, 1998, p. 2):

Use effective reading strategies to achieve their purposes in reading

- Use a variety of strategies and word recognition skills including rereading, finding context clues, applying knowledge of letter–sound relationships, and analyzing word structures
- Infer the meaning of unfamiliar words in the context of a passage by examining known words, phrases, and structures

- Demonstrate phonemic awareness by using letter–sound relationships as aids to pronouncing and understanding unfamiliar words and text
- Comprehend reading by using strategies such as activating prior knowledge, establishing purpose, self-correcting, self-monitoring, rereading, making predictions, finding context clues, developing visual images, applying knowledge of text structures, and adjusting reading rate according to purpose and difficulty
- Read aloud with age-appropriate fluency, accuracy, and expression
- Discern how written texts and accompanying illustrations connect to convey meaning
- Identify and use organizational features of texts, such as headings, paragraphs, and format to improve understanding
- Identify a purpose for reading such as gaining information, learning about a viewpoint, or appreciating literature

This is only the first standard! There are three more, and each one is also accompanied by a list of skills or expectations.

One cannot quarrel with the purpose behind standards and lists of student performance expectations. They provide goals for teaching and learning. However, just as the scope and sequence chart overwhelmed me years ago, so can today's standards and expectations overwhelm a teacher or tutor. I recently worked with a district that had carefully matched its pupil performance expectations for each grade to the state standards. At one grade alone, there were 50 different pupil expectations to be assessed! Let's do a bit of arithmetic and determine whether this is even possible. With one student and 50 expectations, the teacher or tutor is responsible for assessing 50 items. With two students, the teacher or tutor is responsible for 100 items. But with 25 students (the average size of many classrooms), the teacher or tutor is responsible for instructing, assessing, and reporting on 1,250 reading behaviors! Is this even reasonable? Can we make it reasonable?

The good reader behaviors listed in Chapter One are the keys. You can take these good reader behaviors and fit them under any standard, no matter how broad it may be. You can also match any minute expectation to a good reader behavior. For example, let's examine the following good reader behavior: "Good readers determine what is important in the text." Of the 50 items on that district list, the following could fit nicely under the good reader behavior of determining importance: "Identifies main idea and details," "Sequences key events," "Retells story events or key facts," "Summarizes text," and "Recognizes elements of plot." Another good reader behavior is this: "Good readers pronounce unfamiliar words accurately". Under this behavior, we could place the following items from the district list of 50 expectations:

"Reads grade-level sight vocabulary," "Knows and applies vowel diphthongs," "Reads multisyllable words," "Uses chunking to decode," "Identifies root/base words," "Recognizes the number of syllables in a word," "Knows and applies plural and possessives," "Knows and applies prefixes," and "Knows and applies suffixes."

Perhaps, at this point, you would like to offer an argument. You may feel that the good reader behaviors, like the standards are too general. Shouldn't teachers or tutors specifically address all those different pupil expectations that I have so casually grouped under one behavior? Of course. Teachers or tutors must teach a variety of word identification strategies and a variety of organizational text patterns. But can they realistically keep track of every student's progress on every one without doing a bit of regrouping?

We have to realize that all those skills or expectations are not necessarily separate entities. For example, suppose a reader comes to an unfamiliar word and pauses, trying to figure it out. If the reader is successful, does he or she use letters and sounds, prefixes and suffixes, syllable patterns, or a combination of all these? The district list that I have described even included specific prefixes (*bi-*, *ex-*, *co-*, *tri-*, *sub-*, and *auto-*) and suffixes (*-ly*, *-ful*, *-ation*, *-ion*, and *-less*) under the expectations. Is it really possible for one teacher or tutor to identify which of these is known or unknown by each individual student? Is it possible even to know for certain which of these the student uses to identify a specific word? And might not this change, depending upon the word itself? That is why it makes more sense to group specific expectations or skills under a manageable number of good reader behaviors, and to use these good reader behaviors to drive instruction, assessment, and reporting to parents on student progress.

There are other difficulties with lists of pupil expectations or skills. On a list, they all tend to take on equal importance. However, they are not equally crucial to successful reading performance. For example, is "Identifies mood" as important as "Summarizes information"? It is difficult to believe that it is. Some pupil expectations lend themselves to rich instructional and assessment options; others do not. For example, not one teacher in the district could tell me how he or she would assess "Identifies mood" beyond asking this simple question: "What is the mood of the selection?" (In addition, there was no clear agreement among the teachers on a definition of *mood*.) Yet all of the teachers could offer a variety of options for assessing "Retells story events or key facts." Though all of the expectations can be assessed in some fashion, how can a teacher or tutor, within the confines of a busy classroom, keep track of the progress of all the students across all 50 expectations?

If assessment is to be effective, it must be manageable. For this reason, it is crucial to have a realistic starting point. The good reader behaviors provide this starting point. By focusing on them, the teacher or tutor can better handle assessment of all students and be accountable for either the standards or the more detailed performance expectations. The role of the teacher or tutor is to match performance expectations to a good reader behavior, and to tie that behavior to the district or state standards. We know that the reading process is much more than the sum of the good reader behaviors, but these behaviors allow us to realistically handle the instruction and assessment of an extremely complex process.

Teaching the Reading Process, Not the Content of the Text

I often ask my students at the university what they are planning to teach. They generally respond by naming a specific story or a chapter in a textbook. As a teacher or tutor, however, you do not teach a story or chapter. Instead, you use that story or chapter to develop good reader behaviors. The good reader behaviors are your focus; the story or chapter is the tool that you will use to develop it. Of course you want your students to understand the selection. Asking questions helps you to determine whether they have. However, what do you want them to get out of reading it? Do you want them to remember that a character lost his brother's football and had to earn money to replace it? Or do you want them to remember that all stories are built around solving character problems, and that good readers focus on this when they summarize what they have read?

Using good reader behaviors as a starting point helps a teacher or tutor focus on the process of reading as opposed to focusing on the content of selections. The reading teacher or tutor does not primarily teach content; that is, the first goal of the lesson is not that students learn how a character built tin can stilts or why another character dug up earthworms. Reading teachers and tutors teach students how to read, and must therefore concentrate "on the processes real readers . . . engage in as they read" (Allington, 1994, p. 23). Content is important, but it is not the principal goal. For example, the teacher or tutor may want students to learn about butterflies. However, even when facilitating content learning, the teacher or tutor still focuses on process—on how the students read, synthesize, and report their knowledge of butterflies. The thinking processes needed to identify words, and to comprehend and remember selections, are the focal points of reading instruction.

The good reader behaviors are not completely separate. They tend to overlap. For example, good readers determine importance and summarize. How can summarizing be completely separate from noting importance? Good readers ask questions and read to find the answers. Very often, finding the answer involves making an inference.

Should we worry about the fact that good reader behaviors are not separate activities? I do not think so. The reading process is too complex to be divided into discrete parts. We made that mistake in the past with our scope and sequence charts, and we are making it again with our long and detailed lists of student expectations. The good reader behaviors are guidelines that help the teacher or tutor choose an instructional focus. Chances are that in developing one good reader behavior, you are developing others. If you show students how to monitor their comprehension, you are probably also helping them to self-question. Good reader behaviors provide you with a manageable frame of reference for designing instruction and assessing reading performance in terms of process as opposed to content. They provide you with a manageable frame of reference for dealing with standards and expectations. In short, they drive instruction and assessment!

Step 2: Collect Evidence That Is Related to the Good Reader Behaviors

If you know what good reader behaviors you are teaching and assessing, you have a better chance of choosing the proper evidence. Evidence should be relevant; that is, the evidence should be clearly related to the good reader behaviors you have chosen as your focus. If you are teaching students to draw inferences, you should collect evidence on their ability to do just that. If you are focusing on increasing reading fluency, your evidence will be something that shows fluency, such as examples of oral reading.

You also need to know how you will record this evidence during the assessment process and afterward. The classroom or tutoring session is a busy place! As a teacher or tutor, you have to pay attention to many things at once. You cannot trust your memory. If your evidence comes from observation of students' activities or comments, you need to set up some manageable system for recording what they say and do, so you won't forget it. "Without some form of documentation, much of what has been seen will be either forgotten, or, more likely, remembered in a form that scarcely resembles the original artifact or event" (Wolf, 1993, p. 519). You also need to maintain an ongoing record of individual student progress. The following account of Jayne's instruction and assessment suggests how all this may be accomplished.

Jayne chose the following good reader behavior as the focus of her lesson: "Good readers recognize the structure of the text." She decided to use focused discussion to develop her fourth-grade students' understanding of story structure. After reading a story, Jayne gave each student four cards. One card contained the word *Character*. *Problem* and *Solution* were written on the second and third cards. The final card contained *Steps*. As Jayne and her students discussed the story, each child held up a card to indicate what he or she wanted to say. If students held up the *Character* card, they were expected to talk about the character; if they held up the *Problem* card, their comments were expected to focus on the problem; and so on. Jayne modeled comments on these elements of story structure and reminded her students that using story parts would help them to remember and retell a story more effectively.

During the discussion, Jayne also collected evidence about her students' understanding of story structure. She used a simple checklist to keep a record of their comments. The checklist had four columns marked *Character*, *Problem*, *Solution*, and *Steps*, and a fifth column with no heading. If a student held up the *Character* card and talked about a character, Jayne placed a check mark in the *Character* column. If a student identified a character's problem or commented about it, Jayne placed a check mark in the column marked *Problem*. If a student talked about the steps that were involved in solving the problem, or its solution, she checked *Steps* or *Solution*. If students made comments that were not directly related to the structure of the story, or if they had difficulty matching their comments to the card they held up, Jayne noted this in the fifth column. During the discussion, Jayne was both instructing and assessing her students' understanding of components that are common to all stories.

During the discussion, Jayne observed that Paola was staring out the window and that Lorne was attempting to grab Hallie's pencil. What did they tell Jayne about the students' understanding of story structure? Perhaps nothing. On the other hand, perhaps lack of involvement signaled lack of understanding, and Jayne noted this on her checklist. She placed question marks next to Paola's and Lorne's names under the fifth column.

Jayne realized that discussion has limitations in assessing all students. Some are shyer or more reticent than others and do not participate eagerly in discussion. Both the amount of time allowed for discussion and the content of the story limit the number of times a student can contribute, as well as what can be said. Only one student can talk at a time, and that student's contribution may be identical to what others would have said if they had been given the chance. Therefore, Jayne collected additional evidence on her students' understanding of story structure. She asked them to choose one of the characters in the story and plan a short story of their own. They should imagine another problem the character might have, devise a solution, and tell how the character solved it. She hoped that this activity might shed insight on the extent to which individual students such as Paola and Lorne understood the role of basic story elements.

Jayne was also concerned about the performance of individual students during the discussion. On the checklist, she highlighted in yellow the names of students who did not participate in the discussion, or whose comments were unrelated to story structure elements or to the cards they held up. Was the discussion performance of these students due to lack of understanding of story elements? Perhaps they just did not have enough chances to participate during the discussion. Perhaps they chose not to contribute because of uncertainty or shyness. Jayne used her highlighted checklist as a guide for paying more attention to these students and perhaps offering them more opportunities for talking in the future. She also used it as a guide when she held conferences with them about their independent reading. If Jayne had not kept some record of the discussion, she might not have noticed these students—or, if she did, she might have easily have forgotten. Again, the classroom is a busy place, and forgetting occurs very easily in the best of circumstances!

In summary, Jayne followed the first two steps of the assessment process. She identified what she was teaching and assessing by selecting a good reader behavior as her focus and choosing appropriate instructional activities to develop it. She then collected evidence that was related to the good reader behavior and used a checklist to record student performance.

Step 3: Analyze the Evidence on the Good Reader Behaviors

"Assessment is always interpretive" (Johnston, 1992a, p. 60). In an attempt to make sense of students' reading performance, teachers and tutors must interpret the evidence they have collected about the good reader behaviors. What did Jayne's evidence reveal about the presence or absence of the good reader behavior that was the focus of her lesson? Jayne's checklist recorded the kinds of comments her students made, but what did it indicate about their understanding of story structure? Jayne also asked her students to plan a story involving one of the characters they had discussed. What did this plan tell Jayne about individual students' understanding of story elements? This is where a rubric comes in.

Jayne's Checklist

Good Reader Behavior _Recognize Structure of Text_

Date _____

Selection _How Beetles Got Their Beautiful Coats_

Activity _Whole-Class Discussion_

	Character	Problem	Solution	Steps	
Joseph	✓	✓			
LaKendra	✓	✓			
Lorne					?
Marva		✓		✓	
Willie	✓✓				
Juan		✓			
Shane	✓	✓			
Paola					?
Rosa	✓		✓		
Hallie		✓✓			
Raoul	✓				✓
Kendall	✓				✓
Brett					✓✓
Altonia	✓	✓			
Brenda		✓			
DeAndra	✓				
Jesse		✓			✓
Tiffany		✓	✓		
Jackie	✓			✓	
Allie		✓	✓		
Jon		✓			
Detura	✓✓		✓		

What Is a Rubric?

A *rubric* provides "criteria that describe student performance at various levels of proficiency" (O'Neill, 1994, p.1). In other words, it offers guidelines for analyzing the evidence. For example, in Chapter One, we have talked about deciding whether you should stop to fill your gas tank. The evidence you would collect is obviously your gas gauge. However, how do you analyze the state of your gauge? What guideline or criterion do you use for filling up? Do you fill your tank if you are at the halfway mark? Do you fill it if you are three-quarters down? I have a friend who never stops for gas until the gauge reads practically empty! On the other hand, I get very nervous when the gauge hits three-quarters empty. Each of us is using different criterion for stopping for gas, and the criterion we are using is a type of rubric—a guideline for analyzing the evidence.

A rubric is a tool for examining student work and for judging the quality of that work. I remember assigning projects and, when it came time to give a grade, choosing the better students' work to examine first. I then used their performance as a guide for evaluating the others. I suppose this was a form of a rubric, but not a very efficient or thoughtful one. Prior to assigning the project, I should have listed what I wanted the students to include in the project and what I expected the project to look like. In other words, I should have constructed a rubric. Then not only would I have had a guideline for evaluation, but I could have shared this with my students—who then would have known exactly what was expected of them.

Why should a teacher or tutor take the time to construct and use a rubric? First, a rubric clarifies the process of analyzing evidence of good reader behaviors. It provides guidelines for judging quality. Second, rubrics "make expectations explicit" (Winograd, 1994, p. 421). If a rubric is shared with students, it can improve the students' performance by making the teacher's or tutor's expectations quite clear. Students can use the rubric as well as the teacher or tutor. They can use the rubric to evaluate themselves, and self-assessment is a powerful instructional tool. In this way, a rubric both instructs and assesses!

A rubric can be written, but it does not have to be. My friend and I use mental rubrics or guidelines to determine whether we should stop for gas. As another example, think about preparing for a vacation. Some of us make lists of what we must pack and what we must do before we leave. We check each item off. Did we notify the post office to stop mail? Yes. We check it off. Did we take a bathing suit? Yes. We check it off. This list is a simple form of written rubric. Others of us perform the same process mentally, checking off in our heads what we have completed and what still needs to be done. This is an example of a mental rubric.

Constructing a Rubric

As a teacher or tutor, how do you construct a written rubric? There is one primary guideline: Keep it simple! Teachers and tutors rarely have time to construct involved rubrics. They do not have time to score long and complex ones. You want a rubric that is easy to use and is focused upon specific good reader behaviors. If the rubric is too complex, you will eventually discard it (and probably feel guilty for doing so!). Avoid the guilt and emphasize simplicity.

A rubric is made up of two elements: It "lists criteria for a piece of work, [and] it also articulates gradations of quality for each criterion from excellent to poor" (Goodrich, 1996–1997, p. 14). Let's construct a simple rubric so you can get an idea of how to work with these two components. Let's build a rubric for assessing a salesperson. We have all had experiences with very efficient and helpful salespeople. We have also had shopping experiences ruined by bad-tempered salespeople who would not or could not answer our questions or provide the help we needed.

First, we need some criteria for what makes a good salesperson. Think about salespersons whom you would describe as good or excellent, and use what you remember about their behavior to generate some criteria. For example, a salesperson should be friendly. This seems self-evident; nobody appreciates a grouch! A salesperson also should know his or her merchandise. Nothing is more annoying than to ask questions about a possible purchase and not receive an answer (or receive the wrong answer). A salesperson should be attentive and not ignore you by chatting with other sales personnel or arranging merchandise. A salesperson should listen to your needs and not try to talk you into something you don't want. A salesperson should be helpful—that is, willing to make suggestions and offer you alternatives if the merchandise you originally wanted is unavailable. We could probably generate many more criteria, but let's keep it simple. We now have five criteria: A good salesperson is friendly, knows the merchandise, is attentive, is a good listener, and is helpful. We have the first element of our rubric—criteria for performance.

Let's move to the second part—degrees of quality. Each criterion needs to be ranked in some way. The simplest ranking is a yes–no rating; for example. the salesperson was either friendly or not friendly. Another form of ranking involves numbers such as 4, 3, 2, and 1, with 4 standing for highest quality. Young children can understand yes–no ratings and numbers very well. Other rankings are more descriptive. Some rubrics use one or two statements to describe each ranking, and this is a point you may eventually reach. In the beginning, however, strive for simplicity. If you want to move beyond yes–no ratings and numbers, use only one or two words to describe your gradations of quality. In assessing a salesperson, you might use these terms: "Very effective," "Effective," "Somewhat effective," and "Not effective." Suppose you are interested in assessing knowledge and understanding. Your descriptors might be "Full understanding," "Some understanding," "Incomplete understanding," and "Misunderstanding." If you are interested in how often something occurs, you might use "Usually," "Frequently," "Sometimes," and "Never."

So, after listing criteria and deciding upon how to rank them, we put the two together to form a simple rubric for assessing a salesperson.

A good salesperson . . .

	4	3	2	1
Is friendly				
Knows the merchandise				
Is attentive				
Is a good listener				
Is helpful				

Let's review the process of constructing a rubric with a reading task. Teachers and tutors often ask students to give book talks. The student chooses a favorite book and presents it to the class. What rubric would be appropriate for assessing the quality of that presentation? The first step is to list criteria. Just as we listed criteria that described a good salesperson, we have to list criteria for a good book talk. What do you want to see in the students' work? First, tie the assignment to a good reader behavior—in this case, "Good readers choose to read for enjoyment and enrichment." Given this good reader behavior, you might decide that the following criteria should be included: an attention-grabbing introduction, a description of a favorite part or character, an explanation of why the book was chosen, and a personal reflection on the value or worth of the book. Remember to keep your rubric simple. In the interests of simplicity, fewer criteria are better than more. Once you have the criteria, move to the rating scale. Will a yes–no rating be sufficient? Do you want to use numbers? What about words to describe quality? Perhaps your rubric might look like this.

Book Talk Rubric

Name _____ Book _____

	Very effective	Effective	Slightly effective	Not effective
Grabbed audience attention				
Described favorite part/character				
Explained why the book was chosen				
Talked about worth of book				
Overall rating of book talk				

How can you, as a busy teacher or tutor, find the time to construct a rubric? You find the time by making it part of your instruction. You don't stay after school to create rubrics on your own! You don't construct them over the weekend! You create rubrics collaboratively with your students. This is a powerful vehicle for sharing good reader behaviors. Explain the assignment to the students, and ask them what would make a good project. Guide them to choose suitable criteria. Work with them to select realistic descriptors. Deciding upon important criteria and choosing descriptors for quality are effective activities for developing the students' understanding and appreciation of good reader behaviors. Involving the students will also help you to keep the rubric simple. You want a rubric that the students understand as well as you do, because they are going to use it too. Once a rubric is created, use it again and again. If it needs to be revised, involve the students in the revision. In fact, it has been my experience that students often take the initiative in revising or expanding rubrics.

Many districts have constructed their own rubrics, and teachers or tutors are required to use them. There are also published rubrics, such as those constructed by Hill, Ruptic, and Norwick (1998). If such measures are helpful, by all means use them. If they seem overwhelming, use parts of them. Start with what you can realistically handle. As you become more experienced in the instruction and assessment of good reader behaviors, your rubrics will naturally become more complex. Allow yourself to grow into the process.

Jayne used two rubrics to assess her class's performance. As Jayne examined the checklist, she used a mental rubric. She decided that if 18 students, or approximately 80% of the class, offered comments tied to story structure elements, she would be well pleased. Someone else might have used a differ-

Jayne's Rubric

Name _____ Date _____

Assignment _____

_____ I chose a main character from the story to write about.

_____ I matched the character to a problem.

_____ I described the problem.

_____ I listed at least two steps in solving the problem.

_____ I described how the problem was solved.

Score

4–5 checks: I did a very good job!

3 checks: I did okay.

1–2 checks: I need to think harder about story parts.

ent cutoff. That is just fine. There are no absolute guidelines here! Establishing a cutoff is your decision. Try it out; you can always change it. Jayne also noted that most of her students talked about the characters, their problems, and the solutions they reached. However, fewer than half commented about the steps that led to problem resolution. She realized that she would need to focus more on this element with the entire class.

Jayne and her class worked together to construct a short individual rubric to use for evaluating the students' story plans. She reminded them of their focused discussion as a guide to choosing criteria. They decided on a simple yes–no rating. If the behavior was present, it would be checked. They agreed that four or five checks would indicate a very good job in story planning. After the students finished planning their story, they filled out the rubric and evaluated themselves. Jayne collected these filled-out forms and wrote her own evaluations on the same papers. She then returned the papers to the students.

Step 4: Make an Instructional Decision about the Good Reader Behaviors

You have now identified the good reader behaviors you are assessing; you have also collected evidence, and you have analyzed the evidence using a written or mental rubric. You know which good reader behaviors were evident and which were not. The fourth step is to decide what you are going to do about this. How will the evidence and your analysis of it indicate future instructional directions? Unfortunately, teachers and tutors often ignore this last step. After they have analyzed the evidence, they record it in a grade book and plan another lesson totally unrelated to what went on before!

Teachers and tutors make several kinds of instructional decisions. One decision involves choosing the focus of the next lesson. What good reader behavior will the teacher or tutor emphasize next? Another decision relates to grouping. Will the next lesson be presented to the class as a whole? Does the class need to be grouped in some way? What kind of grouping will best achieve the teacher's or tutor's objectives? Should the teacher or tutor set up some form of collaborative or cooperative grouping where children of different abilities work together on a common project? Should the teacher or tutor form groups composed of children of like abilities and offer differentiated instruction? Another instructional decision relates to individual students. Which individuals need additional support? How best can that support be given?

Jayne decided to continue with a focus on story structure for the entire class and to focus on the important steps that lead to solving the problem. She planned a variety of different activities to use with several more stories. She also decided to form a smaller group of children made up of those who did not demonstrate an understanding of story structure. She planned to use the same simple checklist and rubric to monitor their progress.

Jayne thus made two types of instructional decisions. First, she made a decision that focused upon the entire class. Her analysis of students' comments led her to plan more activities for developing an understanding of story structure, particularly the steps that lead to problem resolution. Her analysis also focused upon individual students. This evaluation of individual progress resulted in a decision to provide additional small-group instruction for several children.

SHARING GOOD READER BEHAVIORS WITH STUDENTS

Who should know about good reader behaviors, the lesson focus, and the assessment evidence to be collected? Should it be just the teacher or tutor? Or should students also be aware of these? Think about how eager students are to participate in sports. Motivation is rarely an issue. Of course, playing basketball or soccer may be more fun than many classroom activities. However, I suspect that part of student motivation has to do with their understanding of the game, their knowledge of its rules, and their awareness of what they need to learn in order to play well.

Do students have that understanding of the reading process? Do they know what good readers do? If a coach requires a specific drill for developing free-throw shooting, students generally know what the coach is doing and why. Do students know why a teacher or tutor asks them to keep a journal, compile a word list, write a reflection, or make inferences about character motivation? I recall a third grader who was busily employed in filling out a worksheet. When he finished, he put down his pencil and announced, "There! It's done. I don't know what it means, but I did it." How sad!

It is important to develop students' awareness of their own thought processes during the reading process. Good reader behaviors are the vehicle for doing this. From the very first day of class, students need to know about good reader behaviors. Put good reader behaviors on bulletin boards, and talk about them every day. Model good reader behaviors for the students. "What all children need, and some need more of, [are] models, explanations, and demonstrations" of how reading is accomplished (Allington, 1994, p. 21). Share the lesson focus with the students, and explain how they can demonstrate these good behaviors. Share how you are assessing their development as good literacy learners. Show students the rubric you are using, and ask them to apply it to their own work. Construct rubrics collaboratively with the students, and use this collaboration as a way to further develop their understanding of good reader behaviors. Finally, ask students to describe their own good reader behaviors. Have them develop learning logs to record these.

Jayne explained the purpose of her checklist to the students before they began their discussion. She told them what she would be looking for and recording. After the discussion, the children were eager to see how many checks they had received and in what categories. Before they began planning their stories, Jayne constructed a simple rubric with the students and asked them to fill it out when they had finished writing their story plans. Self-assessment

Sharing Good Reader Behaviors with Students

Describe good reader behaviors to students.
Model good reader behaviors for students.
Share good reader behaviors that are the focus of the lesson.
Share the rubric for assessing good reader behaviors.
Have students describe their own good reader behaviors.

is a powerful tool for focusing students' attention on their own good reader behaviors.

In the past, assessment was the sole prerogative of the teacher or tutor, and to students it was often a mysterious and confusing process. Have you ever received a grade and had no idea why you received it? Teachers or tutors assessed and assigned grades, but the students often had no idea what they did or did not do to earn the grades. Assessment today is a more collaborative venture. Teachers, tutors, and students all assess. They engage in evaluation "so that students can take control of their own learning and teachers can improve their instruction" (Winograd, 1994, p. 421).

MATCHING ASSESSMENT AND INSTRUCTION TO STANDARDS

Some time ago, a former student of mine asked whether I could help her with her reading instruction. When she arrived in my office, she was carrying an extremely large tote bag. It contained the teacher manual of her basal reading anthology; four novels, which were part of the fourth-grade reading curriculum; the district curriculum guide; and a copy of the state standards for reading and language arts. Almost in tears, she piled it all on my desk and confided, "I have no idea where to start! None of this fits together for me. How can I do everything that the district and the state require? Nothing in the manual seems to match the state standards or the curriculum guide. And I will never cover everything in the basal, let alone the four novels! What do I do first?"

I suspect that her feelings were quite representative of many new teachers and tutors who find it impossible to juggle state and district mandates, teacher manuals, curriculum requirements, and all the different forms of text available to a classroom teacher or tutor. We have reading textbooks, storybooks, and novels to use in our instruction. We have social studies and science textbooks. We have newspapers and magazines and selections on the Internet. Teacher manuals offer a wealth of possible activities and projects to use with any one selection. How do we choose what to do? How do we tie all this to state and district standards and to good reader behaviors?

Do we begin with the standards? Do we begin with the good reader behaviors? Do we begin with activities in the teacher manual? Do we begin with the story or novel? The actual beginning point is less important than tying it all together. We need to connect our instruction and assessment to standards and to good reader behaviors. We can move forward from a standard or outcome to the reading selection or activity, or can move backward from the selection or activity to the standard. Let's discuss this in more detail.

You can select a standard or outcome and, if it is quite general, choose a more specific good reader behavior that matches it. Because many standards or outcomes are quite general, this is easy to do. Don't agonize at this point. Remember that the good reader behaviors are not separate and discrete things; neither are the standards. Then you can decide on an appropriate selection and activity for developing the good reader behavior. Another way is to work backward from the selection or activity to the standard or outcome. Choose the selection and select the specific good reader behavior that you want to develop. Decide on an appropriate activity for developing the good reader behavior, and tie all this to district or state standards and outcomes.

Some districts and schools make the decision for you. You are expected to follow the basal reading anthology in a sequential manner, or to teach a specific novel at a certain time of the year. Some tutoring programs provide the activities or selections to use. If you must follow a somewhat prescribed sequence for choosing reading selections or activities, then work backward to the standard or outcome. In other words, look at the selection or activity, and then decide which good reader behavior would be facilitated by having students read or engage in it. In other cases, the decision about which selection to read or write rests with you as the teacher or tutor. In that case, it may make more sense to begin with the standard or outcome and to choose a selection or activity that matches it.

A typical teacher manual contains many possible suggestions for instruction. Novels also come with suggestions for instructional activities. How do you decide which ones to choose? Evaluate in terms of the good reader behaviors. What are you attempting to develop in your students? If you want them to make inferences, asking them to answer literal questions would not be relevant. Neither would a word-sorting activity. On the other hand, focusing discussion on character motivation might be a wonderful device for showing students how to match clues in the text to what they already know. You don't have to use every instructional activity that comes in the teacher manual. Select those that are relevant to the good reader behavior you want to develop

The focus of good reader behaviors also allows you to choose the evidence you will use to evaluate student performance. Sometimes your evidence is an integral part of the activity itself. For example, you have your class engage in repeated and choral reading to develop the good reader behavior of fluent (i.e., accurate, quick, and expressive) reading. Your evidence consists of the increased fluency you note in your students as the repeated and choral reading continues. Sometimes the evidence comes from how you examine ongoing student work—journals, for example. You can read journals to determine whether your students express an appreciation of reading and writing. You can read the same journals to determine whether students can summarize. It all depends on the good reader behavior that is your focus.

Alan chose a poem in his basal reading textbook because it was about winter. The first snow had just fallen, and his second graders were wild with excitement. The manual suggested a variety of activities for developing the poem, such as recognizing rhythm and rhyme, creating visual images, and writing poems. Alan checked his list of good reader behaviors and decided that his second graders needed to work on reading fluently more than they needed to work with visual imagery or poetry composition. Having selected a good reader behavior as a focus, Alan chose repeated choral reading of the poem as his instructional activity for developing fluency. He then decided what his assessment evidence would be. He tape-recorded the class during their first reading of the poem. After several days of choral reading and individual practice, he taped them again. He also asked individual students to read parts of the poem and noted their performance on a checklist. Alan attached this good reader behavior to the state standard "Read aloud with age-appropriate fluency, accuracy, and expression." To summarize, Alan began with a selection, selected a good reader behavior, chose an appropriate instructional activity, decided how to collect and record evidence, and finally tied everything to a state standard. Alan could have done this in a different order. He could have started with the standard or outcome, moved to the good reader behavior, and then chosen an appropriate text and instructional and assessment activities. The important thing is not the order, but the alignment of instruction and assessment with specific good reader behaviors and with state and district standards. It is not enough for teachers and tutors to know what they are teaching and assessing. They must also know why they are doing so!

MAKING READING ASSESSMENT MANAGEABLE

Classrooms and tutoring sessions are very busy places. As a teacher or tutor, you do not have unlimited time to plan and assess instruction. Even if you tie your instruction to good reader behaviors, it is easy to become hopelessly bogged down in planning instruction, assessing student behavior, recording evidence, designing and scoring rubrics, and making decisions about the next steps. There are some shortcuts that are available to teachers or tutors, and you should use them. Teacher and tutor burnout is a very real thing; it often occurs because

---

Making Reading Assessment Manageable

Don't assess everything.

Assess important activities.

Focus on a small number of students each day.

Involve students in self-assessment.

Use simple procedures for recording observations.

Tie anecdotal records to the four-step assessment process.

---

individuals attempt to do too much and, as a result, have no sense of accomplishing anything. "The meaningful assessment of reading results from an often under-appreciated but always skillful balancing act" (Kapinus, 1993, p. 62). Take as many shortcuts as you can to achieve that balance!

• *First, don't feel that you have to assess everything students do*. Teachers and tutors often go on guilt trips if they don't correct every paper, look at every worksheet, keep track of every discussion, and read every journal entry. Why should you? There are some activities that students do just for practice. They don't need more than your awareness that the students actually worked on them. There are some activities that develop classroom climate and student collaboration. Again, they do not need detailed analysis. And there are some activities that are just plain fun and make the reading classroom or tutoring session a happy place to be.

Look for shortcuts and do not feel guilty about using them. Ryan, a middle school English teacher, required his students to keep literature response journals. They generally did this three times a week. Ryan taught five different classes a day, and each class contained approximately 30 students. Reading 450 journal entries each week presented a formidable task, especially since the students welcomed and actually expected some sort of written response from him. Ryan created a shortcut. He focused on journal entries from one class each week. He handed out Post-it Notes and asked the students to mark the entry they wanted him to read. It could be an entry made during that week or one written earlier. This limited Ryan's responses to a more manageable 30 entries per week, and it allowed him to respond more thoughtfully and at greater length—something very much appreciated by his students.

• *Choose important activities to assess, and limit these to two or three a week*. It takes time to develop a rubric, use it for scoring, and record the results. One or two thoughtfully chosen pieces of evidence will give you more input than six or eight hastily developed ones. You have nine months of school. This translates into approximately 36 weeks. If you assess two or three activities each week, you will have between 72 and 108 pieces of data on each child! These will be more than enough for you to determine the presence or absence of good reader behaviors and to document individual progress.

• *Choose a small number of students to focus on each day*. If you have 25 students in your classroom, directing specific attention to each of them on a daily basis may be very difficult. Cunningham (1992) suggests dividing the number of students in your class by 5. Each day, pay special attention to 5 students as opposed to 25. On Monday, focus on the Monday students. Examine their work very carefully. Spend individual time with them. Watch them and write notes about their behavior and performance. On Tuesday, do this with the Tuesday students; on Wednesday, focus on the Wednesday students, and so on. This allows you as a teacher or tutor to realistically concentrate on a manageable number of students each day.

• *Involve students in self-correction and self-assessment*. Have students correct their own work whenever possible. This works well for worksheets, homework assignments, and similar activities where an answer is either right or wrong. However, don't give the students an answer key. Nobody ever learned anything using an answer key. Students concentrate on matching their answers to the key and pay little or no attention to why an answer was right or wrong. Instead, put the students in small groups. Have them compare their answers without an answer key and come to some agreement as to the correct answer.

What about work that does not necessarily have one right answer? Ask the students to discuss their answers and come to some agreement. For example, after reading a folk tale, Faye asked her students to write in their journals about the character they felt was the greediest and to tell why they thought so. Obviously, different students chose different characters. Faye placed the students in groups and asked them to discuss their choices and come to a consensus. She moved around, listening to their deliberations and occasionally offering suggestions. The class then voted on the greediest character. As a result, Faye did not have to read everyone's journal. The small-group discussions and the voting gave her a good idea of their contents.

• *Set up simple procedures for recording your observations*. For example, use a common template (such as the one provided here) for recording observations about student performance. Jayne's checklist used a similar template. Place the names of your students in the first column on the left. Divide the rest of the sheet into four or five columns. Leave a blank space at the top of the template for writing in the good reader behavior that is your focus, and leave blanks at the tops of the columns for writing in the aspects of this behavior that you want to assess. (Again, look back at Jayne's checklist to see how this is done.) You can duplicate multiple copies of this template. Whenever you want to observe your students or evaluate their work, fill in the *Good Reader Behavior* blank and the blank column heads, and you are ready to go! Purchase a clipboard to hold the checklist, and attach a pencil or pen to it with a string. It is easy to drop or misplace a pencil, and it is annoying to have to locate one. A sturdy string prevents this.

Your clipboard and template should be as much parts of you as your own hands. Together, they provide a tool for continuous assessment and recording of student performance. Sara regularly used the activity of "Making Words" (Cunningham & Allington, 1999) to focus her first graders' attention on letter–sound matching. Each student received a series of cardboard letter tiles. They manipulated these to form a series of words as directed by Sara. They started with two-letter words and moved on to three-, four-, and five-letter words. The process culminated with the spelling of a "mystery word" that used all the letter tiles and the sorting of all the words according to common letter patterns. During the entire process, Sara continually moved around the room and watched what her students did. She noted their performance on her template, using a simple coding system of plus and minus signs. In this way, she was able to pay attention to almost every child at some point during the process.

• *Tie anecdotal records to the four-step assessment process.* What about recording observations that are longer than a simple check mark? We call these *anecdotal records*. Anecdotal records are short descriptions of student behavior, and they can be wonderful assessment tools. Unfortunately, many teachers and tutors do not use them. Part of the problem is actually finding the time to write anecdotal records in a busy classroom or tutoring session. Time for writing anecdotal records is closely tied to student independence. In other words, if your students are relatively independent as they read, engage in practice sessions, and prepare projects, it allows you more time for observing and recording. A second problem with anecdotal records is that many teachers or tutors are unsure what to do with them after they are written.

If you apply the four-step assessment process to the use of anecdotal records, they will become more manageable. First, know what you are assessing. Very often, a teacher or tutor records a student's behavior that seems pertinent, but then does nothing with it. This often occurs because the teacher or

Sample Template

Good Reader Behavior _____

Date _____

Selection _____

Activity _____

tutor does not have a clear rationale for recording it in the first place. Certain behaviors can tell you a lot about a student, but only if you know what you are looking for.

Let the classroom activity indicate what you are looking for. For example, if students are reading orally, you might record brief descriptions of their accuracy, fluency, and eagerness to read. During self-selected silent reading, you can look for evidence of motivation for reading or lack of motivation. A child who is misbehaving during self-selected silent reading may be a child who does not like to read. Self-selected silent reading also provides an opportunity to jot down notes on student interests as indicated by book choice. What can you look for during class discussion? Lack of participation may suggest lack of motivation, inability to function effectively in a group, or lack of comprehension. During group work, you can observe the ways students interact with each other and the extent of their ability to collaborate. Individual work provides an opportunity to note such things as persistence and self-directed behavior. The idea is to know what you are looking for during each activity.

A good idea is to compile an observation guide (Rhodes & Nathenson-Mejia, 1992). An observation guide is a list of possible things to look for and record. Constructing the guide forces you to think about student behaviors that are relevant for reading assessment. It helps to construct your guide in the form of questions. What reading behaviors are you looking for? If you know the questions, you have a better chance of finding the answers! Once

---

Observation Guide for Anecdotal Records

Is the student involved in reading?

Does the student independently choose books for personal reading?

How does the student interact with his or her peers?

Can the student work independently?

What are the student's interests?

What peers does the student work with most effectively?

Does the student participate positively in group activities?

Does the student join in class discussions?

What comments does the student make about a specific text or assignment?

What activities seem to motivate the student?

the guide is finished, post it in a prominent place, where it will act as a constant reminder to observe and record what students say and do in the reading classroom or tutoring session. An observation guide might resemble the accompanying box.

The second step of the assessment process is to collect and record evidence. Sometimes the opportunity to write an anecdotal record is lost because of the absence of a pencil or paper. One possible solution is to attach a pad of Post-it Notes to your clipboard and use these to write brief notes about students' reading behaviors. Set up a notebook with a sheet of paper for each child in the class, or if you use portfolios (see below), place a blank piece of paper in each portfolio. Simply remove the Post-it Note at a convenient time, date it, and stick or staple it onto the student's page. You can then examine it later and decide what it reveals about the student's reading behavior.

The third step is to analyze the anecdotal record. If you know what you are looking for, analysis will be much easier. Many anecdotal records remain forgotten in a folder because a teacher or tutor did not have the time to analyze them or was unsure what they revealed about the student. Use your observation guide to help you. It is a reminder of your reason for constructing the anecdotal record in the first place. Do your analysis as soon as you can, but make it brief and simple—no more than a few sentences. If at all possible, analyze an anecdotal record the day you record it, while the memory of the incident is still fresh in your mind.

The fourth step is to make an instructional decision. Again, unfortunately, many anecdotal records are placed in a folder and never looked at again. At the end of the grading period, you should review any anecdotal records you have written and analyzed. They provide evidence for comments made to parents at conferences or comments made on the narrative section of a report cord. You might consider sharing the record with parents and using it as a catalyst for discussion.

USING READING PORTFOLIOS

A *portfolio* is a "systematic collection by students and teachers that could help both consider effort, improvement, processes, and achievement across a diverse range of texts" (Tierney, Carter, & Desai, 1991, p. x). To put it simply, a portfolio is a collection of student work that spans a grading period or year. Portfolios take many forms, from random collections of student work to systematic and organized samples tied to clearly defined student and teacher/tutor goals (the good reader behaviors). Work included in portfolios can be teacher-chosen, student-chosen, or a combination of both. Portfolios come in a variety of formats (file folders, albums, binders, notebooks, etc.). A portfolio is a wonderful way to document an individual student's progress for everyone—the teacher or tutor, the student, and the parents. Unfortunately, portfolios can also involve a lot of work on the part of the teacher or tutor, and they can easily become overwhelming. Like rubrics, they only work if they are manageable.

If you decide to set up student portfolios, ease in gradually. Don't try to do too much too soon. Begin by choosing the items that you want students to include. Of course, these should be related to good reader behaviors. Later on, when students are familiar with the portfolio process, you can ask them to choose what they want to include. Realistically, a portfolio should contain both teacher-selected and student-selected items. If students select items, their portfolios become more meaningful to them. Be sure that all items in a portfolio are dated. This will allow you and the student to compare earlier work with later work and note growth. Assessment is an ongoing process. "Learning is never completed; instead it is always evolving, growing, and changing" (Valencia, 1990b, p. 338). Assessment must reflect this development, and a portfolio is an effective vehicle for doing so.

Decide where you will keep the portfolios. They will be of manageable size in September, but won't be for long—portfolios have a nice habit of growing! Decide where you will keep the portfolios, so that both you and the students have easy access to them. Decide on the portfolio format as well. Expandable file folders are easier to handle than binders that require hole punching in order for artifacts to fit into the binder. Pocket folders tend to become easily tattered, and the contents of the portfolio often outgrow the size of the folder.

Once you begin to feel comfortable with selecting portfolio items, share with the students why you selected them. Students need to know about good reader behaviors. They need to see how a particular activity demonstrated that they were good readers or writers. When students begin to select items, ask them to give reasons based upon the good reader behaviors. Vukelich (1997) recommends attaching an entry slip to each work sample. The entry slips can be preprinted and kept where students can easily locate them. They provide a wonderful explanation for parents during conference sessions; they also provide a focus for teacher and student discussion. Entry slips represent a key component of the portfolio process—"active, collaborative reflection by both teacher and students" (Valencia, 1990b, p. 339).

Portfolio Entry Slip

Name _____ Date _____

Work sample was selected by _____

Work sample is evidence of this good reader behavior _____

_____

Student or teacher comments _____

_____

What can go into a portfolio to document good reader behaviors? Just about any activity that can be related to such behaviors can be part of a portfolio (student writing samples, student word lists, journal entries, audio- or videotapes, tests or quizzes, reading lists or records, reading reviews, workbook pages, teacher checklists, student checklists, drawings, descriptions of projects, etc.). The list is endless. The important point is to be selective; portfolios need to be of manageable size. Only include important items, those that are very clearly tied to good reader behaviors. Periodically do some weeding out of portfolio items. This can be an individual exercise on the part of the student, a small-group activity, or a special conference time between student and teacher or tutor.

Portfolios provide evidence of individual student progress across time. Portfolios document for teachers, tutors, students, and parents growth in good reader and writer behaviors. They "empower teachers to make instructional and assessment decisions, provide useful information to facilitate the development of grade reports, and enhance the teachers' knowledge about their students" (Bergeron, Wermuth, & Hammer, 1997, p. 552).

DEALING WITH REPORT CARDS AND GRADE BOOKS

Teachers and tutors rarely have input into the format of the report card. The school or district decides this, and the teachers or tutors are required to use the format whether or not they agree with it. Most report cards have very limited formats. They require a single letter grade for reading and offer minimal space for teacher or tutor comments. A teacher or tutor may feel that it offers little in the way of substantive information to the parents or the students. If this is so, the teacher or tutor may want to insert a checklist with the report card. The checklist could list the good reader behaviors that were stressed during the grading period.

Some teachers or tutors may prefer a narrative report. Be aware, however, that these can be very time-consuming. If you choose to write a narrative, it helps to divide the report into categories of reading behavior and keep the same categories for all students (Afflerbach, 1993). Some examples of such categories are as follows: "Development of good reader behaviors," "Using reading for projects and assignments," "Reading to pursue personal interests," and "Valuing reading."

Reporting each student's progress in developing good reader behaviors can seem a monumental task if your grade book does not lend itself to such assessment. I suspect that many teachers and tutors still do what I did some years ago. I entered a lot of grades into my grade book, and I did this on the same page in the order in which they occurred. At the end of the grading period, I averaged the grades and transferred this to the report card. I hesitate to admit this, but I gave all grade book entries the same weight. A workbook page counted as much as a written summary!

It makes more sense to divide your grade book into pages for each good reader behavior that you emphasize. Suppose you work on vowel patterns. You and your students make lists of words that contain *eck*, *ump*, and *ake*. You then ask the students to individually sort the words according to their pattern. You would record the student's performance on the grade book page entitled "Good readers pronounce words accurately and automatically." Perhaps you recorded a student's reading rate; that could go there as well. You have another page in your grade book labeled "Good readers learn new words and refine the meanings of known ones. On this page, record any evidence of new word learning such as vocabulary tests, dictionary work, and word usage activities. This allows for a more fine-tuned evaluation of a student's performance. Instead of assessing "reading" in a vague and general way, as I once did, you can see a pattern of student strengths and weaknesses. This can be easily translated into a report card checklist or narrative.

Grade books should not just contain number grades or percentage. This tends to limit the kind of information that you can include. How can you describe fluent reading or the quality of a retelling in terms of a number? Describing student performance in terms of letters such as A, B, C, and D can also be somewhat limiting. Do you really want to evaluate a student's participation in discussion as a letter grade? Consider using a simple coding system in addition to numbers and letters: A plus mark means good performance, a check mark means adequate performance, and a minus signals below-average work. If your rubrics include a point system, record the student score with the total number of points that could be earned. For example, if a rubric has a total of 10 points, and a student achieved 6, do not take the time to translate this into a percent score. Simply record it as 6/10. Record rubric ratings that are descriptive as opposed to numerical. For example, if you used "Very effective," "Effective," "Slightly effective," and "Not effective" on a rubric, abbreviate these and record them in your grade book. This allows you to record many more good reader and writer behaviors in your grade book—and, as a result, to arrive at a more complete picture of a student's strengths and weaknesses.

MAKING TIME
FOR INDIVIDUAL READING ASSESSMENT

Assessment is the basis for making decisions about the whole class as well as individual students. At the close of an instructional activity, a teacher or tutor generally has an idea of the progress of the class and can pinpoint which students are having difficulty. The problem is finding time in a busy day to assess those individuals who are struggling, to determine what is the problem, and to decide how it can be remedied. How can a busy teacher or tutor concentrate on one student? What about the rest of the class? Won't they get out of control?

These are very valid questions, whether you are talking about a class of 27 students or a tutoring group of 5. An important component of assessment is establishing methods of classroom management that give teachers and tutors time to deal with individuals. Although there are no easy answers, teachers and tutors can employ two management practices to provide time for individual assessment. The first is to set up the practice of individual silent reading. The second is to construct student interest centers throughout the classroom.

Setting Up the Practice of Individual Silent Reading

If all the students are engaged in silently reading books of their own choosing, the teacher or tutor can use this time to work with a single student. Unfortunately, many students are not used to reading on their own. They may sit still for a short period of time, but then they begin to act up. The teacher or tutor becomes the disciplinarian who maintains order, and thus has no time to work with individuals. This can be avoided if teachers or tutors include individual silent reading as a daily activity beginning with the very first day of class. Set up rules for acceptable behavior during this period and enforce them. If your students are not used to reading for long periods, begin with very short time segments and then gradually increase these. For example, Glenn began with five-minute silent reading periods for his third graders, because a very short period was all they could manage. He gradually increased the time, and by November, the students were happily occupied for 20 minutes at a time.

Stock your room with all sorts of reading materials at all sorts of difficulty levels. Students who might not read a book might become engrossed in magazines, store catalogues, brochures, programs from sports events, comic books, or newspapers. And don't forget the computer and all the materials that students can find to read on the World Wide Web. Allow students to choose what they want to read. Perhaps there is a wonderful book that you loved and nobody has picked it up. Or perhaps your students are reading some books that you find trivial, and you feel driven to move them to more challenging material. Resist the temptation to force a change, however. Just be happy they are reading! Offer and promote other books as choices, but allow the students to say "no." When students are ready for more challenging material, they will make that step on their own. The whole point is to have students quietly occupied in a worthwhile endeavor to give you some time for interacting with individual students.

Constructing Student Interest Centers

Let me describe a fifth-grade classroom I recently visited. In addition to the typical accessories of desks, bookcases, bulletin boards, and so forth, there were four centers located in different parts of the room. First, there was a writing center stocked with different styles and colors of writing paper, and with a variety of pens and markers. The writing center also contained heavier paper for making book covers and for providing illustrations. An index card file contained many ideas for writing stories or nonfiction selections. A computer and printer were prominent parts of the writing center. Second, there was a sports center stocked with books and magazines about many different sports—familiar ones as well as less known ones, such as rugby and curling. The sports center included biographies of sports figures and was decorated with their pictures. The third center was a travel center stocked with books and travel brochures about foreign countries. There was information about modes of travel ranging from riding camels to space travel. A computer was part of the travel center, and a booklet listed a variety of travel Web sites that students could access. The fourth center was an animal center filled with information about wild and domestic animals. Several stuffed animals adorned this center, which was appropriately located next to the class aquarium.

Centers like these provide motivating activities for students to engage in, thereby freeing a teacher or tutor for other things. As for individual silent reading, the teacher or tutor needs to set up and enforce rules for center use. It is also unrealistic to believe that centers like the ones I described can be set up right at the beginning of school. A teacher or tutor needs to "start small" with one center, and gradually add to the number of centers and the materials included in each.

I asked Emory, the fifth-grade teacher, where he had acquired all the materials that stocked his centers. He laughed and admitted that he and his wife were "rummage sale junkies," and that most of the materials had been bought for very little at rummage sales and flea markets. He also explained that the four centers had evolved over a period of two years. As peers and acquaintances learned what he was doing, they contributed materials. The students also donated books and items to the centers. The class members wanted a fifth center (although Emory admitted he had no idea where he would put it) and were involved in deciding its theme. The two most popular choices were jungles and music stars. I often wonder what was the final decision!

SUMMARY

- Assessment and instruction cannot be separated. Both are based upon an understanding of good reader behaviors.
- The teacher or tutor identifies what is being taught and assessed (i.e., the goal of the lesson) in terms of good reader behaviors. A reading selection is not the goal of a lesson; it is the tool that the teacher or tutor uses to develop good literacy behaviors. The teacher or tutor identifies, collects, and records evidence about student performance. This evidence is relevant to the good reader behavior that is the focus of the lesson.
- The teacher or tutor analyzes the evidence using either written or mental rubrics. Rubrics are procedures used to analyze evidence; they function best if they are simple in design and application. Teachers and tutors should construct rubrics with their students. As a result of analyzing evidence, a teacher or tutor makes instructional decisions about future class activities and about the progress of individual children.

• The teacher or tutor should share good reader behaviors, the lesson focus, and the assessment with students. The teacher or tutor should model the thinking processes that underlie good reader behaviors.

• Teachers and tutors align their instruction and assessment with district or state standards or outcomes. They work either forward from district or state standards to the reading selection or activity, or backward from the reading selection or activity to the district or state standards. They match general district or state standards to specific good reader behaviors and choose appropriate activities for developing them.

• There are various ways of making assessment manageable. For example, do not assess everything students do. Assess only important activities and limit these to two or three a week. Set up simple procedures for recording your observations.

• Maintain reading portfolios for noting individual student progress.

• If a report card format is limiting, consider adding a checklist or a narrative report. Organize the grade book into good reader and writer behaviors.

• A teacher or tutor can arrange time for individual assessment by setting up daily individual silent reading and by providing student interest centers.

ACTIVITIES FOR DEVELOPING UNDERSTANDING

• Choose a selection in a basal reading textbook. Use the four-step process to design and assess a lesson.

• Examine the various instructional activities provided in a basal reading anthology manual. Tie these to the good reader behaviors.

• Obtain a list of state or district standards. Match the good reader behaviors in Chapter One to these standards.

• Locate a list of grade-specific pupil performance expectations. Match these to the good reader behaviors in Chapter One.

• Design a rubric for assessing a good reader behavior.

• Choose a specific grade level and discuss with your peers which good reader behaviors would be most important at that level.

• Complete the self-evaluation form provided on the next page.

Teacher or Tutor Self-Evaluation

I focus my instruction and assessment on good reader behaviors.

> Regularly   Occasionally   A future goal

I plan what kind of evidence I will use to document good reader behaviors.

> Regularly   Occasionally   A future goal

I use rubrics to analyze evidence of good reader behaviors.

> Regularly   Occasionally   A future goal

I construct rubrics with my students.

> Regularly   Occasionally   A future goal

I tie instructional decisions about the class and about individuals to my evidence.

> Regularly   Occasionally   A future goal

I share good reader behaviors with students.

> Regularly   Occasionally   A future goal

I share my lesson focus and my assessment plans with students.

> Regularly   Occasionally   A future goal

I model good reader behaviors for my students.

> Regularly   Occasionally   A future goal

I use shortcuts to make literacy assessment manageable.

> Regularly   Occasionally   A future goal

I use a reading portfolio to document individual student progress in good reader behaviors.

> Regularly   Occasionally   A future goal

I report student performance in terms of good reader behaviors.

> Regularly   Occasionally   A future goal

I foster the practice of individual silent reading to allow time for individual assessment.

> Regularly   Occasionally   A future goal

I use student interest centers to allow time for individual assessment.

> Regularly   Occasionally   A future goal

THREE

The Informal Reading
Inventory Process

How Does It Address the Three Purposes
of Reading Assessment?

OVERVIEW OF THE INFORMAL READING
INVENTORY PROCESS

Teachers and tutors have always listened to students read orally. They have always asked questions after silent reading to decide whether the students understood what they read. In fact, it would be difficult to imagine a reading classroom where teachers or tutors did not listen to their students read and did not evaluate their comprehension.

Joy called Billy, a second grader, to sit next to her at a cozy table tucked into a corner at the front of the room. The other children were all busy at various tasks. Some were illustrating a story that the class had composed that morning. Others were engaged in reading books. Still others were gathered around a computer and eagerly interacting with a motivating piece of software. This gave Joy an opportunity to focus on an individual child.

Joy asked Billy to read aloud part of a story from their second-grade basal anthology. The story was called "One, Two, Three—Ah-Choo!" (Allen, 1989). After Billy finished, Joy asked him to retell what he had read, thanked him for reading to her, and sent him back to join his classmates at the computer.

A similar scenario occurred in David's fifth-grade classroom. The children were independently reading books of their choice, a daily event. As they did so, David moved around the room stopping occasionally to chat with a student. He paused at Cissy's desk and inquired whether she was enjoying her book, *Walk Two Moons* by Sharon Creech (1994). She enthusiastically said that she was. David then told her to continue silently reading the next several pages. When she finished, he asked Cissy to retell the events on those pages, thanked her for talking with him, and moved on to another student.

Larissa met with Carl, a seventh grader, during his study period. She chose an upper middle school selection from a published collection of passages at different grade levels. She asked Carl to read aloud a selection entitled "Biddy Mason," a true account of a slave who gained her freedom and became a wealthy and respected citizen (Leslie & Caldwell, 2001). After asking Carl questions to evaluate his comprehension, Larissa chose an easier passage about the soccer star Pélé, and repeated the process.

These are not unusual situations to encounter in a reading classroom. In fact, listening to students read and asking them about their reading are very common occurrences. Why are they so common? Because teachers and tutors realize that these are powerful assessment tools that can offer valuable information on the three purposes of reading assessment discussed in Chapter One: identifying good reader behaviors, determining a student's reading level, and documenting evidence of progress on the part of the student.

Joy and Billy

Let's return to Joy and Billy. What was Joy assessing as Billy orally read the selection "One, Two, Three-Ah-Choo!"? There were several things. Joy was interested in Billy's accuracy in pronouncing words. Was he able to pronounce words appropriate for second grade? Joy was also concerned about his fluency. Did he read the selection not only accurately, but at an appropriate pace and with some expression? Finally, and perhaps most importantly, she wanted to know whether Billy was able to understand what he read.

What criteria did Joy use to evaluate Billy's fluency? She paid attention to his rate of reading and his voice intonation. Although Billy paused before some words, most of his reading was smooth and expressive. He paid attention to punctuation signals and was quite animated when reading dialogue. Did Billy make the text sound meaningful? He did. Was he enjoyable to listen to? He was.

What about Billy's pronunciation accuracy? Let's look at how Billy read the text. I have divided the selection into short segments. On the left, I provide the original text; on the right, I show how Billy read it. To make it easy for you to notice the difference between the actual text and Billy's reading, I have also underlined Billy's mispronunciations, word additions, and word omissions.*

Text	**Billy's Reading**
Fur and Feathers	*Fun and Feathers*
Wally Springer had a problem. He had many allergies. Dust made him sneeze. Feathers made him sneeze. Now he had just found out his puppy made him sneeze.	Wally Spriger had a problem. He had many I don't know that word so I'll skip it. Dust made him snooze no it's sneeze. Feathers made him sneeze. Now he had found out his puppy made him sneeze.
"The doctor says you are allergic to animal fur," said his mother. "And I'm afraid your allergy shots won't help."	"The doctor says you are algic to animal fur," said his mother. "And I'm afraid your _____ shots won't help."
"Why me?" he groaned. "Other people can have dogs or cats. But not me. I'm allergic to pets." He took his medicine and made a face.	"Why me?" he grumbled. "Other people can have dogs or cats. But I can't not me. I'm allegic to pets." He took his medicine and made a face.
"Not all pets have fur and feathers," said his mother. "We'll just have to find one that won't make you sneeze."	"Not all pets have fur and feathers," said his mother. "We'll just have to find one that won't make you sneeze."

*The selection is from Allen, M. N. (1989). One, two, three—ah-choo! In D. Alvermann, C. A. Bridge, B. A. Schmidt, L. W. Searfoss, & P. Winograd (Eds.), *Come back here, crocodile* (pp. 92–100). Lexington, MA: Heath. Copyright 1989 by Marjorie N. Allen. Reprinted by permission.

No More Sneezes

Wally stared at the fishbowl. Inside, four tadpoles wiggled and swam. They swam around and around. "Tadpoles," said Wally, "are boring."

"Just wait," said his mother. Wally waited and waited. At least tadpoles didn't make him sneeze.

After a few weeks the tadpoles began to sprout legs.

Their tails became shorter and shorter. They changed color. After a few more weeks, they stopped swimming and sat on a rock in the fishbowl.

Now they were frogs. Singing frogs. Jumping frogs. "I can't stand it," said Wally's father. "They sing all night long. They sound like fingernails scratching on a blackboard."

Wally didn't like the noise either. The frogs had kept him awake the whole night.

"Frogs are all right," said Wally. "But snakes are better."

He found a home for his frogs in the pond. There he picked up a beautiful banded Water Snake. She was creamy white with dark bands. She wrapped herself around Wally's arm. Wally called her Sheila. "Snakes don't eat in winter," he told his parents. "They sleep all winter."

When winter came, Wally took Sheila out of her terrarium and put her in a cloth bag. He put the bag in the refrigerator.

No More Sneezes

Wally stared at the fishbowl. Inside, four tadpoles <u>wigged</u> and <u>swimmed</u> swam. They swam around and around. "Tadpoles," said Wally, "are boring."

"Just wait," said his mother. Wally waited and waited. At <u>lease</u> tadpoles didn't make him sneeze.

After a few weeks the tadpoles began to <u>sprut</u> legs.

Their tails became shorter and shorter. They changed <u>their</u> color. After a few more weeks, they stopped <u>their</u> swimming and sat on a rock in the fishbowl.

Now they were frogs. <u>Stinging</u> frogs. Jumping frogs. "I can't stand it," said Wally's father. "They <u>sting</u> all night long. They sound like <u>fingers</u> scratching on a blackboard."

Wally didn't like the noise either. The frogs had kept him awake the whole night.

"Frogs are all right," said Wally. "But snakes are better."

He found a home for his frogs in the pond. There he picked up a beautiful <u>banding</u> Water Snake. She was <u>cremmy</u> white with dark bands. She <u>wound</u> herself around Wally's arm. Wally called her <u>She-eye-la</u>. "Snakes don't eat in winter," he told his parents. "They sleep all winter."

When winter came, Wally took Sheila out of her <u>terrium</u> and put her in a <u>clothes</u> bag. He put the bag in the <u>referator</u>.

"A snake in my refrigerator!" his mother cried.

"It's all right," said Wally. She's way in the back. You'll forget she's there. She'll sleep all winter." Wally was right.

"A snake in my <u>refregator</u>!" his mother cried.

"It's all right," said Wally. "She's way in the back. You'll forget she's there. She'll sleep all winter." Wally was right.

What criteria did Joy use to assess Billy's accuracy in reading the selection? As Billy read, Joy recorded his errors on her copy of the text. After Billy returned to his computer activities, Joy counted the number of words in the selection. There were 328. She also counted Billy's mispronunciations, word omissions, and word additions. Billy made a total of 28 errors. Joy translated this into a percentage. She subtracted 28 from 328 and then divided 300 by 328. Billy's percentage of accuracy on this second-grade selection was 91%. Based upon this, Joy determined that this selection and others like it probably represented an instructional reading level for Billy. That is, Billy could read second-grade words, but not independently. He would need some instructional support if second-grade material were to represent a truly meaningful and enjoyable experience for him.

Joy also noted some good reader behaviors on Billy's part. For example, many of Billy's errors did not change the meaning of the text, but actually reflected his understanding of it. For example, Billy inserted *their* before *color* and *swimming*. He inserted *I can't* after *but* in the phrase *But not me*. He substituted *grumbled* for *groaned*. Clearly Billy was attending to meaning. Good readers always focus on meaning even when attempting to pronounce an infamiliar word. Billy also attempted to match letters and sounds. He was not a wild guesser who offered any alternative for an unknown word. His mispronunciations contained many of the same letters and sounds as the original word, such as *allegic* for *allergic*, *wigged* for *wiggled*, and *sprut* for *sprout*.

After Billy read, Joy assessed his comprehension. She asked him to retell the selection and took brief notes on what he said. Here is Billy's retelling.

"Wally wanted a pet but he couldn't have a dog 'cause he sneezed. He got tadpoles and they just went round and round. Then they got legs. Then they turned into frogs. They began stinging people so he dumped them in a pond. Then he got a snake and put her in a bag to sleep during the winter."

Joy felt that Billy demonstrated acceptable understanding of the selection. He described Wally's problem and recalled the sequence of pets from tadpoles to frogs to snake. He also remembered why Wally did not like the tadpoles and frogs, even though describing the frogs as "stinging people" was the result of his mispronunciation of *singing*.

Joy spent approximately 15 minutes listening to Billy read. She spent another 10 minutes counting errors, determining a percentage, reviewing his errors, and rereading his retelling. What did Joy gain from these 25 minutes? She had an approximate reading level for Billy—second grade. She could compare this level with later efforts in order to document progress. She also noted some important good reader behaviors on Billy's part.

David and Cissy

What did David learn about Cissy's reading as a result of his brief pause at her desk during independent reading? The book that she was reading, *Walk Two Moons*, was part of the classroom library. No grade level was attached to the book, but David considered it appropriate for fifth graders, many of whom had already read and enjoyed it. Cissy was reading Chapter 15 when David asked her to retell what she had read. As Cissy retold the events that spanned several pages, David skimmed these same pages as he listened to Cissy.

> "They were sitting in the river because it was real hot and this boy told them it was private property and he was kind of like threatening them. Then a snake bit Gram. It was a water moccasin. And Gramps cut the bite and the boy helped to suck out the poison. They went to the hospital and Gramps gave the boy some money. Gramps stayed with Gram right in the hospital bed. And Sal and the boy start making up to be friends."

David asked Cissy how she would have felt at that point. She replied that she couldn't understand how Gram could be so calm and keep holding the snake. She also predicted that Gram might die, and that would be terrible for Sal, who loved her grandparents so much. She obviously wanted to keep on reading, so David thanked her and moved on to another student. In the few minutes that David spent with Cissy, he learned that she could silently read text that was appropriate for fifth grade; that she understood what she read; and, perhaps most importantly, that she was deeply involved with the characters in the novel.

Larissa and Carl

What did Larissa want to learn about Carl's reading? Carl was not doing well in many of his classes, and Larissa wanted to determine whether this could be due to difficulties with reading. Like Joy, Larissa noted Carl's fluency. For the most part, Carl read very slowly, stopping often to figure out unfamiliar words. He read in a low monotone and often ignored punctuation signals. Larissa was also interested in his ability to identify words at an upper middle school level. Like Joy, she marked Carl's word pronunciation errors, word omissions, and word additions on her copy of the text. She used the number of words in the selection and the number of Carl's errors to arrive at an accuracy level. Carl made a total of 95 errors while reading a 750-word passage. His accuracy level was 87%, a frustration level. This suggested to Larissa that Carl could not yet successfully handle upper middle school text. Carl's comprehension after reading also verified that this level of material was too difficult for him. He was only able to answer three of ten questions correctly, for a comprehension score of 30%. Few good reader behaviors were evident as Carl struggled with "Biddy Mason." For this reason, Larissa decided to repeat the process with an easier selection. Larissa had indeed discovered that reading difficulties were probably contributing to Carl's problems in school. Now she had to determine the level of text that Carl could read and understand.

Joy, David, and Larissa all used elements of what is known as the *informal reading inventory process* to assess their students' reading growth. Each asked the student to read, orally or silently; each asked the student to retell or to answer questions about the reading; and each used criteria to evaluate fluency, word pronunciation, and comprehension.

The informal reading inventory process (abbreviated from here on as the IRI process) is generally used with an individual student. The student reads a passage at a specific grade level, either orally or silently. For example, Billy read second-grade text, Cissy read text appropriate for fifth grade, and Carl struggled through an upper middle school selection. If the student reads orally, the teacher or tutor records and counts any oral reading errors, as Joy and Larissa did. After reading, the student retells the selection and/or answers questions about its content. Both Joy and David employed retelling, and Larissa asked specific questions.

The IRI process is what its full name implies—an informal assessment tool. Therefore, it allows for flexibility on the part of the teacher or tutor who can adapt administration to meet their needs. The IRI process can be an effective and sensitive measure for collecting evidence about a student's reading. A teacher or tutor can use the process to address all three categories of reading assessment. The teacher or tutor can determine the level of text that a student can read successfully. Both Joy and David were able to do this. On the other hand, Larissa discovered that Carl was unable to read at his middle school level, and she had to probe further. The IRI process can be used to suggest the presence or absence of good reader behaviors. Again, both Joy and David observed good reader behaviors in their students, while Larissa did not because of the difficulty level of the text. The IRIR process can also be used to measure an individual student's progress. It allows a teacher or tutor to compare student performance at different points in time, such as before tutoring begins and later on during the tutoring process.

DIFFERENCES BETWEEN THE IRI PROCESS AND AN INFORMAL READING INVENTORY

We must distinguish between the *IRI process* and an *Informal Reading Inventory*. The IRI process can be used with any passage to determine whether a student can read and comprehend it, to indicate good reader behaviors, and to note student progress. A teacher or tutor can use selections from a basal reading anthology, as Joy did, or a trade book, as David did. The teacher or tutor can also use a content area textbook. The IRI process allows a teacher or tutor to evaluate a student in an authentic reading situation. The student reads selections that represent what he or she encounters daily in the classroom or in personal reading. In this chapter, we are primarily focusing on the IRI process.

An informal reading inventory (abbreviated from here on as an IRI) is a published instrument that consists of a variety of passages at different grade levels. Larissa used a published IRI to assess Carl's reading. Each passage is followed by questions to ask the student. IRI grade levels usually span preprimer, primer, and first through sixth or eighth grades. Some IRIs contain high school passages. All IRIs offer detailed directions for recording and scoring student responses.

You can use the IRI process with a published IRI, as Larissa did, or you can use it with a passage that you select, as Joy and David did. You may find that a published IRI is more convenient. It includes a copy of the passage for the student to read and a copy for you to write on. It provides scoring guidelines on each teacher copy. Appendix 3.3 provides a list of published IRIs that you may wish to examine. On the other hand, using the IRI process with selections that you choose allows you to evaluate a student's performance in the materials you are actually using in your classroom. Graded passages from an IRI may or may not parallel your classroom materials. For example, the "Biddy Mason" passage that Carl read was probably representative of the general difficulty level of upper middle school selections. However, it may not have been similar in content and format to the literature selections that Carl was expected to read and understand.

Published IRIs offer different assessment options. Some provide graded word lists. Others include procedures to determine whether the passage is about a familiar topic. Most IRIs offer some process for analyzing the oral reading errors that a student makes. Some IRIs assess comprehension by scoring the student's retelling as well as scoring answers to questions. As you become more familiar with the IRI process, you will be able to use these options with any passage as a possible source of evidence about a student's reading. The more options you use, the more you learn. Unfortunately, it is also true that the more options you use, the more time these take. A short focused assessment may offer more information than a detailed series of IRI options.

USING THE IRI PROCESS TO DETERMINE READING LEVELS

Can a student successfully read the content area textbook used in his or her classroom? Can the student read a selection from a basal anthology or a novel that is part of the class curriculum? The IRI process allows to you to determine whether a student can successfully read and comprehend the material used in his or her classroom. You can ask the student to read a representative selection from the textbook, anthology, or novel, and use the IRI process to find out whether he or she is successful in doing so.

The IRI process also allows you to determine whether a student can read and comprehend passages at higher or lower levels of difficulty than the classroom materials. You can use the IRI process to determine the highest level of text that the student can handle successfully. Many students can read material that is more difficult than their classroom texts. Unfortunately, many others can only handle passages that are much easier than their classroom materials. It is important for you as a teacher or tutor to know this. It helps you to decide whether a student has a reading problem. Students who are unable to read selections appropriate for their grade level may have difficulties with reading that can have a negative impact on their school performance.

Knowing your students' reading levels also allows you to effectively group students of like ability. You can then offer instruction that is clearly targeted to their needs. Perhaps you want to set up a book club format where a small group of students reads the same text and discusses it among themselves. The IRI process can help you to determine if all group members can successfully handle the material.

There are basically two purposes for using the IRI process. Most teachers and tutors use the IRI process to find out whether students can read and com-

---

IRI Process Levels

Independent: The student can read and comprehend without assistance.

Instructional: The student can read and comprehend with assistance.

Frustration: The student is unable to read with adequate word identification accuracy and comprehension.

---

prehend material at their chronological grade level. A teacher or tutor chooses a selection that is appropriate for that grade level and uses the IRI process to determine whether a student can handle it successfully. The second purpose is to determine the highest level that a student can manage. Of course, asking a student to read several passages of different difficulty levels takes much more time, and busy teachers or tutors often leave this more detailed assessment to reading specialists or other diagnosticians in their school or district. However, it is important for teachers and tutors to understand the full scope of the IRI process.

The IRI process provides two possible scores: a score for *word identification accuracy* when the student reads orally, and a *comprehension* score. Word identification accuracy scores and comprehension scores are then used to determine three possible levels for the student: the *independent* level, the *instructional* level, and the *frustration* level. The independent level is the grade level at which the student can read without teacher or tutor guidance. You are probably reading at an independent level when you choose a novel for pleasure reading. *Walk Two Moons* (Creech, 1994) probably represented an independent reading level for Cissy. The instructional level is the level at which a student can read with teacher or tutor support. Second-grade text was an instructional level for Billy. Usually the instructional level is the level used for reading instruction. Perhaps sections of this book represent your instructional reading level. They may contain some concepts that are new to you. Because of their unfamiliarity, you may need to reread certain pages at a slower pace and pose questions about their content. The frustration level is the level that is too difficult and results in a frustrating experience for the student. I would guess that the directions for an income tax form or the contents of an insurance policy represent a frustration level for you, as they do for me.

If a student reads a passage orally, the IRI process provides two scores: an independent, instructional, or frustration level for word identification accuracy, and an independent, instructional, or frustration level for comprehension. If the student reads the passage silently, there is only one score: an independent, instructional, or frustration level for comprehension.

Most published IRIs use similar scoring criteria. A word identification accuracy score of 98%–100% represents an independent level. If all word identification errors are counted, as Joy and Larissa did, a score of 90%–97% represents an instructional level (Leslie & Caldwell, 2001). If you only count errors that change meaning, 95%–97% represents an instructional level. A score below 90% indicates a frustration level. For comprehension, a score of 90%–100% on the questions suggests an independent level, and a score of 70%–89% represents the instructional level. A score below 70% signals a frustration level.

Where do the numbers above come from? You get the numbers for word identification accuracy by counting the number of errors (often called *miscues*) the student makes while orally reading the passage. You get the num-

---

Scoring Guidelines for the IRI Process

Word Identification Accuracy

Independent level:
   98%–100% word identification accuracy

Instructional level:
   90%–97% word identification accuracy if all errors are counted
   95%–97% word identification accuracy if only meaning change
      errors are counted

Frustration level:
   Less than 90% word identification accuracy if all errors are
      counted
   Less than 95% word identification accuracy if only meaning
      change errors are counted

Comprehension

Independent level: 90%–100% accuracy in answering questions

Instructional level: 70%–89% accuracy in answering questions

Frustration level: Less than 70% accuracy in answering questions

bers for comprehension by counting the number of questions that the student answers correctly. If you ask a student to retell, as Joy and David did, you do not get a numerical score from the retelling; you must evaluate the quality of the retelling on your own.

How does the IRI process play out? To determine whether a student can read classroom materials, choose a representative passage from your content textbook, your basal anthology, or tradebooks used for instruction. If the student is successful in identifying words and comprehending the selection, you have your answer. If, on the other hand, the student is unsuccessful, you know that classroom materials may be too difficult.

Denis was in third grade and newly arrived in his school. His teacher wanted to determine whether he could handle materials that were used in the classroom. She asked him to orally read several pages of a third-grade selection from the school's basal reading anthology. She recorded his word identification errors. When he finished reading, she asked him several questions about the selection. Denis was successful, scoring at an instructional level for both word identification accuracy and comprehension. His teacher was relieved that Denis would probably be able to keep up with his peers.

Perhaps you are interested in finding the highest level that a student can read successfully. Choose a beginning passage. If this passage represents an independent level for the student, move to the next higher passage. Keep moving up until the student reaches a frustration level. This does not take as long as you might think. Usually two to three passages are sufficient to establish the highest instructional level.

After several weeks of school, it became evident to Holly's teacher that she was not able to keep up with her third-grade peers. The teacher asked Holly to read a short third-grade selection. Holly scored at a frustration level for both word identification accuracy and comprehension. The teacher then selected a second-grade selection for Holly to read. Holly scored at a frustration level for word identification accuracy and at an instructional level for comprehension. The teacher then chose a first-grade passage. Holly was successful at this level scoring at an instructional level, for word identification accuracy and at an independent level for comprehension. Holly's teacher placed Holly at a first-grade reading level. This represented a difference of two years from Holly's chronological grade placement, and her teacher immediately contacted the school reading specialist to arrange for additional reading instruction.

As you can see, one purpose of the IRI process is to determine whether a student can read and comprehend material that is appropriate for his or her grade level. A second purpose is to have the student read increasingly difficult passages to find his or her highest instructional level.

Finding the Highest Instructional Level

Choose a passage of suitable length.

If the student reads orally:

    Record word identification errors.

    Record comprehension.

    Determine independent, instructional, or frustration levels for word identification accuracy, for comprehension, and for the total passage.

If the student reads silently:

    Record comprehension.

    Determine independent, instructional, or frustration levels for comprehension.

If the student scores at an instructional level, move up to the next highest passage.

If the student scores at a frustration level, move down to the next lowest level.

Continue until the highest instructional level is reached.

Scoring Word Identification Accuracy

Finding the Accuracy Score

In order to score word identification accuracy and arrive at an independent, instructional, or frustration level, you must know the number of words in the passage. If you have a passage of 100 words and the student makes 5 errors, his or her word identification score is 95%—an instructional level. Unfortunately, few passages are so considerate to have exactly 100 words. If you are using a published IRI, the number of words in each passage is stated. If you are using your own passage, you have to count the number of words. When you are scoring word identification accuracy, the first step is to subtract the number of errors from the total number of words to arrive at the total number of correct words. Then divide the number of words read correctly by the total number of words. For example, Gloria read a 243-word passage and made 26 errors. She read 217 words correctly. Dividing 217 by 243 gives us .89 or 89%, a frustration level.

Types of Oral Reading Errors

What kind of errors do students make? They substitute or mispronounce words. For example, Ellie read *He helped to fix the bus* as *He hoped to find the bus*. Ellie made two errors, substituting *hoped* for *helped* and *find* for *fixed*. As noted earlier, such errors are often called miscues. Sometime these miscues are nonwords, such as *aminals* for *animals* or *hovy* for *heavy*. Remember Billy's attempts to pronounce *allergies* and *refrigerator*? Students often omit or add words. Glen read *They like to be in the sun* as *They like the sun*. Glen omitted three words: *to*, *be*, and *in*. Each omission counts as an error. Later on, he read *There are fish in lakes* as *There are a lot of fish in lakes*. Glen added three words: *a*, *lot*, and *of*. Each addition counts as an error. Each substitution, mispronunciation, omission, or addition counts for 1 point.

Counting Errors That Do Not Change Meaning

What if a substitution, omission, or addition does not alter the meaning of the passage? For example, a student reads *They saw a hen and cows* as *They saw hens and cows*. Is the omission of *a* and the substitution of *hens* for *hen* errors? The meaning of the passage is not really distorted. Some people feel very strongly that you should only count those errors that do change passage meaning, such as substituting *looked* for *liked* in the sentence *They liked petting the kittens*. Some people feel that you should not count any errors that are self-corrected. You have to decide how you feel about this. I recommend that you count all deviations from the text even if they do not change meaning. First, this represents a faster and more reliable scoring system. Deciding whether a miscue really changes meaning can take more time than you might like. And two people can violently disagree! What about self-corrections? Again, whether you count these is up to you. I generally count them as errors because each represents an initial misreading of a word.

What if Joy and Larissa had only counted errors that changed meaning? Billy made 16 errors that changed meaning, for an accuracy score of 95%. Carl made 53 errors that significantly changed meaning, for an accuracy score of 93%. If you only count meaning change errors, you have to adjust your scoring system. An instructional level is signaled by scores between 95% and 97%. So Billy still fell within the instructional range, and Carl was still at a frustration level.

Recording Oral Reading Errors with Check Marks

How do you record these errors or miscues on your copy of the student's text? The easiest and fastest way is simply to make a check mark when a miscue occurs. If the student omits two words, use two check marks; if a student adds three words, make three check marks; and so on. This will give you the total number of miscues, and you can figure out the word identification accuracy level.

Let's look at some of Billy's errors as described by check marks.

| | **Billy's Errors Marked** |
| **Billy's Reading** | **with Checks** |

Fun and *Feathers*

Wally <u>Spriger</u> had a problem. He had
many <u>I don't know that word so I'll</u>
<u>skip it</u>. Dust made him <u>snooze no it's</u>
sneeze. Feathers made him sneeze. Now
he had found out his puppy made him
sneeze.

   "The doctor says you are <u>algic</u> to
animal fur," said his mother. "And I'm
afraid your _____ shots won't help."

   "Why me?" he <u>grumbled</u>. "Other
people can have dogs or cats. But <u>I</u>
<u>can't</u> not me. I'm <u>allegic</u> to pets." He
took his medicine and made a face.

✓
Fur and Feathers

Wally Spri✓nger had a problem. He h✓ad
many all✓ergies. Dust made him snee✓ze.
Feathers made him sneeze. Now he had
just found out his puppy made him
sneeze.

   "The doctor says you are all✓ergic to
animal fur," sai✓d his mother. "And I'm
afraid your all✓ergy sh✓ots won't help."

   "Why me?" he groaned. "Other✓,
people can ha✓ve dogs or cats. But not✓
me. I'm all✓ergic to pets." He took his
medicine and made a face.

Recording Oral Reading Errors with a Coding System

The more traditional way to record errors is to indicate the type of each miscue. Was it a mispronunciation, a substitution, an omission, or an insertion?
All published IRIs suggest a coding system for indicating the type of miscue.
Let's return to Billy's reading and mark it with a more detailed recording system. Mispronunciations and substitutions are written above the word. Omissions are circled. Additions are written above the line and indicated with a
caret. Self-corrections are marked with a C.

Miscue Coding System

Omissions: Circle.

   It was a ⦸cold⦸ winter day.

Insertions: Insert the added word above a caret.
                        all
   John looked at ⌃ the toys in his room.

Substitutions or mispronunciations: Write above the word.
                                                well
   He knew the mouse lived in the wall.

Self-corrections: Mark with a C.
              holding C
   He was having ⌃ a birthday party.

Billy's Reading	Billy's Errors Marked with Traditional Coding

Fun and Feathers

Wally Spriger had a problem. He had many I don't know that word so I'll skip it. Dust made him snooze no it's sneeze. Feathers made him sneeze. Now he had found out his puppy made him sneeze.

"The doctor says you are algic to animal fur," said his mother. "And I'm afraid your _____ shots won't help."

"Why me?" he grumbled. "Other people can have dogs or cats. But I can't not me. I'm allegic to pets." He took his medicine and made a face.

Fun
Fur and Feathers

Spriger
Wally Springer had a problem. He had
snooze C
many (allergies) Dust made him sneeze.
Feathers made him sneeze. Now he had
(just) found out his puppy made him
sneeze.

algic
"The doctor says you are allergic to
animal fur," said his mother. "And I'm
afraid your (allergy) shots won't help."
grumbled
"Why me?" he groaned. "Other
I can't
people can have dogs or cats. But not ^
allegic
me. I'm allergic to pets." He took his
medicine and made a face.

Which system of recording errors is better? If you use check marks, should you feel guilty about not using a more descriptive recording system? I do not think so. Use the system that makes you comfortable. You have an entire professional career to grow into a descriptive recording system. The important thing is that you use the IRI process often. If you are uncomfortable or unsure of yourself, you probably won't. And you will miss an important method of assessing reading.

Students do other things while reading orally. They often repeat a word. Sometimes they hesitate before pronouncing a word. They often ignore punctuation. Should you code these as errors? Some published IRIs suggest that you should, but I do not agree. They do not alter the text, so they really do not represent errors (McKenna, 1983). You may note them if you wish, but you do not want the IRI process to become so detailed that you avoid using it. Arranging time for the IRI process with an individual student is often very difficult, so you want a process that is both effective and efficient.

Scoring Comprehension

The scoring process for comprehension questions is quite easy. Mark each question as correct or incorrect. Find out the total number correct, and divide by the total number of questions. Karla answered seven questions correctly out of possible eight. This translated into a score of 87%—an instructional level. Sometimes a student will answer part of a question. For example, Jake was asked to name two ways in which a virus differs from a cell. He was only able to name one. Should he receive half credit? Again, in the interests of an efficient IRI process, I suggest that you score an answer as either correct or incorrect and do not score partial credit. Of course, the best way is to avoid asking questions that require multiple answers!

Issues Regarding the IRI Process

Different Levels for Word Identification Accuracy and Comprehension

Students often score at different levels for word identification accuracy and comprehension, and a teacher or tutor needs to determine what is the total passage level. For example, when reading second-grade material, Holly scored at a frustration level for word identification accuracy and at an instructional level for comprehension. In first-grade text, her level was instructional for word identification accuracy and independent for comprehension. When this happens, choose the lower level as Holly's teacher did, determining that second grade represented a frustration level for Holly and first grade represented an instructional level.

It is always better to underestimate a student's reading level than to overestimate it. If you assign a level that is too high, you may miss the existence of a reading problem. For instance, Jerome consistently scored higher on comprehension than on word identification accuracy. If his teacher had assigned the comprehension level as his overall level, Jerome would have been placed as reading at his chronological level of fourth grade. However, he was at a frustration level for word identification accuracy in second-grade text. Assigning a fourth-grade level would have masked Jerome's very real problem with word identification.

There is another reason for underestimating reading level. You may be choosing instructional materials based upon that level. If a student cannot read the chosen material, substituting an easier book can be quite embarrassing to the student. It is much nicer to be able to say, "This book is too easy for you. Let's try one that is more difficult." The problem of under or overestimating levels will not be an issue if you assign total passage levels based upon the lower level attained in word identification accuracy and comprehension. It is my experience that this results in a realistic reading level in most cases.

Familiarity of Topic

The IRI process works most effectively with text on topics that are familiar to the student. You are trying to find the student's highest level. You can expect that the student will not perform as successfully when reading selections on unfamiliar topics. For example, Rosemary attained a strong third-grade level when reading about a birthday party. She did less well when reading an expository third-grade selection about the procedure of carding and spinning wool. Similarly, students tend to do better when reading stories or narratives than when reading textbooks or other expository materials. For these reasons, begin with narrative selections on familiar topics, unless you are specifically interested in a student's ability to read a content-area textbook.

How can you tell whether a passage is about a familiar topic? Preprimer, primer, first-grade, and second-grade selections tend to be written on topics familiar to that age group. This is true of published IRIs as well as textbooks written for younger students. By third grade, however, more and more unfamiliar topics are introduced to students. Many IRIs suggest various prereading procedures, such as asking a student to define key concepts or to predict from the title what the selection will be about. Sometimes the easiest way is to simply ask the student what he or she knows about the topic. When asked what she knew about sheep and wool, Rosemary responded, "Not very much. I know a sheep is an animal, and I think wool goes into a sweater." Often a teacher or tutor will know a student so well that it will be easy to select a passage on a familiar topic.

Length of Passage

If you are using a published IRI, the length of the passage is not an issue. However, if you are selecting a passage from a trade book or a basal reading textbook, you need to be conscious of how long it is. As always, classrooms are busy places, and you will not have unlimited time for individual assessment! It is probably better to choose only part of a selection for the IRI process instead of the entire selection. How much should you select? A long passage requires more administration time, and some students are threatened by having to read lengthy selections on their own. On the other hand, too short a selection does not provide enough evidence to make valid instructional decisions. The accompanying box suggests guidelines for selecting passages of appropriate length. These are not rigid guidelines. Remember that the IRI process is an informal procedure, and you are free to adapt it to your own needs.

> ## Guidelines for Passage Length
>
> *Preprimer level*: 40–60 words
> *Primer level*: 60–100 words
> *First-grade level*: 100–200 words
> *Second-grade level*: 200–300 words
> *Third-grade level and above*: 300–400 words

Materials and Preparations for the IRI Process

You will need a student copy of the selection and a copy for you to record word identification errors and answers to comprehension questions. If you are using a published IRI, examiner copies are provided for you to duplicate. If you are using your own selection, you will need to duplicate the student's copy. Published IRIs provide questions for you to ask, with space for you to record the student's answers. If you are using your own selection, you should write the questions beforehand. A clipboard to write on is also convenient.

Many teachers and tutors like to tape IRI sessions, so they can go back and verify their marking of students' errors and answers to questions. I have used the IRI process many times, and I still find that a tape is helpful. Does this make a student nervous? If you explain that you are doing this because you can't remember everything, this often helps to reduce any concern on the part of the student. If you place the tape recorder off to one side, students quickly forget about it. Many students enjoy "playing" with the recorder for a short time—saying their name and the date into the recorder, and playing it back as a test.

Where should you test a student? Obviously a quiet place is most desirable. Noise can be distracting to both you and the student. Many teachers and tutors test students at the back of a classroom while the other students are engaged in relatively quiet activities. How long does the process take? This varies quite a bit from student to student, depending upon your purpose for using the IRI process. If you are using it to determine whether a student can read a specific text, as Joy did, it probably won't take too long. If you are attempting to find the student's highest reading level, it will take longer. Sometimes you only need to administer one or two passages in order to find that level. Sometimes you will have to administer more. The nice thing about the IRI process is that you can adapt it to your needs. There is no reason why you can't stretch the process over several short sessions. In fact, for some students, that might be most desirable.

USING THE IRI PROCESS TO IDENTIFY GOOD READER BEHAVIORS

Fluency

As noted in Chapter One, good readers read fluently—that is, accurately, quickly, and expressively. When a teacher or tutor asks a student to read orally, this presents a wonderful opportunity for evaluating the presence or absence of fluency. Students who are not fluent are choppy readers. They pause often, repeat words, and stumble over them. They read in a monotone and use little expression. Other students race through the text, ignoring punctuation marks and sentence breaks. Their goal seems to be to complete the reading as soon as possible. You can judge the presence of absence of fluency simply by listening to a student read orally. You will know a fluent reader when you hear one!

Another opportunity offered by the IRI process to evaluate fluency is to determine reading rate as measured by words per minute. Determining rate of reading is discussed in Chapter Six.

Retelling

Some published IRIs ask a student to retell the contents of the selection before answering questions. They generally provide scoring grids of some sort where the examiner marks the ideas that the student recalled. You can use this option with any passage. After the student has finished reading either orally or silently, ask the student to tell all that he or she can remember. Underline on your copy the parts that the student remembered. If you have tape-recorded the session, you can listen to the retelling to verify your initial impressions.

How should you evaluate a retelling? You can do this by asking yourself several questions about the retelling. Was it complete? In other words, did the student remember the important ideas? You can't expect a student to remember everything, but he or she should be able to recall the main points. In the case of narratives, the student should remember the main character, the problem, and how the problem was resolved. In the case of expository text, the student should remember the main ideas and a few supporting details. Retelling as an assessment option is discussed more fully in Chapter Seven.

A retelling can suggest the presence of good reader behaviors. For example, good readers determine what is important in the text; they summarize and reorganize ideas in the text; and they make inferences and predictions. Usually a retelling does not add a lot of time to the IRI process. A retelling is certainly more authentic than answering questions, because it represents what people actually do when they read. Using simple checklists such as the ones provided here to evaluate retelling helps to remind you what you are looking for.

Retelling Checklist for Narrative Text

_____ Identified main character (or characters)

_____ Identified the character's problem

_____ Identified the setting

_____ Described the resolution

_____ Included steps for arriving at the resolution

_____ Made inferences

_____ Retold sequentially

_____ Retold accurately

_____ Offered personal reaction

Retelling Checklist for Expository Text

_____ Identified main ideas

_____ Identified supporting details

_____ Made inferences

_____ Retold sequentially

_____ Retold accurately

_____ Offered personal reaction

Look-Backs

In many published IRIs, the student is expected to answer the comprehension questions without looking back in the text. However, for students who are in third grade or above, this might underestimate their comprehension ability. Think about why a student might not be able to answer a question. Perhaps the student did not comprehend during reading. On the other hand, perhaps the student comprehended but then forgot what he or she read. Using *look-backs* can help you distinguish between the two. If a student does not know an answer or provides an incorrect one, ask him or her to look back in the text to locate the missing information. If a student can do this, you can assume that the initial error was due to forgetting, not lack of comprehension. However, if the student is unsuccessful in looking back, the problem is probably lack of comprehension.

Good readers use look-backs most of the time. In particular, look-backs reflect the good reader behavior of monitoring comprehension and repairing comprehension breakdowns. Rarely are people expected to read something once and then answer questions. Even on standardized tests, students are allowed to look back in paragraphs while they choose their answers. For this reason, I suggest that you employ look-backs as a regular part of the IRI process. Look-backs are discussed more fully in Chapter Seven.

USING THE IRI PROCESS TO DETERMINE PROGRESS

In order to determine whether a student has made progress, you need a starting point. You need to know the student's beginning level so you can compare this with the student's level at a later time. Many districts are designing tutoring programs for students who are having difficulties in reading. The IRI process can be used for an analysis of reading status prior to an intervention program and of gains made following the program. The IRI process can also be used by a classroom teacher to measure growth throughout the school year. Several studies suggest that the IRI process is sensitive to both immediate and long-term change (Leslie & Allen, 1999; Caldwell, Fromm, & O'Connor, 1997–1998; Regner, 1992; Glass, 1989).

You can use the IRI process in two ways to measure student growth. One way is to administer the same passage for the pre- and postintervention assessment. The teacher or tutor should find the student's highest instructional level and then readminister the same passage later. A second option is to use two different passages that are as similar as possible. The passages should be at the same readability level, have the same structure (narrative or expository) and be of the same level of familiarity.

Two reading teachers designed a tutorial program for second- through fifth-grade students who were experiencing difficulties in reading (Caldwell et al., 1998). They began by finding the highest instructional level for each student in familiar narrative text. The highest instructional levels ranged from preprimer through second grade, although several children could not successfully read at the preprimer level. The tutoring program consisted of four 30-minute sessions each week and lasted from October to May.

In May, the students were asked to reread the initial passage that represented their highest instructional level in October. If they were successful, they were then asked to read a passage at the next highest level. This process was continued until they reached their highest instructional levels following eight months of tutoring. The average gain was two levels for both word identification accuracy and comprehension!

Some school districts are using the IRI process to measure individual growth at the beginning of the year, at the midpoint, and at the end. Admittedly, this takes a lot of time on the part of classroom teachers, but the benefits are well worth it. Some schools use creative ways to find time for the IRI process. For example, combining two classrooms for a project of some sort frees one teacher to work with individual students. Some districts have trained parents or aides to administer the passages and ask the questions. In one school, university undergraduates in a reading practicum course administered the IRI process to students.

GROUP ADMINISTRATION OF THE IRI PROCESS

The IRI process is primarily used with individuals; however, it can be adapted for group use. A teacher or tutor will not find it as sensitive a process when employed with groups, but it can provide information about students' probable reading levels.

Jeanne, an enterprising fourth-grade teacher with a large class, knew that she would have to find some sort of shortcut in order to evaluate the progress of all her students. She did not have an aide, and there were few parent volunteers in her classroom. Also, there was no support system in the school to help her with the IRI process. She reasoned that if students could silently read a passage and successfully answer questions on their own, she could assume that they were reading at an instructional level. Accordingly, in September, Jeanne duplicated a passage at the fourth-grade level and a list of questions for the entire class. She asked her students to read the passage silently, look back to find answers to the questions, and write down their answers. Jeanne scored the questions, and a few days later she repeated the process. However, some children were given higher-level passages, and some were asked to read an easier passage. She continued in this way until she had determined the highest instructional level for each child at the beginning of the school year.

Jeanne did not totally abandon working with individuals. She spent some time with the children who did not succeed with the fourth-grade passage, asking them to read orally so she could evaluate their word identification accuracy and fluency. Jeanne repeated this process in January and at the end of the school year. Each time, she compared an individual child's levels and noted the amount of growth. Parents were very appreciative of her efforts, and the students were proud of how much they had grown. This group adaptation of the IRI process considerably lessened the amount of time Jeanne had to spend with single students. She admitted that she would have preferred to spend individual time with each student, but in the absence of any school support, she did the best she could. She felt that the results presented a valid picture of her students' progress across a school year.

Another group adaptation involves oral reading. Linda chose a second-grade selection and divided it into five relatively equal parts. She counted the number of words in each part. Linda then assembled a group of five second graders and told them that they would be taking turns reading orally and answering questions. Each child read in turn, and Linda recorded errors on her copy of the text. After each child finished reading his or her part, Linda asked two or three questions to evaluate comprehension and then moved on to the next child. Linda used the number of errors that each child made to assign a probable reading level for word identification accuracy. Linda knew that this was perhaps a poor substitute for an individual IRI process assessment, but she felt it was better than nothing. She repeated this process regularly throughout the school year, using different levels of text.

SUMMARY

- The informal reading inventory (IRI) process is an individual assessment that allows a teacher or tutor to determine reading level, identify good reader behaviors, and determine individual progress. An informal reading inventory (IRI) is a published instrument containing passages at different grade levels.

- The IRI process provides two possible scores: a score for word identification accuracy and a score for comprehension. The scores are then used to determine a student's independent, instructional, and frustration reading levels.
- Word identification accuracy scores are determined by counting the number of oral reading errors or miscues that a student makes while reading orally. Comprehension scores are determined by counting the number of questions that are answered correctly.
- Students may have different levels for word identification accuracy and comprehension on the same passage. The teacher or tutor should assign a total passage level by choosing the lowest of the two.
- The IRI process works best with familiar text.
- The IRI process can be used to identify several good reader behaviors: reading fluently and expressively, determining what is important in the text, summarizing ideas in the text, making inferences and predictions, and monitoring comprehension. Fluency evaluation, answering questions, retelling, and look-backs are ways of assessing these behaviors.
- The IRI process can be used to determine student progress at different points in time. The teacher or tutor compares levels prior to instruction with levels attained after instruction.
- The IRI process can be amended for group administration; however, this provides a less sensitive measure of student ability.

ACTIVITIES FOR DEVELOPING UNDERSTANDING

- Use Appendices 3.1 and 3.2 for practice in using the IRI process with a selection from a basal reader (Appendix 3.1) and with a published IRI (Appendix 3.2).
- Choose a selection of suitable length to use with the IRI process. Count the total number of words. Compose five to ten questions. Ask a student to read this orally, and determine levels for both word identification accuracy and comprehension.
- Use a published IRI and administer the passages to find a student's highest instructional level. Score oral reading, comprehension, and retelling according to the IRI guidelines.
- Complete the self-evaluation form provided at the end of this chapter (following the Appendices).

Practice in Scoring Word Identification Accuracy and Comprehension Using the Informal Reading Inventory Process

Donny read the following second-grade selection from a basal anthology.* Two copies of this selection have been provided. On the first copy, score Donny's performance using check marks. Then, on the second copy, score his performance using the traditional coding system. Decide whether Donny's word identification accuracy suggests an independent, instructional, or frustration level for second-grade material. After you have finished, compare your scoring to mine. Then go on to evaluate Donny's retelling. Compare your evaluation to mine.

The selection is from Emerson, F. (1977). Nobody comes to dinner. In D. Alvermann, C. A. Bridge, B. A. Schmidt, L. W. Searfoss, & P. Winograd (Eds.), *Come back here, crocodile* (pp. 248–256). Lexington, MA: Heath. Copyright 1977 by F. Emerson Andrews (Text); Copyright 1977 by Lydia Dabcovich (Illustrations). Reprinted by permission of Little, Brown and Company, Inc.

DONNY'S READING

Nobody Comes to Dinner

Oscar was hoping having a bad day. The arm didn't go off, so he got up late. He couldn't find his flavor blue sneakers, and after a long time he rembered he left them in the yard. But it was raining and they might be wet. Oscar had to put on his black cowboy boots. When he got to school, the boys and girls pointed to his black boots and gagged.

After school was even worser. Oscar went over to his friends' house, but they said, "Go away. We're playing. We don't need you."

Oscar went home and waited for a call, but nobody came. He went to the playground, and sitting alone on the slide in the rain is not funny.

Now it was dinner. Oscar was mad and he was not going to eat. He told that to his mother formly. His mother took him by the hand and put him to the table. His older sister Jane was there and little Chrispher was sitting in his chair with the plowers on it.

His mother came in carrying a tray with three bowls of stimming soap soup.

"It's good vegble soup tonight," she said, "the kind you all like."

"I hate vegble soup," said Oscar as his bowl was placed before him. "I hate all vegbles."

"Just try a little," said his mother.

Oscar closed his lips and scored up his face. "I don't like you."

Jane recked over and took the spoon.

"Come on now, Oscar."

"I don't like you. I don't like Chripher. I like nobody."

Everyone at the table looked at Oscar. He glored back.

YOUR RECORDING USING CHECKMARKS

Nobody Comes to Dinner

Oscar was having a bad day. The alarm didn't go off, so he got up late. He couldn't find his favorite blue sneakers, and after a long search he remembered he must have left them in the yard. But it was raining and they would be soaked. Oscar had to put on his black cowboy boots. When he got to school, the boys and girls pointed to his big boots and giggled.

After school was even worse. Oscar went over to his friends' house, but they said, "Go away. We're playing and we don't want you."

He went home and waited for a telephone call, but nobody called. He went down to the playground, but sitting alone on the swings in the rain is no fun.

Now it was dinner time. Oscar was mad and decided he was not going to eat. He told that to his mother firmly. His mother took him by the hand and pulled him to the table. His older sister Jane was already there and little Christopher was sitting in his chair with the pillow on it.

His mother came in carrying a tray with three bowls of steaming soup.

"It's good vegetable soup tonight," she said, "the kind you all like."

"I hate vegetable soup," said Oscar as his bowl was placed before him. "I hate all vegetables."

"Just try a little," said his mother.

Oscar closed his lips and screwed up his face. "I don't like you."

Jane reached over and took the spoon.

"Come on now, Oscar."

"I don't like you either. I don't like Christopher. I like nobody."

Everyone at the table looked at Oscar. He glared back.

281 words

Number of errors: _____

Subtract the number of errors from 281: _____

Divide this number by 281 to arrive at a percentage for word identification
   accuracy: _____

Level (circle one): Independent, Instructional, Frustration

YOUR RECORDING USING THE TRADITIONAL
CODING SYSTEM

Nobody Comes to Dinner

Oscar was having a bad day. The alarm didn't go off, so he got up late. He couldn't find his favorite blue sneakers, and after a long search he remembered he must have left them in the yard. But it was raining and they would be soaked. Oscar had to put on his black cowboy boots. When he got to school, the boys and girls pointed to his big boots and giggled.

After school was even worse. Oscar went over to his friends' house, but they said, "Go away. We're playing and we don't want you."

He went home and waited for a telephone call, but nobody called. He went down to the playground, but sitting alone on the swings in the rain is no fun.

Now it was dinner time. Oscar was mad and decided he was not going to eat. He told that to his mother firmly. His mother took him by the hand and pulled him to the table. His older sister Jane was already there and little Christopher was sitting in his chair with the pillow on it.

His mother came in carrying a tray with three bowls of steaming soup.

"It's good vegetable soup tonight," she said, "the kind you all like."

"I hate vegetable soup," said Oscar as his bowl was placed before him. "I hate all vegetables."

"Just try a little," said his mother.

Oscar closed his lips and screwed up his face. "I don't like you."

Jane reached over and took the spoon.

"Come on now, Oscar."

"I don't like you either. I don't like Christopher. I like nobody."

Everyone at the table looked at Oscar. He glared back.

281 words

Number of errors: _____

Subtract the number of errors from 281: _____

Divide this number by 281 to arrive at a percentage for word identification
        accuracy: _____

Level (circle one): Independent, Instructional, Frustration

MY RECORDING USING CHECK MARKS

Nobody Comes to Dinner

Oscar was having a bad day. The alarm didn't go off, so he got up late. He couldn't find his favorite blue sneakers, and after a long search he remembered he must have left them in the yard. But it was raining and they would be soaked. Oscar had to put on his black cowboy boots. When he got to school, the boys and girls pointed to his big boots and giggled.

After school was even worse. Oscar went over to his friends' house, but they said, "Go away. We're playing and we don't want you."

He went home and waited for a telephone call, but nobody called. He went down to the playground, but sitting alone on the swings in the rain is no fun.

Now it was dinner time. Oscar was mad and decided he was not going to eat. He told that to his mother firmly. His mother took him by the hand and pulled him to the table. His older sister Jane was already there and little Christopher was sitting in his chair with the pillow on it.

His mother came in carrying a tray with three bowls of steaming soup.

"It's good vegetable soup tonight," she said, "the kind you all like."

"I hate vegetable soup," said Oscar as his bowl was placed before him. "I hate all vegetables."

"Just try a little," said his mother.

Oscar closed his lips and screwed up his face. "I don't like you."

Jane reached over and took the spoon.

"Come on now, Oscar."

"I don't like you either. I don't like Christopher. I like nobody."

Everyone at the table looked at Oscar. He glared back.

281 words

Number of errors: _39_

Subtract the number of errors from 281: _242_

Divide this number by 281 to arrive at a percentage for word identification
accuracy: _86_

Level (circle one): Independent, Instructional, (Frustration)

MY RECORDING USING THE TRADITIONAL CODING SYSTEM

Nobody Comes to Dinner

hoping C   *arm*
Oscar was having a bad day. The alarm didn't go off, so he got up late. He couldn't find
flavor   *time*   *rembered*
his favorite blue sneakers, and after a long search he remembered he (must)(have) left
might   *wet*
them in the yard. But it was raining and they would be soaked. Oscar had to put on
black
his black cowboy boots. When he got to school, the boys and girls pointed to his big
gagged
boots and giggled.

worser
After school was even worse. Oscar went over to his friends' house, but they said,
need
"Go away. We're playing (and) we don't want you."
Oscar   *came*
He went home and waited for a (telephone) call, but nobody called. He went (down)
and   *slide*   *not funny*
to the playground, but sitting alone on the swings in the rain is no fun.

Now it was dinner (time). Oscar was mad and (decided) he was not going to eat. He
formly   *put*
told that to his mother firmly. His mother took him by the hand and pulled him to the
Chrispher
table. His older sister Jane was (already) there and little Christopher was sitting in his
plowers
chair with the pillow on it.
stimming soap C
His mother came in carrying a tray with three bowls of steaming soup.
vegble
"It's good vegetable soup tonight," she said, "the kind you all like."
vegble
"I hate vegetable soup," said Oscar as his bowl was placed before him. "I hate all
vegbles
vegetables."

"Just try a little," said his mother.
scored
Oscar closed his lips and screwed up his face. "I don't like you."
recked
Jane reached over and took the spoon.

"Come on now, Oscar."
                               Chrispher
"I don't like you (either.) I don't like Christopher. I like nobody."
                               glored
Everyone at the table looked at Oscar. He glared back.

281 words

Number of errors: __39__

Subtract the number of errors from 281: __242__

Divide this number by 281 to arrive at a percentage for word identification

     accuracy: __86__

Level (circle one): Independent, Instructional, (Frustration)

EVALUATING RETELLING

Use the retelling guideline to evaluate Donny's retelling. Then compare your evaluation to mine.

DONNY'S RETELLING

"Oscar lost his sneakers and he got wet looking for them. He went to his friends and played. He went on the slide. Oscar wouldn't eat his soup and he said he hated his mother and his sister. And nobody likes him."

YOUR EVALUATION OF DONNY'S RETELLING

Retelling Checklist for Narrative Text

_____ Identified main character (or characters)

_____ Identified the character's problem

_____ Identified the setting

_____ Described the resolution

_____ Included steps for arriving at the resolution

_____ Made inferences

_____ Retold sequentially

_____ Retold accurately

_____ Offered personal reaction

MY EVALUATION OF DONNY'S RETELLING

Retelling Checklist for Narrative Text

✓   Identified main character (or characters)

no   Identified the character's problem   *only identified lost sneakers*

✓   Identified the setting   *one setting*

no   Described the resolution

✓   Included steps for arriving at the resolution

?   Made inferences   *inferred that nobody likes Oscar*

✓   Retold sequentially

no   Retold accurately   *said Oscar got wet, played with friends, and went on the slide. These were inaccurate.*

no   Offered personal reaction

APPENDIX 3.2

Practice in Scoring Word Recognition Accuracy and Comprehension Using a Published Informal Reading Inventory

Paul read the following fourth-grade selection from a published IRI.* His errors are recorded, and his retelling and answers to the questions are included. Count his errors and determine his level for word identification accuracy. Score his answers to the questions and determine his level for comprehension. Then use the Retelling Checklist and evaluate his retelling. What good reader behaviors did you note? Then compare your scoring and evaluation to mine.

This IRI allows for two word identification accuracy scores: one for all errors (called Total Accuracy) and one only for errors that change meaning (called Total Acceptability). I placed an × in the margin for errors that I did not believe changed meaning. Then I figured out both scores.

You will note that this IRI evaluates topic familiarity before the student reads the passage by asking several questions about the concepts in the passage. Answers are scored on a 3-point scale. Paul's answers suggested familiarity with the topic of the passage.

You will also note that there is a place for the teacher or tutor to record the student's performance following a look-back. When Paul was asked to look back in the text for an answer, I recorded this by writing in *Look-Back*.

The scored selection and checklists (except for the Retelling Checklist) are from Leslie, L., & Caldwell, J. S. (2001). *The Qualitative Reading Inventory 3*. New York: Addison Wesley Longman. Copyright 2001 by Addison Wesley Longman. Reprinted by permission. As noted within the Appendix, the "Johnny Appleseed" selection itself is from Armbruster, B. B., Mitsakas, C. L., & Rogers, V. R. (1986). *America's history*. Lexington, MA: Ginn. Copyright 1986 by Ginn. Reprinted by permission of the publisher.

YOUR SCORING OF PAUL

Level: Four

Narrative

Concept Questions:

Who was Johnny Appleseed?

he went west and planted
apple trees

_____ (3-2-1-0)

Why do people plant fruit trees in certain places?

they look good there or
they grow best there

_____ (3-2-1-0)

Why do people plant apple trees?

they like apples — you get
food

_____ (3-2-1-0)

What does "making apple cider" mean to you?

just making it from
apples

_____ (3-2-1-0)

Score: _10_ /12 = _83_ %

✓ FAM _____ UNFAM

Prediction:

_____

_____

Johnny Appleseed

John Chapman was born in 1774 and grew
up in Massachusetts. He became a farmer and
learned how to grow different kinds of crops

and trees. John especially liked to grow and eat
[*espickly*]
apples. Many people were moving west at that
[*the*]
time. They were heading for Ohio and Penn-
sylvania. John knew that apples were a good
food for settlers to have. Apple trees were
[*sett ling ers*]
strong and easy to grow. Apples could be eaten
raw and they could be cooked in many ways.
They could also be dried for later use. So in
[*drod*]
1797, John decided to go west. He wanted to
plant apple trees for people who would build
[*were building*]
their new homes there.
John first gathered bags of apple seeds. He
[*gattered*]
got many of his seeds from farmers who
squeezed apples to make a drink called cider.
[*squashed*]
Then, in the spring, he left for the western
frontier. He planted seeds as he went along.
[*front*]
Also, he gave them to people who knew how
valuable apple trees were.

John walked many miles in all kinds of
weather. He had to cross dangerous rivers and
[*dan grous C*]
find his way through strange forests. Often he
was hungry, cold, and wet. Sometimes he had
to hide from unfriendly Indians. His clothes
[*some*]
became ragged and torn. He used a sack for a
[*raggy*]
shirt, and he cut out holes for the arms. He
wore no shoes. But he never gave up. He
guarded his precious seeds and carefully
[*garted*] [*pregnant*]
planted them where they had the best chance
[*put*]
of growing into strong trees.

Level: Four

John's <u>fame</u> spread. He was nicknamed Johnny Appleseed. New <u>settlers</u> welcomed him and ~~gratefully~~ *grat ply* accepted a gift of apple seeds. Many *leg ons* legends grew up about Johnny Appleseed that were not (always) true. However, one thing is true. Thanks to Johnny Appleseed, apple trees now grow in parts of America where they (once) never did. (308 words)

From *America's History* by B. B. Armbruster, C. L. Mitsakas, and V. R. Rogers (1986). Copyright © 1986 by Ginn. Reprinted by permission of the publisher.

Number of Total Miscues
(Total Accuracy): _____

Number of Meaning-Change Miscues
(Total Acceptability): _____

Total Accuracy		Total Acceptability
0–7 miscues ____	Independent ____	0–7 miscues
8–32 miscues ____	Instructional ____	8–16 miscues
32+ miscues ____	Frustration ____	17+ miscues

Rate: 308 × 60 = 18,480 / *204* seconds = *91* WPM

Retelling Scoring Sheet for Johnny Appleseed

Setting/Background

____ John Chapman was born
____ in 1774.
____ He became a farmer
____ and grew crops.
____ John liked
____ to grow

____ and eat apples.
____ People were moving west.
____ Apples were a good food
____ for settlers to have.

Goal

____ John decided
____ to go west.
____ He wanted
____ to plant apple trees.

Events

____ John got many seeds
____ from farmers
____ who squeezed apples
____ to make a drink
____ called cider.
____ He left
____ for the frontier.
____ He planted seeds
____ as he went along.
____ He gave them away.
____ John walked miles.
____ He crossed rivers
____ and went through forests.
____ He was hungry
____ and wet.
____ He had to hide
____ from Indians
____ unfriendly Indians.
____ His clothes were torn.
____ He used a sack
____ for a shirt
____ and he cut out holes
____ for the arms.
____ He wore no shoes.

Resolution

____ John's fame spread.
____ He was nicknamed
____ Johnny Appleseed.
____ Settlers accepted seeds
____ gratefully.
____ Thanks to Johnny Appleseed,
____ apple trees grow

It's about this guy who went west. He liked to eat apples so he planted them. He had problems like he was hungry and he crossed rivers and hid from Indians and he planted seeds as he went. He went across forests and he use sacks for shirts and he got famous.

Level: Four

____ in many parts
____ of America.

Other ideas recalled, including inferences:

Questions for Johnny Appleseed

1. What was John Chapman's main goal?
   Implicit: to plant apple trees across the country

   *plant a lot of apple
   trees all over the west*

2. Why did John choose apples to plant in-stead of some other fruit?
   Implicit: the trees were easy to grow; the fruit could be used in a lot of ways; he es-pecially liked apples

   he liked apples

3. Where did John get most of his seeds?
   Explicit: from farmers or from people who made cider

   farmers

4. Why would John be able to get so many seeds from cider makers?
   Implicit: cider is a drink and you don't drink seeds; apples have a lot of seeds and you don't use seeds in cider

   *there aren't seeds in
   cider*

5. How do we know that John cared about planting apple trees?
   Implicit: he suffered hardships; he guarded the apple seeds carefully

   *he went through a lot — he
   didn't give up*

6. How did John get to the many places he visited?
   Explicit: he walked

   walked

7. Name one hardship John suffered.
   Explicit: being hungry, cold, wet, lost, in danger from unfriendly Indians

   *Indians who were unfriendly —
   he was cold — he didn't
   have clothes*

8. Why should we thank Johnny Appleseed?
   Explicit: apple trees now grow in parts of America where they once never did

   *why would we want to
   thank him — he's dead*

Without Look-Backs

Number Correct Explicit: ____

Number Correct Implicit: ____

      Total: ____

____ Independent: 8 correct

____ Instructional: 6–7 correct

____ Frustration: 0–5 correct

With Look-Backs

Number Correct Explicit: ____

Number Correct Implicit: ____

      Total: ____

____ Independent: 8 correct

____ Instructional: 6–7 correct

____ Frustration: 0–5 correct

Retelling Checklist for Narrative Text

_____ Identified main character (or characters)

_____ Identified the character's problem

_____ Identified the setting

_____ Described the resolution

_____ Included steps for arriving at the resolution

_____ Made inferences

_____ Retold sequentially

_____ Retold accurately

_____ Offered personal reaction

MY SCORING OF PAUL

Level: Four

Narrative

Concept Questions:

Who was Johnny Appleseed?

he went west and planted
apple trees

(3)-2-1-0)

Why do people plant fruit trees in certain places?

they look good there or
they grow best there

(3)-2-1-0)

Why do people plant apple trees?

they like apples — you get
food

(3)-2-1-0)

What does "making apple cider" mean to you?

just making it from
apples

(3-2-(1)-0)

Score: _10_ /12 = _83_ %

✓ FAM _____ UNFAM

Prediction:

_____
_____

Johnny Appleseed

John Chapman was born in 1774 and grew

up in Massachusetts. He became a farmer and

X learned (how) to grow different kinds of crops

and trees. John ~~especially~~ *espickly* liked to grow and eat

apples. Many people were moving west at that *the* X

time. They were heading for Ohio and Penn-

sylvania. John knew that apples were a good

food for settlers *sett ling ers* to have. Apple trees were

strong and easy to grow. Apples could be eaten

raw and they could be cooked in many ways.

They could also be dried *drod* for later use. So in

1797, John decided to go west. He wanted to

plant apple trees for people who would build *were building* X X

their (new) homes there. X

John first gathered *gattered* bags of apple seeds. He

got many of his seeds from farmers who

squeezed *squashed* apples to make a drink called cider. X

Then, in the spring, he left for the western

frontier. *front* He planted seeds as he went along.

Also, he gave them to people who knew how

(valuable) apple trees were.

John walked (many) miles in all kinds of X

weather. He had to cross dangerous *dan grous C* rivers and X

find his way through strange forests. Often he

was hungry, cold, and wet. Sometimes he had

to hide from some unfriendly Indians. His clothes X

became ragged *raggy* and torn. He used a sack for a

shirt, and he cut out holes for the arms. He

wore no shoes. But he never gave up. He

guarded *garted* his precious *pregnant* seeds and carefully

planted *put* them where they had the best chance X

of growing into (strong) trees. X

Level: Four

John's <u>fame</u> spread. He was nicknamed Johnny Appleseed. New <u>settlers</u> welcomed him and ~~grat ply~~ 'gratefully accepted a gift of apple seeds. Many ~~leg ons~~ legends grew up about Johnny Appleseed that were not (always) true. How-**X** ever, one thing is true. Thanks to Johnny Appleseed, apple trees now grow in parts of America where they (once) never did. (308**X** words)

From *America's History* by B. B. Armbruster, C. L. Mitsakas, and V. R. Rogers (1986). Copyright © 1986 by Ginn. Reprinted by permission of the publisher.

Number of Total Miscues
(Total Accuracy): _____ **24**

Number of Meaning-Change Miscues
(Total Acceptability): _____ **11**

Total Accuracy		Total Acceptability
0–7 miscues _____ Independent		_____ 0–7 miscues
8–32 miscues **24** Instructional	**11**	8–16 miscues
32+ miscues _____ Frustration	_____	17+ miscues

Rate: 308 × 60 = 18,480 / **204** seconds = **91** WPM

Retelling Scoring Sheet for Johnny Appleseed

Setting/Background

_____ John Chapman was born
_____ in 1774.
_____ He became a farmer
_____ and grew crops.
✓ John liked
_____ to grow

✓ and eat apples.
_____ People were moving west.
_____ Apples were a good food
_____ for settlers to have.

Goal

_____ John decided
✓ to go west.
_____ He wanted
_____ to plant apple trees.

Events

_____ John got many seeds
_____ from farmers
_____ who squeezed apples
_____ to make a drink
_____ called cider.
_____ He left
_____ for the frontier.
✓ He planted seeds
_____ as he went along.
_____ He gave them away.
_____ John walked miles.
✓ He crossed rivers
✓ and went through forests.
✓ He was hungry
_____ and wet.
✓ He had to hide
✓ from Indians
_____ unfriendly Indians.
_____ His clothes were torn.
✓ He used a sack
✓ for a shirt
_____ and he cut out holes
_____ for the arms.
_____ He wore no shoes.

Resolution

✓ John's fame spread.
_____ He was nicknamed
_____ Johnny Appleseed.
_____ Settlers accepted seeds
_____ gratefully.
_____ Thanks to Johnny Appleseed,
_____ apple trees grow

It's about this guy who went west. He liked to eat apples so he planted them. He had problems like he was hungry and he crossed rivers and hid from Indians and he planted seeds as he went. He went across forests and he use sacks for shirts and he got famous.

Level: Four

____ in many parts
____ of America.

Other ideas recalled, including inferences:

Questions for Johnny Appleseed

C
1. What was John Chapman's main goal?
   Implicit: to plant apple trees across the
   country

   plant a lot of apple
   trees all over the west

C
2. Why did John choose apples to plant instead of some other fruit?
   Implicit: the trees were easy to grow; the
   fruit could be used in a lot of ways; he especially liked apples

   he liked apples

C
3. Where did John get most of his seeds?
   Explicit: from farmers or from people who
   made cider

   farmers

C
4. Why would John be able to get so many
   seeds from cider makers?
   Implicit: cider is a drink and you don't
   drink seeds; apples have a lot of seeds and
   you don't use seeds in cider

   there aren't seeds in
   cider

C
5. How do we know that John cared about
   planting apple trees?
   Implicit: he suffered hardships; he guarded
   the apple seeds carefully

   he went through a lot — he
   didn't give up

C
6. How did John get to the many places he
   visited?
   Explicit: he walked

   walked

C
7. Name one hardship John suffered.
   Explicit: being hungry, cold, wet, lost, in
   danger from unfriendly Indians

   Indians who were unfriendly —
   he was cold — he didn't
   have clothes

✓
8. Why should we thank Johnny Appleseed?
   Explicit: apple trees now grow in parts of
   America where they once never did

   why would we want to
   thank him — he's dead
   Look back: *C*

Without Look-Backs

Number Correct Explicit: _3_

Number Correct Implicit: _4_

Total: _7_

____ Independent: 8 correct

✓ Instructional: 6–7 correct

____ Frustration: 0–5 correct

With Look-Backs   4

Number Correct Explicit: _4_

Number Correct Implicit: _8_

Total: ____

✓ Independent: 8 correct

____ Instructional: 6–7 correct

____ Frustration: 0–5 correct

Retelling Checklist for Narrative Text

  ✓ Identified main character (or characters)

  ✓ Identified the character's problem

  ✓ Identified the setting

  _____ Described the resolution

  ✓ Included steps for arriving at the resolution

  _____ Made inferences

  ✓ Retold sequentially

  ✓ Retold accurately

  _____ Offered personal reaction

APPENDIX 3.3

Published Informal Reading Inventories

———————

Bader, L. A. (1998). *Reading and Learning Inventory*. Upper Saddle River, NJ: Merrill.

 The inventory provides graded word lists. Passages span preprimer through grade 12. There are three passages at each level. Comprehension is assessed by questions and retelling. Additional diagnostic measures are included, such as measures of phonics and structural analysis, semantic and syntactic cloze tests, a preliteracy assessment, and measures of writing and arithmetic.

Burns, P. C., & Roe, B. D. (1989). *The Burns/Roe Informal Reading Inventory*. Boston: Houghton Mifflin.

 The inventory provides graded word lists. There are three forms with passages that range from preprimer through grade 12. Comprehension is assessed by questions.

Johns, J. J. (1997). *Basic Reading Inventory*. Dubuque, IA: Kendall-Hunt.

 The inventory contains graded word lists. There are five forms. Three forms provide passages ranging from preprimer through grade 8. Two additional forms provide narrative and expository passages from grades 3 through 12. Comprehension is primarily assessed through questions. The inventory also contains a variety of other diagnostic measures, such as alphabet knowledge, wordless picture reading, phonemic awareness, phonemic segmentation, and writing.

Leslie, L., & Caldwell, J. S. (2001). *The Qualitative Reading Inventory 3*. New York: Addison Wesley Longman.

 The inventory contains graded word lists. At the preprimer through upper middle school levels, there are both narrative and expository passages, three of each type at levels 3 and above. At preprimer through grade 2, passages are presented with pictures and without pictures. At the high school level, there are single, intact literature, social studies, and science passages, each divided into three parts. Comprehension is assessed through questions and through retelling. Above level 3, the inventory provides the option of using look-backs to assess comprehension. The inventory provides the options of modeling and using the think-aloud process for further assessment at the high school level.

Shanker, J. L., & Ekwall, E. E. (2000). *The Ekwall/Shanker Reading Inventory* (4th ed.). Boston: Allyn & Bacon.

The inventory provides graded word lists. There are four forms. Each form contains passages that range from preprimer through grade 9. The inventory provides additional diagnostic measures focusing on such components as phonics, structural analysis, contractions, and reading interests.

Silvaroli, N. J. (1994). *Classroom Reading Inventory*. Madison, WI: Brown & Benchmark.

This inventory has graded word lists. There are four forms. Form A passages range from preprimer through level 8. All are accompanied by pictures. Form B passages are literature-based and appropriate for an elementary school audience. They are accompanied by pictures and span levels 1 through 6. Form C is appropriate for a junior high audience and spans levels 1 through 8. There are no pictures. Form D is suitable for an adult audience and spans levels 1 through 8. Comprehension is assessed through questions except for the literature-based passages, which are evaluated through retelling.

Stieglitz, E. L. (1997). *The Stieglitz Informal Reading Inventory*. Boston: Allyn & Bacon.

This inventory has graded word lists as well as words presented in the context of a single sentence. The passages span levels 1 through 9. At each level there are two narrative passages and two expository passages. Comprehension is assessed through questions and through retelling. The inventory also contains a process for evaluating emergent literacy through stories dictated to the examiner.

Swearington, R., & Allen, D. (1997). *Classroom Assessment of Reading Processes*. Boston: Houghton Mifflin.

The inventory provides graded word lists. There are four forms, two focusing on narrative passages and two focusing on expository passages. The passages range from grades 1 through 6. Narrative comprehension is assessed by retelling. Expository comprehension is assessed by questions asked at specific points during the reading process.

Teacher or Tutor Self-Evaluation

I use the informal reading inventory (IRI) process to determine whether students can read classroom materials.

        Regularly   Occasionally   A future goal

I use the IRI process to determine students' highest reading levels.

        Regularly   Occasionally   A future goal

I am comfortable using any text for the IRI process.

        Regularly   Occasionally   A future goal

I am comfortable using a published IRI.

        Regularly   Occasionally   A future goal

I am comfortable recording and scoring oral reading errors.

        Regularly   Occasionally   A future goal

I am comfortable scoring comprehension.

        Regularly   Occasionally   A future goal

I am comfortable identifying good reader behaviors through the IRI process.

        Regularly   Occasionally   A future goal

I am comfortable using the IRI process to determine individual student progress.

        Regularly   Occasionally   A future goal

I adapt the IRI process for group administration.

        Regularly   Occasionally   A future goal

FOUR

Early Literacy
What Do We Need to Know about Beginning Readers?

OVERVIEW OF EARLY LITERACY

Just a few days ago, I ran into a friend and her young son, Steven, at a local store. Steven was happily engaged in picking out school supplies, and he had amassed a rather formidable pile of notebooks, tablets, pencils, crayons, scissors, and glue sticks. When I arrived, he was attempting to decide on a book bag to hold all his treasures. The presence of different cartoon characters and movie heroes on the bags was making this a difficult choice. When Steven finally selected his book bag, I asked him whether he was excited about school, and he solemnly assured me he was. I asked him why. Without hesitation, Steven mentioned new friends and riding the school bus as reasons for his positive anticipation. Then he exclaimed, "And I'm going to learn how to read all by myself! I won't have to ask Mom or Jessie [his sister] to read to me. I can't wait!" Like Steven, many people think that learning to read begins in school, but this represents a limited concept of early literacy (or what has come to be called *emergent literacy*).

The development of literacy begins long before a child enters a classroom or tutoring session. It begins with the development of oral language. Spoken language and written language are much alike. They share the same sound system, the same vocabulary, and the same structure. For example, the sounds that form the spoken word *dog* are the same sounds that are represented by the letter sequence *d-o-g*. The meaning of the word *dog* is the same, whether we are talking, writing, or reading. The structure of sentences in spoken and written language remains basically the same. The spoken sentence "I saw a big dog" will be represented in print in the same way (*I saw a big dog*). It will not be twisted or altered to another form, such as *dog big saw I a*. This means that if children are to learn to read and write their language, they must first acquire that language. They must learn the sounds that stand for meaning. They must learn the underlying concepts. They must learn how to string sounds together to form words and words together to form sentences. They must learn certain language conventions, such as adding *-ed* to signify what happened in the past.

Any language represents an extremely complex system. Think about all the grammar books that have been written. Consider the size of an unabridged dictionary. These are attempts to describe a system that children seem to learn quite effortlessly. Why and how do they do this? Children learn almost immediately that language brings rewards. It brings attention. It brings food and toys. It brings comfort and knowledge. It helps to establish and maintain relationships that can be very satisfying. Perhaps the most important thing is that language brings meaning into their world. Language allows them to describe their feelings and experiences and share them with others. Language in childhood develops through interaction with parents, caregivers, siblings, and peers. Language expands when parents and caregivers talk with a child, encourage the child's verbalizations, and use language to support problem-solving efforts (such as deciding whether to go to the zoo on Saturday or discussing what present to take to a party).

Oral language is absolutely necessary for literacy development, but it is not sufficient. There are children with adequate oral language skills who unfortunately lack a basic requirement for learning to read and write. That basic requirement is preschool literacy experiences. The amount and quality of literacy experiences in a preschooler's life will positively or negatively affect later literacy development. What do we mean by *literacy experiences*? Let's go back to Steven. Steven's home environment is filled with a wide variety of books, magazines, newspapers, and other examples of print. Steven's parents and grandparents all enjoy and value reading. Steven was given books from the very beginning of his life—sturdy books that defied destruction by chewing, bending, or tearing. Steven also had pencils, crayons, and paper. He was encouraged to write, even if that writing looked more like scribbles. He played with alphabet blocks and magnetic letters. He listened to songs and nursery rhymes on a tape recorder, and he watched computer videos that visually portrayed his favorite stories. And what is probably most important, Steven's parents, grandparents, and sister read to him every day almost from the time of his birth.

"The single most important activity for building the knowledge and skills eventually required for reading appears to be reading aloud to children" (Adams, 1990, p. 46). Effective storybook reading involves the child and the reader in a conversation about the book, the characters, and the plot. The reader and the child ask questions together. They relate the book to their own lives. The reader offers information to the child and responds to the child's questions and comments. The reader draws the child out, encourages verbalization, and expands on the child's comments. Children learn a lot about their language and about literacy from storybook reading. They learn new vocabulary words and new concepts. They learn new sentence structures and new ways of saying things. They learn new language conventions, such as question words, dialogue patterns, and word endings like -*er*, -*est*, and -*ly*. They learn that print matches the sounds of speech, and that reading is a meaningful and enjoyable activity.

In summary, literacy development begins when oral language development begins. Literacy development is fostered by active oral language interactions with parents and caregivers. It is further supported by caregivers who value and model literacy activities, and who make literacy materials such as books and writing easily accessible (Pressley, 1998).

WHAT CHILDREN NEED TO KNOW ABOUT LANGUAGE

Engaging in oral language and participating in many and varied literacy experiences help a child to become aware of such language elements as words, syllables, and phonemes or sounds (Adams, 1990). Children must pay attention to these if they are to succeed as readers and writers. Some children develop this awareness on their own. Others need more structured experiences with individual sounds. It is impossible to identify and spell words without a consciousness of words as individual units composed of syllables and phonemes. Let's briefly examine each.

Word and Syllable Awareness

As proficient readers, we know that any utterance is made up of different words, and if we were asked to, we could count and keep track of the number of words in any spoken message. Of course, we probably would not comprehend very much while doing this, because when we listen, we focus on the meaning of the entire message—not the number of words it contains. However, we can count the number of spoken words because we are aware of words as separate entities. This word awareness is not readily apparent to young children. In print there are spaces between words, but in speech there are no pauses to separate one word from another. We speak in one continuous speech stream. Have you ever heard someone speaking an unfamiliar foreign language? Can you tell how many words they are saying? Probably not, because speakers do not separate words with pauses, and your ignorance of that language prevented you from distinguishing individual units of meaning. Children gradually learn to attend to individual words as they develop oral vocabulary and as they interact with print. "As children become aware of the one-by-oneness of words in print, they begin to notice and isolate words in speech" (Adams, 1990, p. 52).

A *syllable* is a speech sound that you can produce in isolation. For example, in the word *hotel* there are two syllables, and you can say each one separately: *ho* and *tel*. Awareness of syllable sounds predicts future reading success (Adams, 1990). How can you identify a syllable if you are not aware of its existence? It is much like expecting people to identify the rules of a game that they have never heard of.

Phonemic Awareness

A *phoneme* is a small sound segment. Phonemes are represented in print by letters. However, just as words are not separated in the speech stream, neither are phonemes. Many phonemes cannot even be spoken in isolation. For example, pronounce the sound represented by the letter *b*. I would guess that you said *buh*. But that is attaching the sound of the short vowel *u* to the sound of *b*. Remove *uh* and pronounce *b* without it. What did you get? Just a puff of air. Children must learn to distinguish phonemes as separate units if they are to match letters and sounds within syllables and words. Distinguishing phonemes is more difficult than becoming aware of words and syllables as separate units.

Phonemic awareness is the preprint awareness that words are made up of separate sounds. It is not the ability to hear the sounds, but the ability to perceive their separateness. It is difficult for literate adults to conceptualize phonemic awareness. If I ask you how many sounds are in the word *hotel*, probably you will mentally compare the spelling of the word with the sounds and arrive at an answer. But phonemic awareness is actually apart from print. It is the awareness of separate sounds in words—even those words that you cannot read, write, or spell.

Let me use an analogy to describe phonemic awareness. Pretend that I am sitting at a piano and you cannot see my fingers on the keys. If I play one chord and then another chord, you would be able to say whether they are alike or different. That is auditory discrimination. But could you tell me how many notes I played in each chord? Unless you were trained in music, I doubt that you could. Being able to say how many notes or sounds in a chord is analogous to phonemic awareness—that is, being able to distinguish and differentiate the sounds in a spoken word.

Much research has demonstrated that a child's ability to identify and manipulate phonemes is highly related to later achievement in reading and spelling (Ball & Blachman, 1991; Byrne & Fielding-Barnsley, 1991; Stanovich, 1988). In fact, next to alphabet knowledge, phonemic awareness is the second best predictor of reading success! How is this determined? Researchers first measure phonemic awareness in preschoolers. They then correlate these preschool scores with later achievement scores in reading and spelling. Preschoolers with high levels of phonemic awareness demonstrate higher reading achievement at the end of first grade and into second grade. Juel (1988) followed a group of children from first grade through fourth grade and determined that phonemic awareness was the best predictor of poor reading achievement in first grade. A low level of phonemic awareness in first grade, in turn, was very predictive of reading problems in fourth grade.

What kind of tasks measure phonemic awareness? Phonemic segmentation tests determine whether a child can break a syllable into phonemes. Children are asked to listen to a spoken one-syllable word and then tap out the number of phonemes they hear. For example, if presented with *cat*, they should tap three times. A phoneme manipulation test asks a child to manipulate phonemes by saying a word without a certain phoneme. For example, the child is asked to say *cat* without the *c*. In blending tests, the examiner presents the child with phoneme segments (*s . . . a . . . t*) and asks the child to blend these into a word (*sat*). Some tests present three or four spoken words, and the child is asked to determine which is different. The difference could be based upon the beginnings or ends of the words. For example, if the words are *cat*, *cut*, *sat*, and *cot*, the odd word would be *sat* because it represents a different beginning sound. If the words were *jump*, *lump*, *damp*, and *dark*, the odd word would be *dark* as representative of a different ending sound.

WHAT CHILDREN NEED TO LEARN ABOUT PRINT

In order to learn to read and write, children must develop basic concepts about how print works. The most important concept is the awareness that print stands for meaning. Those little black squiggles on the page represent spoken language. They hold information, but they are different from pictures. Another important concept is the understanding that print comes in many forms and can be found in many places (such as billboards, television screens, books, road signs, soup cans, etc.). The form or size of the letters or words, and the places where they may be found do not change their meaning. The meaning of *stop* remains the same, whether it is printed on an octagonal red sign, in a book, or on a warning label. Children need to learn that print can be produced by anyone, including themselves. How do children develop these concepts? "Such development does not occur in a vacuum. It depends upon growing up in an environment where print is important. It depends upon interactions with print that are a source of social and intellectual pleasure for the individual children and the people who surround them" (Adams, 1990, p. 61).

Children must also learn the conventions of print. Books have a beginning and an end. Print goes in a certain direction. In English, we begin at the top of the message or page and move to the bottom. We begin reading on the left side and move to the right side. Print is made up of words, and words have spaces between them. Words are made up of letters, and there are no spaces between the letters.

Children must learn to identify the letters of the alphabet. This is not as easy as it sounds. The alphabet is probably the first thing in a young child's life that changes with direction. A chair is a chair no matter what direction it is facing. It is a chair whether it is upside down, right side up, or lying on its side. Mother is Mother, whether she is standing up, lying down, or standing on her head. This is called *object constancy*. But consider the alphabet. If you reverse the direction of the letter *b*, you have the letter *d*. The letter *n*, turned upside down, becomes the letter *u*. Letters are also very abstract, that is, they do not resemble a concrete object in any way. There are very small differences between two letters. The only difference between the letter *c* and the letter *o* is the closed loop. The letter *b* and the letter *h* look similar. Only the horizontal crosspiece distinguishes the letter *l* from the letter *t*.

Research indicates that the ability to identify and name alphabet letters is a powerful predictor of later success in literacy (Adams, 1990). Many children who have lived in a print-rich environment enter school already knowing the names of the letters. They can sing the alphabet song and discriminate among written letters. This is an important first step to learning the letters' sounds and learning to read words. Unfortunately, some children enter school with little understanding of the purpose of print or the conventions of print, including the letters of the alphabet.

FIRST STAGES OF READING WORDS

What do beginning readers look like? What strategies do they use to identify words and construct meaning from text? Children progress through different stages as they learn about print and develop their ability to recognize words (Ehri, 1991; Gough & Juel, 1991; Spear-Swerling & Sternberg, 1996).

Let's consider four-year-old Zachary, who climbs into his grandmother's lap and announces, "I'm going to read you a story." He settles himself comfortably and opens *The Three Little Pigs*. "It's about these pigs, and they are going to leave their mother. It says so right here." Zachary points to the words. "And this is the word *pig*. I can tell because it has a tail on the end just like a pig." He carefully turns the page. "One pig made a house. He used straw. The middle pig made a stick house." Zachary points to the print and carefully turns another page. "The last pig made a house of bricks, and then this mean old wolf came. Here's a picture of the wolf." Zachary turns the page and continues. "The wolf said he was going to huff and puff and blow down the straw house. And he did! See how it all came down!" Zachary continues in this fashion until he finishes the book. "I'm a good reader, aren't I, Grandma?" Zachary's proud grandmother assures him that he is.

Now Zachary is obviously telling the story to his grandmother and using the pictures as guides. The words he uses are not an exact match for the words on the page. Is Zachary really reading? Not in the sense that you are reading this book right now. But Zachary has grasped a key concept. He knows that print stands for meaning, for something that he can say (Adams, 1990). And he knows that he can't just say anything as he "reads" a book. What he says must match what is on the page, and Zachary matches his words to the pictures of the pigs, their houses, and the wolf

Zachary is in the first stage of reading words, called the *logographic* stage (Ehri, 1991) or the stage of *visual cue reading* (Spear-Swerling & Sternberg, 1996). In this stage, children identify words using visual cues. They do not try to match letters and sounds. They can identify the word *McDonald's*, but only in the presence of the familiar logo, the golden arches. Zachary is confident that he can recognize the word *pig* because it has a tail at the end. Chances are that Zachary will identify any word ending in *y* as *pig*. (In a similar fashion, a youngster once confided to me that he could always recognize *dog* because the dog was barking. Its mouth was open in the middle of the word! Of course, he confidently pronounced *got* and *from* as *dog* and was quite proud of himself for doing so.) Still, Zachary has made a fine beginning.

Cyntha, a first grader, selects *Mrs. WishyWashy* by Joy Cowley (1999) to read. She first looks at the picture and then points to each word with her finger. " 'Oh, lovely mud,' said the cow," Cyntha reads. She looks at the next page and goes on, "And she jumped in it." Cyntha turns the page, looks at the picture, and continues. " 'Oh, lovely mud,' said the pig, and she jumped in it. No! She rolled in it." Like Zachary, Cyntha uses the pictures to help her recognize the words and comprehend the story. Seeing the pig rolling as opposed to jumping, she changes *jumped* to *rolled*; unlike Zachary, however, she basically reads the words as they are on the page. Later, when Cyntha goes through a set of word cards, she attempts to use letters and sounds as opposed to visual cues, but identifies *down* as *day* and *out* as *over*. Cyntha is in the *alphabetic* stage (Ehri, 1991) or the stage of *phonetic cue recoding* (Spear-Swerling & Sternberg, 1996).

Children in this stage try to match letters and sounds, but they depend heavily upon context and pictures to help them pronounce words and understand what they read. Cyntha reads *jumped* in the context of *Mrs. Wishy-Washy*, but misses it on the word card. She correctly identifies *mud* during her reading of the story, but calls it *man* on the word card. Readers in this stage focus on the beginning and the ends of words and tend to ignore vowels. Gradually, however, children begin to pay attention to vowels and to note sound and spelling patterns in words. They move into later stages of reading development. They are no longer beginning readers. They become more confident and proficient in identifying words. They develop strategies for remembering and understanding what they read. We discuss the later stages of reading development in Chapters Five, Six, and Seven.

PURPOSES OF EARLY LITERACY ASSESSMENT

Any teacher or tutor who works with young children should be aware that certain factors are very important to the development of literacy. These include oral language, phonemic awareness, print awareness, alphabet knowledge, and early reading strategies. The teacher or tutor cannot assume that all are in place when a child enters school, but must carefully assess the child's awareness and knowledge of each. "The ability to read does not emerge spontaneously, but through regular and active engagement with print. For a child who is well prepared to learn to read, the beginning of formal reading should not be a abrupt step, but a further step on a journey well under way" (Adams, 1990, p. 71). For the child who is not well prepared, sensitive and timely assessment by a teacher or tutor may provide the first steps in his or her journey to literacy.

ASSESSING ORAL LANGUAGE

There are many tests for assessing oral language that can identify a child's level of development and his or her language strengths and needs. These tests measure a variety of skills (such as the length of a child's utterance, the use of different language conventions, the clarity of articulation, the depth of the child's concept base, etc.). Such comprehensive measures are administered and scored by trained individuals. It is not the role of the teacher or tutor to do so. Many schools and districts assess oral language prior to school entrance, and a teacher or tutor should know whether such an assessment has taken place. If not, the teacher or tutor has a very important function, and that is to identify any child whose language development may be questionable and refer that child for more in-depth assessment.

As a teacher or tutor, how do you do this without special training? If you carefully listen to all the students in your class or group over a period of several weeks, you will soon notice language differences. Children whose language is not as developed as their peers just do not sound right. You do not need extensive checklists to figure this out. Just listen to children and engage them in dialogue. If you are unsure about a specific child, ask a more experienced teacher or tutor to listen with you. Like many teachers and tutors, you may be afraid of making a wrong identification—that is, sending a child for more assessment only to find out that no problem exists. Because of the importance of oral language, it is better to refer for assessment when none was needed than not to refer when assessment was actually warranted.

ASSESSING PHONEMIC AWARENESS

There are many ways to assess phonemic awareness. There are also a variety of published assessment measures. Because phonemic awareness is an unfamiliar concept to most teachers and tutors, I suggest that such teachers or tutors use an already constructed assessment rather than making their own.

The Yopp–Singer Test of Phonemic Segmentation

The Yopp–Singer Test of Phonemic Segmentation (Yopp, 1995/1999) "measures a child's ability to separately articulate the sounds of a spoken word in order" (p. 167). For example, if the examiner says *dog*, the child should respond with three sounds, /d/, /o/, and /g/. Correct responses are based upon sounds not letters. If the spoken word is *race*, the child should give three sounds, /r/, /a/, and /ce/. The Yopp–Singer Test is made up of 22 words that represent a combination of two and three sounds. The test is administered individually and takes about five to ten minutes.

Before the test is administered, the child practices breaking words apart with three sample items. During this part, the examiner models the process for the child. During the administration of the 22 items, the examiner indicates whether a response is correct and corrects incorrect segmentation by providing the correct answer. The child's score is the number of correctly segmented words. High scores indicate that the child is probably phonemically aware. Emerging phonemic awareness is indicated by the ability to segment some items. A child who can segment no words or only a few words can be considered to be lacking in phonemic awareness.

According to Yopp (1995/1999), performance on the Yopp–Singer Test predicts reading and spelling performance in grades 2 through 6. The test is a valid, reliable, simple, and quick measure of phonemic awareness. Teachers and tutors can use the Yopp–Singer Test to identify children who lack phonemic awareness and who may therefore experience difficulty in learning to read and spell. The teachers or tutors can then provide instructional support in developing phonemic awareness. Research suggests that phonemic awareness can be trained, with subsequent gains in reading and spelling (Bradley & Bryant, 1983; Lundberg, Frost, & Petersen, 1988; Ball & Blachman, 1991).

The Test of Awareness of Language Segments

The Test of Awareness of Language Segments (TALS; Sawyer, 1987) is another individual test that measures a child's segmentation ability. The child is asked to break sentences into words, words into syllables, and words into sounds.

Like the Yopp–Singer Test, the TALS provides a practice session prior to formal administration of the items. Unlike the Yopp–Singer Test, the TALS has the examiner present the child with blocks and ask the child to push forward one block for every word, syllable, or sound he or she hears. On the Yopp–Singer Test, all 22 items are administered; the TALS differs in that the child's performance determines whether or not the examiner administers all three parts of the test. Segmenting sentences into words is the first part. If successful, the child moves on to segmenting words into syllables. If successful with this second task, the child is asked to segment words into sounds. The TALS provides a more comprehensive measure of phonemic awareness by including three different tasks.

The Assessment Test

The Assessment Test (Adams, Foorman, Lundberg, & Beeler, 1998) is part of a textbook that provides a phonemic awareness curriculum based upon language games and sound activities. The games involve a variety of components: listening, rhyming, word and sentence awareness, syllable awareness, initial and final sounds, phonemes, and an introduction to letters and spelling. The Assessment Test is a group test that allows a teacher or tutor to evaluate individual phonemic awareness. It also suggests an appropriate placement level for the classroom activities described above.

The Assessment Test is made up of six subtests: Detecting Rhymes, Counting Syllables, Matching Initial Sounds, Counting Phonemes, Comparing Word Lengths, and Representing Phonemes with Letters. It is a paper-and-pencil test. The authors recommend that it be administered to no more than 15 first graders at one time or 6 kindergartners at one time. They also suggest that two teachers administer the test, to ensure that children follow directions and pay attention.

In the Detecting Rhymes subtest, children look at pictures and connect those that rhyme with a line. Children count syllables by looking at pictures and making tally marks to indicate the number of syllables they hear. Children match initial sounds by drawing a line between pictures that begin with the same sound. They count phonemes by looking at pictures and using tally marks to indicate how many sounds they hear. Children compare word lengths by deciding which one of two pictures represents a word that has the most phonemes. In the Representing Phonemes with Letters subtest, children spell words represented by five pictures. Each subtest has a total of 5 points, with a maximum score of 30 points.

A teacher or tutor can use this measure to evaluate individual students or to evaluate an entire group of students. By adding together the scores of each child on a specific subtest and dividing this total by the number of children who took the test, the teacher or tutor arrives at a class average for that subtest. The authors suggest that a score of less than 4 indicates a need for instructional support in that particular area of phonemic awareness. Dividing phonemic awareness into separate categories allows the teacher or tutor to assess phonemic awareness specifically as opposed to generally. It also suggests defined areas for instructional emphasis.

ASSESSING PRINT AWARENESS

The teacher or tutor can purchase a published test, the Concepts about Print (CAP) Test (Clay, 1972, 1979, 1993) to assess a child's emerging understanding of print concepts. The teacher or tutor can also evaluate this understanding quite simply by sharing a book with a student.

Concepts about Print Test

In administering the CAP Test, the examiner and the child read a book together. Clay provides two little books, *Sand* (Clay, 1972) and *Stones* (Clay, 1979), for this purpose. The CAP Test evaluates whether the child can recognize the front of the book, the beginning of the text, and whether the book is right side up. It assesses the child's understanding that print (not pictures) carries the message, and that English text is read in a certain direction (from top to bottom and from left to right). The CAP Test also evaluates whether the child can match a spoken word to a written word and whether the child recognizes letters, words, and punctuation. The book used in this test presents words in the wrong order, upside-down pictures, and misplaced lines. If the child recognizes such errors, the examiner can assume concept knowledge.

Sharing a Book

As a teacher or tutor, you can also learn about a child's developing print awareness simply by asking the child questions and by observing his or her behaviors. Choose a simple book with one or two lines per page. Tell the child, "We are going to read this book." Note the child's reaction to this. Does he or she exhibit interest and enthusiasm? Ask the child to pick it up. Does the child hold it right side up? Does the child hold it so the front of the book is facing him or her? Ask the child to point to the title and the author. Open the book and ask the child to point to "what we will be reading." The child should point to print, not pictures. Ask the child to point to "where we begin" and "where we will go next." Does the child point to the beginning of the first line and move from right to left? Does the child return to the second line? Ask the child to point to a word. Read the text on the first page, moving your hand under the lines so the child can see. After reading, pronounce one of the words and ask the child to point to it. Ask the child to point to a letter. Can the child identify any letters by name? Can the child identify a sentence by noting beginning capitalization and ending punctuation? Use the accompanying checklist to keep track of the child's performance.

Assessing print awareness works best with individual children. It does not take long. However, it can also be done with a very small group. The nice thing about assessing print concepts in the fashion described here is that it represents a very natural and authentic literacy situation—an adult and a child interacting together about print and enjoying the process. Assessing print concepts lets a teacher or tutor know the specific type of instructional support that is needed to move the child on his or her journey toward literacy.

Print Awareness Checklist

___ Regards print with enthusiasm

___ Holds book right way up

___ Identifies front of book

___ Points to title

___ Points to author

___ Points to print, not pictures

___ Recognizes top–bottom direction

___ Recognizes left–right direction

___ Can point to a word

___ Can point to two words

___ Can match spoken word with printed word

___ Recognizes an upper-case letter

___ Recognizes a lower-case letter

___ Can identify letters by name

___ Can identify a sentence

ASSESSING ALPHABET KNOWLEDGE

Assessing alphabet knowledge involves three components: Can the child recognize individual letters? Can the child differentiate between upper- and lower-case letters? And can the child write these letters? Alphabet knowledge, like phonemic awareness, is a sensitive predictor of early reading achievement (Adams, 1990).

As a teacher or tutor, you do not need a formal test to assess alphabet knowledge. Simply type the alphabet letters in lower case at the top of a page and in upper case at the bottom. Mix the letters up (i.e., do not type them as *a*, *b*, *c*, etc.). Ask your student to identify the lower-case letters first. They tend to be more common and therefore more familiar. Then ask the student to identify the upper-case letters. Finally, say a letter and ask your student to write it. You can record answers on a duplicate of the student's sheet.

You can also use this sheet to determine whether the student knows the sound that is represented by a letter. Point to the letter and ask the student what sound it makes. What about letters that can stand for more than one sound, like the vowels and the consonants *c* and *g*? Don't worry about whether the student knows all the sounds. Knowledge of one sound is enough to indicate the student's understanding that alphabet letters represent sounds.

ASSESSING EARLY EFFORTS
IN WORD IDENTIFICATION

When children begin reading text, it is important for teachers and tutors to evaluate individual progress. Is a child becoming more skilled in identifying words and gradually moving from success in very easy selections to success in increasingly difficult ones? A running record allows a teacher or tutor to assess a child's performance in any selection. The teacher or tutor counts the number of word identification errors that a child makes and uses this count to determine whether the text was easy, difficult, or appropriate for the child.

It can also be very helpful to attempt to get inside a child's head to determine what strategies he or she uses in attempting to identify words. Is the child using meaning cues, as Zachary does in the earlier example? Is the child trying to match letters and sounds, as Cyntha does? Is he or she predicting from the sentence structure? What behaviors indicate that the child is progressing as a reader? Does the young reader hesitate before words or repeat words, perhaps stalling for time as he or she attempts to figure out the next word? Does the young reader skip unknown words, ask for help, or attempt to identify the word on his or her own? Does the child self-correct errors? A teacher or tutor can employ the *running record* process to find answers to these questions. This is probably not something that you as a beginning teacher or tutor will do immediately. First, you should become confident in recording word identification errors and in determining whether the text is easy or difficult for a child. Later, when you feel comfortable with the basic elements of a running record, you can move to analyzing the child's strategies for identifying words.

Running Records

A *running record* is a way to record what an individual child does while reading orally. The primary purpose of a running record is to determine whether a specific text is easy, difficult, or appropriate for a child.

A running record is very similar to the informal reading inventory (IRI) process (discussed in Chapter Three). Both are used with a single child, and both involve the recording of oral reading performance. However, there are differences. In the IRI process, the teacher or tutor records oral reading errors on a duplicate copy of the text that is being read by the child. In a running record, the teacher or tutor records oral reading performance on a blank sheet of paper. In the IRI process, only errors or deviations from the text are marked. In a running record, the teacher or tutor places a check mark on the paper for each word read correctly.

The IRI process employs miscue analysis to determine what strategies the student uses in attempting to identify words. This involves rewriting the miscues on a separate sheet of paper and examining each one according to several categories. (Miscue analysis is explained in Chapter Five.) When using a running record, the teacher or tutor records possible word identification strategies on the original record sheet. Both the IRI process and the running record code the child's errors as to type, and use the number of errors to arrive at some evaluation of the difficulty level of the text for the student.

Because a running record does not demand that the teacher or tutor duplicate the text that will be read by the student, it is, in a sense, a more flexible process. A teacher or tutor can decide to use a running record on the spur of the moment, because no advance preparation is required. However, unless the teacher or tutor records oral reading performance in an orderly and uniform way, later interpretation of the running record can be difficult.

Taking a running record is not easy. Like the IRI process, it requires practice and takes time to examine and score. Scoring can involve determining the difficulty level of the text for a child, or it can be more complex and include an analysis of word identification strategies. As a beginning teacher or tutor, you will probably find that a running record is most helpful in determining which book a child can read with comfort and success. If this is the only use that you make of a running record, it is a very helpful one. Don't feel guilty about not engaging in more detailed strategy analysis. Chances are that you will not have the time. However, it is a good idea for you to be aware of the scope and power of the running record, even if you do not use it to its full extent.

Coding Oral Reading Performance in a Running Record

As the child reads, record what he or she says. Transcribe each separate line that the child reads as a separate line on the blank record sheet. Once the child is finished, return to the coding sheet and make additional notations. These notations are indicated below as "Later analysis."

You may choose to mark only those words that are correctly identified, as opposed to identifying, coding, and analyzing errors. The process of identifying and coding errors is much more time-consuming and complex. If you mark only the correctly identified words, this will be sufficient to determine how difficult the text is for the child. Identifying, coding, and analyzing errors may represent too great an expenditure of time for you as a busy teacher or tutor. However, I illustrate below how it is done, so that you can understand the power of a running record. Ideally, when you become adept at recording correctly identified words, you can move on to a more detailed analysis.

- *Words read correctly*. Mark words read correctly with a check.

Text:	Who do I see on the log?
Student:	Who do I see on the log?
Running record:	✓ ✓ ✓ ✓ ✓ ✓

- *Omissions*. Mark omitted words with a dash. After the running record is completed, return to the record and write in the omitted word.

Text:	Oh! I bet it is a frog.
Student:	I bet it is a frog.
Running record:	— ✓ ✓ ✓ ✓ ✓ ✓
Later analysis:	$\frac{-}{oh}$ ✓ ✓ ✓ ✓ ✓ ✓

• *Substitutions*. If a student substitutes words, write in the substitution and later fill in the text word.

Text: Who do I see on the plant?
Student: What do I see on the plant?
Running record: *what* ✓ ✓ ✓ ✓ ✓
Later analysis: $\underline{what}$ ✓ ✓ ✓ ✓ ✓
                         who

• *Insertions*. If a student adds a word, write in the addition. Later on, when you return to the record, simply place a dash under the word to indicate that there was no matching word.

Text: Oh! I bet it is an ant.
Student: Oh! I bet it is a big ant.
Running record: ✓ ✓ ✓ ✓ ✓ *big* ✓
Later analysis: ✓ ✓ ✓ ✓ ✓ $\underline{big}$ ✓
                         —

• *Self-corrections*. When readers self-correct, write the original word and follow it with an SC. Later, indicate the text word.

Text: Who do I see on the rug?
Student: Who do I see on the rag rug?
Running record: ✓ ✓ ✓ ✓ ✓ *rag SC*
Later analysis: ✓ ✓ ✓ ✓ ✓ $\underline{rag\ SC}$
                         rug

• *Repetitions*. When readers repeat a words or several words, mark each word with an R. If they repeat an entire line, draw a line and mark the line R. If they repeat a word or words twice, indicate that this happened with a 2.

Text: Oh! I bet it is a bug.
Student: Oh! Oh! I bet it is is is a bug bug.
                         Oh! I bet it is a bug.
Running record: ✓ R ✓ ✓ ✓ ✓ R^2 ✓ ✓ R
                         ——————————————R

• *Attempts*. Children often attempt several different pronunciations before they settle on the one that satisfies them. Coding their attempts can often indicate what strategies they are using. Record each attempt and draw a vertical line between each one.

Text:	Who do I see in the truck?
Student:	Who do I see in the to/ter/trick/truck?
Running record:	✓ ✓ ✓ ✓ ✓ ✓ *to /ter /trick*
Later analysis:	✓ ✓ ✓ ✓ ✓ ✓ <u>*to /ter /trick*</u> *truck*

• *Try again.* Sometimes a child becomes hopelessly confused and makes so many errors that he or she either stops reading or asks for help. Feel free to ask the child, "Why don't you try that again?" Code the new effort, but mark that line with a bracket; then you can compare the second reading to the first one.

Text:	And who is dancing that happy jig?
Student:	And what who is decing the silly happen decking I don't know that word And who is decing that happen happy jug jig?
Running record:	✓ *what SC* ✓ *decing the silly happen decking* (✓ ✓ ✓ *decing* ✓ *happen SC jug SC*)
Later analysis:	(✓ ✓ ✓ *decing* ✓ *happen SC jug SC*) <u>*dancing*</u> <u>*happy*</u> <u>*jig*</u>

Let's try another example and see how you do. We will take it line by line. Record Amanda's performance in the space provided. Then check my recording and my explanation of what I did.*

Text:	It was a warm spring day.
Student:	It was a super day.
Your running record:	
My running record:	✓ ✓ ✓ — <u>*super*</u> ✓ *spring*
Explanation:	Amanda omitted *warm*, so I indicated this with a dash. She substituted *super* for *spring*, so I wrote *super* and later filled in the missed word below the substitution.

---

*The selection read by Amanda, "A Trip" (which is also the selection read by Jamael in Appendix 4.1), is from Leslie, L., and Caldwell, J. S. (2001). *The Qualitative Reading Inventory 3.* New York: Addison Wesley Longman. Copyright 2001 by Addison Wesley Longman. Reprinted by permission.

Text: The children were going on a trip.
Student: The children were gone on a trip.
Your running record:

My running record: ✓ ✓ ✓ _gone_ ✓ ✓ ✓
                                 going

Explanation: Amanda substituted *gone* for *going*, so I wrote in
                         the substitution and later indicated the original
                         word.

Text: The trip was to a farm.
Student: The trip was to the a farm.
Your running record:

My running record: ✓ ✓ ✓ ✓ _the_ SC
                                   _a_

Explanation: Amanda substituted *the* for *a* but corrected it. I
                         recorded *the* as a substitution, and marked it SC
                         to indicate that she corrected it.

Text: The children wanted to see many animals.
Student: The children were to see many animals there.
Your running record:

My running record: ✓ ✓ _were_ ✓ ✓ ✓ ✓ _there_
                               wanted   _—_

Explanation: Amanda substituted *were* for *wanted*, so I wrote
                         in *were*. She inserted *there*, so I wrote in *there*,
                         but indicated with a dash that it was an inser-
                         tion.

Text: They wanted to write down all they saw.
Student: They wanted to write down to write down all
                         they saw.
Your running record:

My running record: ✓ ✓ ✓ ✓ ✓ R R R ✓ ✓

Explanation: Amanda repeated *to write down*, so I indicated
                         this with an R for each repeated word.

Text:	They were going to make a book for their class.
Student:	They were going to make a book for their class.
Your running record:	

My running record: ✓ ✓ ✓ ✓ ✓ ✓ ✓ ✓

Explanation: Amanda made no errors. I recorded each word that she correctly pronounced with a check.

Text:	On the way to the farm the bus broke down.
Student:	On their way to the farm the bug broke down.
Your running record:	

My running record: ✓ $\frac{their}{the}$ ✓ ✓ ✓ ✓ $\frac{bug}{bus}$ ✓ ✓

Explanation: Amanda substituted *their* for *the* and *bug* for *bus*. I wrote in the substitutions and later indicated the original words.

Text:	The children thought their trip was over.
Student:	The children threw their trip their trip was over.
Your running record:	

My running record: ✓ ✓ $\frac{threw}{thought}$ ✓ ✓ R R ✓ ✓

Explanation: Amanda substituted *threw* for *thought*, so I wrote in *threw*. She repeated *their trip*, and I indicated this with an R for each word repeated.

Text:	Then a man stopped his car.
Student:	Then a man his car.
Your running record:	

My running record: ✓ ✓ ✓ $\frac{—}{stopped}$ ✓ ✓

Explanation: Amanda omitted *stopped*. I indicated this with a dash and later wrote in the omitted word.

Text:	He helped to fix the bus.
Student:	He hoped helped to fix to fix the bus.

Your running record:

My running record: ✓ *hoped* SC ✓ ✓ R R ✓ ✓
                   $\overline{helped}$

Explanation: Amanda substituted *hoped* for *helped*, but she
                   then corrected her error. I wrote down the origi-
                   nal substitution and indicated that it was cor-
                   rected by SC. Amanda also repeated *to fix*, and I
                   indicated this with R for each repeated word.

Text: The bus started again.
Student: The bus started up again.
Your running record:

My running record: ✓ ✓ ✓ $\underline{up}$ ✓

Explanation: Amanda inserted *up*, and I wrote down her in-
                   sertion. Later I placed a dash under it to indi-
                   cate that there was no matching word.

Text: The children said, "Yea!"
Student: The children said, "Yea!"
Your running record:

My running record: ✓ ✓ ✓ ✓

Explanation: Amanda made no errors. Each word that she
                   correctly pronounced was indicated with a
                   check.

Text: The children got to the farm.
Student: The children thought got to the farm to the farm.
Your running record:

My running record: ✓ ✓ *thought* SC ✓ ✓ ✓ ✓ R R R
                       $\overline{}$

Explanation: Amanda substituted *thought*, but corrected her
                   error. I wrote down the substitution, but indi-
                   cated the self-correction with SC. She repeated
                   to the farm. I indicated the repetition of each
                   word with an R.

Text: They saw a pig.
Student: They saw pigs.
Your running record:

My running record: ✓ ✓ $\frac{a}{-}$ $\frac{pigs}{pig}$

Explanation: Amanda omitted *a*, and I indicated this with a
                             dash. She substituted *pigs* for *pig*, and I wrote in
                             the substitution.

Text: They saw a hen and cows.
Student: They saw a hen and they saw cows.
Your running record:

My running record: ✓ ✓ ✓ ✓ ✓ $\frac{they}{-}$ $\frac{saw}{-}$ ✓

Explanation: Amanda inserted *they saw*, and I wrote in each
                             inserted word. Later I indicated with a dash that
                             there was no matching word in the text.

Text: They liked petting the kittens.
Student: They liked po/pit/putting/petting the kittens.
Your running record:

My running record: ✓ ✓ $\frac{po/pit/putting}{petting}$ SC ✓ ✓

Explanation: Amanda attempted several pronunciations of *pet-
                             ting*. I recorded each attempt and indicated with
                             SC that she eventually arrived at the correct pro-
                             nunciation. Later I indicated the word that she
                             was attempting to pronounce.

Text: They learned about milking cows.
Student: They leaned about making cows about milking
                             cows.
Your running record:

My running record: ✓ $\frac{leaned}{learned}$ ✓ $\frac{making}{milking}$ ✓ R ✓ R

Explanation: Amanda substituted *leaned* for *learned*. She sub-
                             stituted *making* for *milking*. Then she repeated

the entire phrase *about milking cows* and self-corrected her original mispronunciation of *milking*. I indicated her later self-correction with a check as opposed to an SC, because she made the correction during a repetition as opposed to immediately after the original substitution.

Text: They liked the trip to the farm.
Student: They liked going on the trip to the farm.
Your running record:

My running record: ✓ ✓ *going on* ✓ ✓ ✓ ✓

Explanation: Amanda inserted *going on* before *the trip to the farm*. I wrote in these two words and later indicated with dashes that there were no matching words in the text.

Text: They wanted to go again.
Student: The they wanted to go there again.
Your running record:

My running record: *The* SC ✓ ✓ ✓ *there* ✓
                   They

Explanation: Amanda substituted *the* for *they*. I wrote in the substitution, but indicated her immediate correction with an SC. She inserted *there*. I wrote this in and indicated with a dash the lack of matching text.

Computing Error Rate and Accuracy Rate

Once you have listened to the child read and you have taken a running record, the next step is to analyze the child's performance. What does the number of errors tell you? It provides a rough estimate of the difficulty level of the text for an individual child. Johnston (1997) offers the following guidelines. A rate of 1 error in 20 words, or a 5% error rate, suggests that the text is easy. An error rate greater than 1 in 10 words, or 10%, indicates that the text is hard. Anything between 1 in 20 (5%) and 1 in 10 (10%) suggests an appropriate level of difficulty for the child.

Guidelines for Error Rates and Accuracy Rates in Running Records

Easy text:
 5% or lower error rate
 95% accuracy rate

Appropriate text:
 Between 6% and 9% error rate
 Between 91% and 94% accuracy rate

Difficult text:
 10% or higher error rate
 90% or lower accuracy rate

Amanda read a total of 119 words. If we count all errors (even those that were self-corrected), and if we do not count repetitions, she made a total of 24 errors. To figure out her error rate, divide the number of errors, 24, by the total number of words, 119. The answer is .20. Multiply .20 by 100 to get rid of the decimal and you have a 20% error rate. Subtract 20% from 100% to get the accuracy rate, which is 80%. According to the guidelines described above, the text that Amanda read was too difficult for her.

Let's try another computation of error and accuracy rate. Claudia made 13 errors in a 76-word text. Figure out Claudia's error rate, and accuracy rate and then check with my scoring.

The number of errors, 13, divided by the total number of words, 76, is .17. If .17 is multiplied by 100, we have an error rate of 17%. If 17% is subtracted from 100%, we have an accuracy rate of 83%. According to the guidelines above, the text that Claudia read was too difficult for her.

These error and accuracy rates roughly correspond to the IRI process levels of independent, instructional, and frustration. An error rate of 5% or less,

Formula for Computing Error Rates and Accuracy Rates

Number of errors divided by total number of words multiplied by 100 equals error rate.
Answer subtracted from 100 equals accuracy rate.

or an accuracy rate of 95% or above, indicates an independent reading level. An error rate of 6%–9%, or an accuracy rate of 91%–94% indicates an instructional level (or what Johnston, 1997, calls a *learning level*). An error rate of 10% or above, or an accuracy level of 90% or below, indicates a frustration level. The difference is that the IRI process levels are attached to a numerical grade level and interpreted in terms of the grade level of the selection that was read. The running record levels are attached to a specific book.

Counting Errors

What do you count as an error? Is repetition or self-correction an error? If the error does not alter the meaning of the text, should it be counted? These are the same questions that plague teachers and tutors who use the IRI process. Make your decision as to what constitutes an error and stay with it. I recommend that you employ the same system for the Informal Reading Inventory Process and for running records. It is easy to get confused if you use different guidelines for the two processes. I have always employed the following guidelines.

• Count all errors, even those that were self-corrected. Many people disagree with me about self-corrections, but I believe that the initial error indicates lack of automatic decoding and should be counted. When you decide whether the text was easy, appropriate, or difficult, you can note the number of self-corrections as one indication that a child is moving toward word identification accuracy.

• Do not count repetitions.

• Count all substitutions, insertions, and omissions even if they do not distort meaning. Again, people disagree with this, but I find the process of determining whether meaning is or is not altered too time-consuming. As I have mentioned in Chapter Three, the difference between errors that distort meaning and those that do not seldom results in a level change.

• If a child encounters the same word in the text and mispronounces it each time, count it as an error each time it is mispronounced.

• If a line is omitted, count each word as an error.

Interpretation of Coding

If you wish to probe further into a child's strategies for identifying words, you can analyze his or her errors. Most teachers and tutors are too busy to do this on a regular basis. I include the procedure to give you an idea of the power of the running record process, but I do not suggest that you attempt this analysis until you are very comfortable with recording errors and with computing error and accuracy rates.

There are basically three sources of information that readers can draw on when faced with an unfamiliar word. These are discussed again in Chapter Five in relation to miscue analysis. First, a reader can use semantics or meaning to identify a word. For example, in the sentence *I fed peanuts to the big elephant*, *peanuts* and *big* might act as powerful meaning clues to the identification of *elephant*. Second, a reader can use syntax or the structure of the language to identify a word. In the sentence *The little cat hid under the bed*, *hid* and *bed* could act as structure clues to *under*. Finally, the reader can use the visual information provided by letters and can attempt to match letters and sounds.

Once the running record is completed, you can examine each deviation from the test to determine which information source the child is using. You can mark each error as M (meaning), S (structure), or V (visual). Sometimes you will be unable to decide which source was used; in that case, mark any that seem probable.

Text:

Once there was a mouse.
He lived in a wall of an old house.
Each night the mouse went to the kitchen.
He wanted to find something to eat.

Student:

Once there went was a mouse.
He lives in a wall of an old house.
Each night the mouse went to the kitten.
He wants to find simming to eat.

Running record:

✓ ✓ went SC ✓ ✓
✓ lives ✓ ✓ ✓ ✓ ✓
✓ ✓ ✓ ✓ ✓ ✓ kitten
✓ wants ✓ ✓ simming ✓ ✓

Later analysis:

✓ ✓ <u>went</u> SC ✓ ✓   M ✓
    was

✓ <u>lives</u> ✓ ✓ ✓ ✓ ✓   S ✓
    lived

✓ ✓ ✓ ✓ ✓ ✓ <u>kitten</u>   M ✓
              kitchen

✓ <u>wants</u> ✓ ✓ <u>simming</u> ✓ ✓   S ✓ ✓
   wanted   something

The substitution of *went* for *was* could be marked as both a meaning cue and a visual cue. The child might have predicted a story action (meaning), and both words began with the same letter (visual). Of course, the error was self-corrected, so the child paid attention to letters and sounds—visual cues. The substitution of *lives* for *lived* could involve both visual and structure cues. The child paid attention to the initial letters (visual), but substituted present for past tense (structure). The present tense is a structure often used in beginning stories, so we can hypothesize that the child may have been drawing upon this. The substitution of *kitten* for *kitchen* involves both meaning and visual cues. Both words begin with the same three letters (visual), but in a story about a mouse, the substitution of *kitten* could be taken as a meaning cue. The substitution of *wants* for *wanted* follows the pattern of *lives* for *lived*. The substitution of *simming* for *something* represents attention to a visual source—the beginning letter and the ending. Because it represents a nonword, we cannot say that meaning was involved.

Beginning readers tend to depend upon meaning for word identification. As they become more knowledgeable about letter–sound matching, they begin to emphasize the visual source. You want a child to emphasize meaning, because reading is, after all, a process of making meaning. But you also want the child to use the visual system to identify words. Good readers identify unfamiliar words by matching letters and sounds, and it is important that young readers learn how to do this. Running records can demonstrate changes over time in the strategies used by young readers.

Which should you as a teacher or tutor use: a running record or the IRI process? It is up to you unless your school or district mandates one or the other. Is one more time-consuming than the other? I do not think so. Both require practice before you feel comfortable and confident in the process. Both can involve a simple counting of errors or a more detailed analysis of oral reading patterns.

The IRI process culminates in a general independent, instructional, or frustration level. It is based on the assumption that a child who experiences success in a specific passage will probably experience success in passages of similar difficulty. The running record indicates that a particular book is easy, hard, or appropriate. Both allow you to evaluate the appropriateness of any text for a particular child. Both can be used with any text, although the IRI process requires more advance notice in order to duplicate the examiner copy. The running record may be more appropriate for shorter and simpler text, and the IRI process may be easier for longer and more complex selections.

SUMMARY

• The development of literacy begins with the development of oral language. Oral language is necessary for literacy development, but it is not sufficient. The amount and quality of preschool literacy experiences, especially reading aloud to children, have a profound effect upon literacy development.

• Children need to acquire an awareness of words and syllables as separate units. They also need to develop phonemic awareness—an awareness of phonemes or sounds as separate units in a word. A child's ability to identify and manipulate phonemes is highly related to later reading and spelling achievement.

• Children must develop basic concepts about how print works, and they must learn the conventions of print. Children must also learn to identify the letters of the alphabet. Alphabet knowledge is a powerful predictor of later reading achievement.

• Beginning readers first identify words using visual cues. Later they begin to match letters and sounds. Early readers rely upon context and pictures to help them identify words and understand text.

• Teachers or tutors must carefully observe the oral language of young children in order to refer them for additional assessment.

• Teachers and tutors may use three published measures to assess phonemic awareness: the Yopp–Singer Test of Phonemic Segmentation, the Test of Awareness of Language Segments (TALS), and the Assessment Test.

• Teachers or tutors may use the Concepts about Print (CAP) Test to assess print awareness. They may also devise their own checklists and assess print awareness while talking to a child about a book.

• Teachers and tutors should assess alphabet knowledge: recognition of individual letters, differentiation of upper and lower case, and ability to write the letters.

• A running record can be used to determine whether a selection is easy, difficult, or appropriate for a child. A running record can also be used to identify word identification strategies.

• The informal reading inventory (IRI) process and a running record are very similar.

ACTIVITIES FOR DEVELOPING UNDERSTANDING

• Administer the Yopp–Singer Test of Phonemic Segmentation. Score the child's performance and make a judgment regarding the child's level of phonemic awareness.

• Use the CAP Test or the Print Awareness Checklist to assess a child's developing understanding in this area.

• Make a letter template and use this to assess a child's recognition of upper-case and lower-case letters. Assess the child's ability to write these letters.

• Listen to a child read a short piece of text. Tape-record this so you can refer to the tape. Take a running record as the child reads. Then go back, listen to the tape, and refine your running record.

• Use the running record to compute the child's accuracy.

• Use Appendix 4.1 for further practice in coding an IRI process and a running record.

• Complete the self-evaluation form provided at the end of this chapter (following Appendix 4.1).

APPENDIX 4.1

Practice in Coding an IRI Process and a Running Record

The following exercise provides more practice in recording and counting oral reading performance. Jamael orally read a first-grade selection entitled "A Trip" (the same selection read by Amanda in the earlier example). Using the transcript of Jamael's reading, record his performance according to the guidelines of the IRI process. Then record his performance as a running record. Afterward, check my recording and compare your results. This exercise points out the similarities between the IRI process and the running record.

JAMAEL'S READING

It was a warm summer day. The children were gone on a trip. The trip was to a farm. The children went to see many aminals animals. They wasn't to write all they was. They were gone to make a book for their kalass. On the way to the farm the bus broke down. The children thogut their trip was over. Then a man stops his car. He here helped to fox fix the bus. The bus started again. He the children said, "Yes!" The children got to the farm. They saw pigs. They saw a hen and cows. They liked pigs petting the kittens. They liked about making cows. They liked the trip to the farm. They went to go again.

YOUR RECORDING

IRI process   **Running record**

It was a warm spring day.

The children were going on a trip.

The trip was to a farm.

The children wanted to see many animals.

They wanted to write down all they saw.

They were going to make a book for their class.

On the way to the farm the bus broke down.

The children thought their trip was over.

Then a man stopped his car.

He helped to fix the bus.

The bus started again.

The children said, "Yea!"

The children got to the farm.

They saw a pig.

They saw a hen and cows.

They liked petting the kittens.

They learned about milking cows.

They liked the trip to the farm.

They wanted to go again. (119 words)

Number of all errors: Number of all errors:

Accuracy level: Error rate:

Level: Text difficulty:

MY RECORDING

IRI process	Running record

IRI process

summer
It was a warm spring day.

gone
The children were going on a trip.

The trip was to a farm.

went   aminals C
The children wanted to see many animals.

wasn't   was
They wanted to write (down) all they saw.

gone   kalass
They were going to make a book for their class.

On the way to the farm the bus broke down.

thogut
The children thought their trip was over.

stops
Then a man stopped his car.

here C fox C
He helped to fix the bus.

The bus started again.
He C   Yes
The children said, "Yea!"

The children got to the farm.

pigs
They saw (a) pig.

They saw a hen and cows.

pigs C
They liked petting the kittens.

liked   making
They learned about milking cows.

They liked the trip to the farm.

went
They wanted to go again. (119 words)

Running record

✓ ✓ ✓ ✓ $\frac{summer}{spring}$ ✓

✓ ✓ ✓ $\frac{gone}{going}$ ✓ ✓ ✓

✓ ✓ ✓ ✓ ✓ ✓

✓ ✓ $\frac{went}{wanted}$ ✓ ✓ ✓ $\frac{aminals\ SC}{animals}$

✓ $\frac{wasn't}{wanted}$ ✓ ✓ $\frac{-}{down}$ ✓ ✓ $\frac{was}{saw}$

✓ ✓ $\frac{gone}{going}$ ✓ ✓ ✓ ✓ ✓ $\frac{kaylass}{class}$

✓ ✓ ✓ ✓ ✓ ✓ ✓ ✓ ✓

✓ ✓ $\frac{thogut}{thought}$ ✓ ✓ ✓ ✓

✓ ✓ ✓ $\frac{stops}{stopped}$ ✓ ✓

✓ $\frac{here\ SC}{helped}$ ✓ $\frac{fox\ SC}{fix}$ ✓ ✓

✓ ✓ ✓ ✓

$\frac{he\ SC}{the}$ ✓ ✓ $\frac{yes}{yea}$

✓ ✓ ✓ ✓ ✓ ✓

✓ ✓ $\frac{-}{a}$ $\frac{pigs}{pig}$

✓ ✓ ✓ ✓ ✓ ✓

✓ ✓ $\frac{pigs\ SC}{petting}$ ✓ ✓

✓ $\frac{liked}{learned}$ ✓ $\frac{making}{milking}$ ✓

✓ ✓ ✓ ✓ ✓ ✓

✓ $\frac{went}{wanted}$ ✓ ✓ ✓

Number of all errors: *21*

Accuracy level:
    119 − 21 = 98 ÷ 119 = 82%

Level: *Frustration*

Number of all errors: *21*

Error rate:
    21 ÷ 119 = .18 × 100 = 18%

Text difficulty: *Hard*

Teacher or Tutor Self-Evaluation

I carefully listen to the oral language of my students in order to identify any children who might need assessment by a specialist.

> Regularly   Occasionally   A future goal

I assess the phonemic awareness of my students using the Yopp–Singer, the TALS, or the Assessment Test.

> Regularly   Occasionally   A future goal

I assess print awareness using the CAP Test.

> Regularly   Occasionally   A future goal

I assess print awareness by sharing a book with a child.

> Regularly   Occasionally   A future goal

I assess alphabet knowledge.

> Regularly   Occasionally   A future goal

I use a running record to determine text difficulty.

> Regularly   Occasionally   A future goal

I use a running record to analyze a student's reading strategies.

> Regularly   Occasionally   A future goal

FIVE

Word Identification

How Can We Assess a Student's Word Identification Ability?

CHAPTER TOPICS

THE ROLE OF WORD IDENTIFICATION
IN THE READING PROCESS

Good readers pronounce words both accurately and automatically. But this is just the beginning. If reading were only saying words, it would be a very dull process. However, readers also construct meaning—and, when they do, wonderful things happen! Readers attach meaning to words, phrases, sentences, and paragraphs. Readers create visual images, become emotionally involved with the characters, and tie the events in the text to their own lives. Readers predict what will happen next and identify what is important. Readers may argue with the author, and accept or reject the author's views. And these are only a few of the activities that go under the general heading of comprehension. But comprehension cannot take place if readers are unable to identify the words both accurately and automatically.

Word identification has often been confused with the reading process as a whole. Even today, there are people with an oversimplified view of the reading process: They believe that teaching students to pronounce words is all that is needed. This is untrue. Word identification is a necessary element in reading, but it is not sufficient. Reading is a process of constructing meaning. Word identification is the key that opens the door to the exciting world of comprehension. Without comprehension, what would be the purpose of reading?

I worked with a second grader whose parents were graduate students at a large university. Aushabell's native language was extremely phonetic; that is, there was an almost exact and perfect match between the letters of her language and the sounds. Using her skill in letter–sound matching, Aushabell was able to identify English words with amazing accuracy. She read a short story to me with very few oral reading errors. However, she had no idea what she read. Although she could say the words, she was not able to attach meaning to them. As a result, Aushabell comprehended little if anything. Unfortunately, Aushabell's teacher—obviously confusing saying words with the reading process as a whole—informed her parents that Aushabell was an excellent reader!

STRATEGIES FOR IDENTIFYING WORDS

How does a reader identify or pronounce a word? Ehri (1997) suggests that there are basically four ways. The most common way for good readers is to identify words from memory. Most of the words that you and I encounter are very familiar to us (words such as *and, mother, club, with,* etc.). We pronounce them immediately, without any analysis and without consciously matching letters and sounds. We call these words *sight words.* Instant recognition of a large store of sight words allows us to read quickly and fluently. We do not have to stop and try to figure out each word. And because

---

Four Ways to Identify a Word

Memory.
Decoding of individual sounds.
Predicting from context.
Decoding by analogy to known words.

---

we do not have to pay attention to word identification, we can focus on comprehension.

What strategies do we use when we meet an unfamiliar word—one we have never before seen in print? In the following sentence, there is a word you have probably never seen before:

**Mary's sudden *tergiversation* surprised all her friends
and especially her family.**

Were you able to pronounce *tergiversation?* I am sure you were. What strategy did you use? Did you match individual sounds to single letters beginning with *t*, moving on to *e*, and continuing until each letter and its accompanying sound was identified? Then did you blend all the individual letter sounds to arrive at the correct pronunciation? This is the second strategy that readers can use. Ehri (1997) calls it *decoding* or *word attack*. However, it does not always work, especially with multisyllabic words or long words.

Did you attempt to predict the pronunciation of *tergiversation* from the context of the sentence? Perhaps you read the sentence and then returned to *tergiversation*. Did the sentence help you with pronunciation? I doubt it. All you know is that the *tergiversation* surprised people, but there were no clues to help you with its pronunciation. Predicting from context is yet another strategy for identifying words but, again, it does not always work. Using context for word pronunciation is very typical of beginning readers. They can pronounce *elephant* when a picture accompanies the text, but are unsuccessful if *elephant* is printed on a word card.

So how did you pronounce *tergiversation?* You probably broke the word into familiar chunks and matched your pronunciation to words you already knew as sight words. Perhaps you knew *ter* because of its similarity to *her* or because you knew *termite*. You had no problem with *give*; it was a sight word for you. And, of course, if you knew *conversation* (and I'm sure you did), the rest was easy. In other words, you quickly analyzed the word using analogies to known words. Let's try another word

twisdorsercleck

See how fast you did this? What known words (called *analogues*) did you use? *Twine* for *tw*? *Horse* for *dorse*? *Heck* for *cleck*? Each reader chooses different analogues. Sometimes the analogue is a syllable, and sometimes it is a whole word. How would you pronounce *souquet* and *fongue*? Did you use *bouquet* or *tongue* (Ehri, 1997)? Using analogues to pronounce unfamiliar words is not a foolproof process. Sometimes it results in inaccurate pronunciation because the wrong analogue was chosen. Consider *disland* (Ehri, 1997). Did you use *is* and *land*, or did you pronounce the word using the analogue *island*? But, for the most part, analyzing unfamiliar words by analogy to known words and word parts works extremely well, especially for long words. It may not result in an exact and complete pronunciation, but it usually gives you enough clues to arrive at an approximate one. If you have heard the word before, that is probably all you need.

For example, suppose you have never seen the word *hotel* in print, but you certainly know what a hotel is. Your eyes meet *hotel*. Now you probably pause and mentally try out two possible pronunciations, *hot el* and *ho tel*. The second matches the word you have heard, so you choose *ho tel* and read on. The process is so efficient that you are hardly aware of your actions. However, success in analyzing by analogy is based upon two things: a large store of sight words to use as analogues, and a large listening vocabulary. A *listening vocabulary* consists of all the words you have heard; when you use analogues to arrive at an approximate pronunciation, you match that pronunciation with a word in your listening vocabulary. Teachers and tutors need to be aware of the importance of sight vocabulary and listening vocabulary in word identification.

Were you a bit troubled with *tergiversation*? I imagine you are fairly confident that you pronounced it accurately, but you were not able to match it to a known word in your head. Therefore, you were not totally certain of your pronunciation accuracy, and you certainly were confused about the meaning. Just saying words is not enough. Remember Aushabell? A reader must know the meanings of the words. If you could not attach meaning to *tergiversation*, the wonderful comprehension process was hampered. However, if you know that a tergiversation is a desertion of a cause (usually a religious or political one), then things change. Read the sentence again. Now what predictions about Mary and her friends and family can you make?

THE ROLE OF CONTEXT IN WORD IDENTIFICATION

One of the strategies that younger readers use is to predict word pronunciation from the context of the story or picture. According to some popular theories, all good readers do this. Such theories propose that good readers are skilled in identifying words because they rely heavily on context to predict word pronunciation. A substantial body of research, however, suggests exactly the opposite: As readers become more skilled, they no longer need or use context to recognize words (Stanovich, 1991, 1993–1994, 2000).

Good readers rarely use context to identify words, because they have a large sight vocabulary and have mastered the letter–sound system of their language. In fact, the ability to identify words accurately and quickly *out of context* is a characteristic of good readers (Perfetti, 1985, 1988; Stanovich, 1980, 1991). Their word recognition is too rapid and automatic for context usage to play a meaningful part. This is true for both familiar and unfamiliar words. Instead, context is a "mechanism in the comprehension process" (Stanovich, 1993–1994, p. 282). For example, readers use context to assign meanings to new and unknown words, as you no doubt attempted to do with *tergiversation.*

Poor readers who have not developed a large sight vocabulary and who have not mastered the letter–sound patterns of their language often overuse context (Perfetti, 1985; Stanovich, 1986). However, context clues do not always work well for them. In order to use context to recognize a word, a reader needs to identify most of the other words accurately. Students with reading problems often cannot recognize enough words to do this (Adams, 1990; Pflaum, Walberg, Karegianes, & Rassher, 1980). In addition, their word analysis skills are so poor that they ignore the sense of what they are reading to focus on laboriously matching individual letters and sounds.

It is important for teachers and tutors to understand the role of context in word identification, in order to choose appropriate evidence for assessing word identification skill. For example, a student's reading of a story with pictures may suggest effective word identification. However, that same student's reading of a text without pictures may offer a very different view. Some people question asking students to read word lists or word cards, because these are not authentic measures. However, comparing performance on a word list with word identification performance while reading a story may indicate the extent to which a student relies on context. Good readers recognize words accurately and automatically, and they do not use context to do this once they have moved through the initial stages of reading development.

LATER STAGES OF READING WORDS

Children tend to move through stages as they learn to identify words. In Chapter Four, I have described the first two stages of learning to read words—the stages of visual cue recoding and phonetic cue recoding (Ehri, 1991; Gough & Juel, 1991; Spear-Swerling & Sternberg, 1996). Remember Zachary, who uses the pictures to tell the story and who recognizes the word *pig* because it has a tail at the end? Remember Cyntha, who attempts to match consonant letters and sounds, but depends heavily upon context and pictures to pronounce words? Ideally, just as Zachary will move into Cyntha's stage of phonetic cue recoding, so too will Cyntha move on and become more competent and confident in reading words.

José, a second grader, chooses a book about turtles to read to his parents. When he meets an unfamiliar word, he knows that the letters and sounds are the clues to word pronunciation. He no longer depends upon pictures. More importantly, he recognizes that not any word will do. The word must fit the meaning of the passage. José has begun to notice word patterns and to use them as analogues. He divides an unfamiliar word between the initial consonant(s) (called the *onset*) and the vowel pattern (referred to as the *rime*). Gough and Juel (1991) estimate that this is the stage when word pronunciation becomes almost effortless. A child who knows *cake* probably also will know *flake, make, bake, fake,* and so on, even if he or she has never seen these words in print before. José is in the stage of *controlled word reading* (Spear-Swerling & Sternberg, 1996)—a very typical stage for second graders. However, his reading is slow and often laborious, and José needs to move into the next stage, where most words are recognized automatically.

Eight-year-old LaKendra's favorite pastime is reading. She eagerly participates in the activities of her school's book club and enjoys regular trips to the library. Each night, LaKendra reads a story to her little brother and then reads to herself before bedtime. However, LaKendra is less enthusiastic about reading science and social studies textbooks. Although she can successfully pronounce most of the words, she does not remember a lot of what she reads. "They're hard books," she complains to her mother, "and I have to read them over and over." LaKendra, like many second and third graders, is in the stage of *sight word reading* (Ehri, 1991) or *automatic word recognition* (Spear-Swerling & Sternberg, 1996). Children in this stage can recognize many words automatically without "sounding out." LaKendra has learned how to identify unfamiliar words. Now she needs to learn strategies for more advanced comprehension, such as identifying important information, summarizing content, synthesizing information, and repairing comprehension roadblocks.

It is important to realize that these stages are not discrete stages. In other words, a child does not approach all words in the same way. The child may use sound–letter matching for the majority of unfamiliar words, have a store of automatically recognized sight words, and still rely on visual cues for other words. In order to understand this, think about how you read. Spear-Swerling and Sternberg (1996) would say that you are in the stage of *proficient adult reading*, where pronunciation of words is seldom an issue. What do you do when you meet a word you have never seen in print before? You revert to letter–sound matching and sound it out! Even though the stages are not discrete, they provide a useful benchmark for describing good reader behaviors, and for choosing activities to move a reader to the next highest stage.

PURPOSES OF WORD IDENTIFICATION ASSESSMENT

This chapter focuses on the word identification process—the process that you used to pronounce *tergiversation* and *twisdorsercleck*. (Chapter Six focuses on assessment of sight word vocabulary.) What does a teacher or tutor need to know about word identification assessment in order to plan future lessons and group students effectively? First, the teacher or tutor needs to know whether a student can accurately pronounce words at an appropriate grade level. Second, the teacher or tutor needs to know what good reader strategies the student uses to do this. Does the student predict from context, as is typical of readers in the early stages of reading development? Does the student match letters and sounds? Does the student note word patterns and recognize words by analogy? Third, what progress in word identification is evident in the student's reading?

ASSESSING WORD IDENTIFICATION LEVELS

The teacher or tutor can assess word identification levels in two ways: listening to students orally read grade-level passages, and asking students to read leveled word lists.

Listening to Students Orally Read Grade-Level Passages

In Chapter Three, the informal reading inventory (IRI) process has been described. The teacher or tutor chooses a graded passage from a published informal reading inventory (IRI), or a passage that is appropriate for the student's chronological grade level. The student reads the passage orally, and the teacher or tutor marks all oral reading errors. The teacher or tutor counts these errors and, based upon the number of words in the passage, determines a percentage score for word identification accuracy. An accuracy score of 98%–100% represents an independent level, and a score of 90%–97% signals an instructional level (if all errors are counted as opposed to only counting those that change meaning). A score below 90% represents a frustration level—evidence that the student does not yet adequately recognize words at the grade level represented by the passage. This process represents an effective way to provide evidence about a student's ability to recognize words accurately.

It admittedly takes time to use the IRI process to collect evidence about a student's word identification ability. Many teachers and tutors tend to avoid it because of difficulty in scheduling time to work with an individual child. However, the IRI process has been successfully used for many years (Johnson, Kress, & Pikulski, 1987). The sensitivity of this measure more than makes up for the inconvenience of scheduling an individual session and arranging activities to occupy the other students in the class or group.

I strongly suggest that the word identification progress of every student in grades 1 through 3 be assessed at least three times during the year using the IRI process. This tells the teacher or tutor whether the student is identifying words at an appropriate grade level. It signals whether there is any problem in this area that needs special attention. If administered at the beginning, middle, and end of the year, it provides evidence of student growth in word identification.

Listening to Students Read Graded Word Lists

Let's admit from the very beginning that reading word lists is not an authentic measure. Authentic measures parallel the actual reading process. Asking a student to read a passage and retell what he or she remembers is an authentic measure. But nobody ever curled up with a good list of words! However, word lists have their place in assessing a student's word identification ability. In the first place, a graded word list is highly predictive of a student's ability to identify words in a passage at a similar grade level (Leslie & Caldwell, 2001). Because of this, a graded word list can provide a quick estimate of grade level with regard to word identification. Of course, using a graded word list says absolutely nothing about a student's ability to construct meaning.

How are graded word lists constructed? Some words in our language are very frequent; that is, they occur over and over. Words like *the*, *of*, and *to* occur much more frequently than words like *system*, *public*, and *water*. There are lists of words arranged from most frequent to least frequent (Carroll, Davies, & Richman, 1971; Sakiey & Fry, 1979). The more frequent words are obviously found in selections at the lower grade levels. *And*, *the*, and *be*, for example, can be found in most preprimer texts. As words become more infrequent, they are assigned higher grade levels.

Where can a teacher or tutor obtain a graded word list? Many published IRIs include graded word lists in their array of assessment options. The contents of different published IRIs are listed in Appendix 3.3 of Chapter Three. IRIs also offer guidelines for determining independent, instructional, and frustration levels for word list performance. For example, the Qualitative Reading Inventory 3 (Leslie & Caldwell, 2001) uses the following scoring system for graded lists of 20 words. A score of 90%–100% (18–20 correct words) represents an independent level. A score of 70%–85% (14–17 correct words) indicates an instructional level. Any score below 70% (14 correct words) suggests a frustration level.

There are other lists available, such as the Dolch list (Johnson, 1971), which ranks words according to their frequency and assigns grade levels to them based upon this. A teacher or tutor could construct a list of words taken from selections appropriate for a specific grade level, but I would not suggest this. First, it can be a very time-consuming process. Second, the teacher or tutor would need a rationale for choosing each word. And, finally, unless some pilot testing of the list was done, there would be no certainty that the list would represent a valid predictive measure of a student's ability to identify other words at that grade level. Teachers and tutors do not have time for this. If you intend to use a graded word list, use one that has been either pilot-tested or shown through extensive use to be a valid predictor.

Using word lists can also help a teacher or tutor determine a student's reliance upon context. It is very natural for students in the stages of visual cue recoding and the phonetic cue recoding to depend upon context for word identification. However, it is important that they move beyond this as quickly as possible. It has been demonstrated over and over that good readers are able to identify words without any supportive context. If a student is more successful pronouncing words in a passage than identifying the same words on a list, this may indicate reliance upon context. A teacher or tutor can choose words that a student has pronounced when supported by context, present them to the student in a list format, and compare the two performances.

Of course, having students read word lists could be as time-consuming as engaging in the IRI process. If a choice between the two is necessary, asking students to read authentic text is always preferable to a word list.

Perhaps of more importance than a graded word list is the student's ability to accurately and quickly read words presented during instruction, such as vocabulary words drawn from a story or textbook chapter. The teacher or tutor can place these words on word cards and ask students to read through the pile. For some time, word cards were frowned upon as lacking authenticity. However, it has been my experience that many students enjoy manipulating word cards and testing their ability to read them. They enjoy placing them into separate piles: known words, unknown words, and almost known words. Teachers and tutors can construct a simple checklist to record individual progress.

ASSESSING GOOD READER STRATEGIES IN WORD IDENTIFICATION

Good readers identify words by analogy to known sight words. They tend to break words and syllables into onsets (the beginning consonant or consonants) and rimes (the vowel pattern). They match the onsets and rimes to known words, as you did with *tergiversation* and *twisdorsercleck*. When they arrive at a possible pronunciation, they match this to a word in their listening vocabulary. Good readers focus upon meaning as they do this. While they pay attention to correct pronunciation, they are primarily concerned with the sense of what they read. How can a teacher or tutor assess what students do when they meet an unfamiliar word?

A process called *miscue analysis* can suggest whether a student is paying attention to meaning during the word identification process. Using word sorts and nonsense words can suggest the extent to which a student is focusing on letter–sound matching and, in particular, upon letter patterns. Asking students how they identify words can also reveal the presence or absence of good reader strategies.

Miscue Analysis

Oral reading errors are often called *miscues*—a term coined by Goodman (1969), who felt that students made errors because they paid attention to the wrong cues. In other words, they were miscued. A reader, influenced by *semantic* or *meaning* cues, might read *My friends gave me birthday presents* as

My friends gave me birthday gifts. One could infer that the substitution of *gifts* for *presents* was due to semantic information, specifically the word *birthday*. A reader might be misled by syntactic cues referring to the grammar structure of our language. The student who reads *He dug up the plant* as *He digged up the plant* is probably paying attention to the grammar of the language. Another cue system identified by Goodman is the *graphophonic* cue system, which focuses attention on letters (graphemes) and sounds (phonemes). The student who reads *house* as *hoose* may be focusing on this cue system.

Goodman devised an extensive system, called miscue analysis, for analyzing reader miscues and attempting to identify the cue systems that were overused or underused. Many variations of miscue analysis exist today, and most published IRIs include some form of miscue analysis as an assessment option.

Engaging in miscue analysis can help the teacher or tutor identify good reader word identification strategies. A good reader focuses both on letter–sound patterns and on meaning. Although good readers do not use context to help them pronounce words, they are very conscious that the words they pronounce make sense in the context of the selection. I remember glancing at a newspaper headline and reading *Mayor blasts urban police.* Intrigued as to what the police department was doing to incur the mayor's wrath, I read on. I quickly discovered that the word I read as *police* was actually *policies!* I misread a word, but as a good reader, I paid attention to meaning and corrected my error.

Miscue analysis takes time—something that few teachers or tutors have enough of. I am not suggesting that teachers or tutors engage in miscue analysis, but it is important for them to know what it is and what it can reveal. In most schools and districts, reading specialists or diagnosticians use miscue analysis as an assessment tool. However, teachers or tutors should know enough about the process to understand the results of such an analysis if it is applied to one of their students.

Miscue analysis helps to determine whether a reader is paying attention to letters and sounds, to meaning, or (ideally) to both. Of course, enough miscues to base the analysis upon are needed. Making judgments on the basis of five miscues is poor practice. A minimum number would be 10 to 12.

Some forms of miscue analysis record word omissions and word insertions as well as word substitutions and mispronunciations. In order to simplify the miscue analysis process, even for a reading specialist (who is also very busy!), it is better to record and analyze just word substitutions (such as *said* for *shouted*) and mispronunciations (such as *orcheds* for *orchards*). The purpose of miscue analysis is to answer two questions. First, is the student paying attention to letter–sound matching? Second, is the student maintaining a focus on meaning? Insertions and omissions do not really say anything about letter–sound matching, but real word substitutions and mispronunciations do. The teacher or tutor records the miscues on a worksheet (such as the one provided here) and uses the following guidelines to suggest attention to meaning and attention to letter–sound patterns.

When the student is focusing on meaning, the student may substitute a word that still makes sense in the passage, such as *looked* for *watched*. The Miscue Analysis Worksheet has a column marked *Keeps Meaning*. If the miscue does not change meaning, a check goes in this column.

Other miscues show that the student is using letter and sound cues. These miscues contain many of the same sounds as the word in the passage. The mispronunciation may not make any sense; in fact, it may not even be a real word. Some examples would be *piloneer* for *pioneer* and *thoree* for *theory*. If the miscue is similar to the actual word in the beginning letters and sounds, place a check in the column marked *Same Beginning*. If the miscue is similar to the end of the text word, place a check in the column marked *Same Ending*. Beginning and ending similarity is enough to determine whether a student is paying attention to letter and sounds. What about the middle of a word? Middle sounds are usually vowels and vowel patterns. Vowel sounds tend to be extremely variable. They are also the last letter–sound elements that students pay attention to as they develop accurate and automatic word identification. In order to keep the miscue analysis simple, you do not need to worry about miscue similarity with regard to vowel sounds.

If a student corrects the miscue, it suggests two things. If the student corrects a miscue that distorted meaning, you can infer that the reader is paying attention to meaning. If the reader corrects an acceptable miscue (one that does not change meaning), the reader is probably paying attention to letter–sound patterns. In each case, place a check in the column marked *Self-Corrected*.

Once the miscues are recorded and evaluated as to letter–sound matching and meaning, how do you determine reader strategies? You look at the pattern of check marks. Use the following guidelines to do this. In the *Strategy* column, mark M if the miscue suggests that the reader was paying attention to meaning. Mark LS if the reader was paying attention to letter–sound matches. Mark both M and LS if both meaning and letter–sound matching were involved. You are not looking for percentages but for patterns. A good reader will pay attention to both meaning and letter–sound patterns.

Miscue Analysis Worksheet

Student name _____

Date _____

Selection _____

Text Word	Miscue (Substitution or Mispronunciation)	Same Beginning	Same Ending	Keeps Meaning	Self-Corrected	Strategy M	LS

Miscue Patterns

Attention to letter–sound matching:
    The miscue is similar in the beginning sound.
    The miscue is similar in the ending sound.
    The miscue did not change meaning but was corrected.

Attention to meaning:
    The miscue did not change meaning.
    The miscue changed meaning but was corrected.

Attention to both letter–sound matching and meaning:
    A miscue that represents any combination of the above.

Do you remember Jamael, whose reading about a class trip is presented at the end of Chapter Four as Appendix 4.1? You have been given the option there to score Jamael's reading using the IRI process guidelines or a running record. Here, Jamael's substitutions and mispronunciations have been recorded on a Miscue Analysis Worksheet. The following are the reasons for how the miscues were coded.

- *spring/summer*: Both began with the sound of *s*, so I marked the error and the text word as having the same beginning. I marked Jamael's word identification strategy LS, as matching letters and sounds. I also marked M for meaning, because Jamael may have used the meaning of *warm* to cue his substitution of *summer*.
- *going/gone*: The miscue and the text word began with the same sound, so I checked *Same Beginning*. The miscue did not change meaning, so I checked *Keeps Meaning*. I marked Jamael as using both a letter–sound strategy and a meaning strategy.
- *wanted/went*: Both were similar in the beginning, and I marked Jamael as using a letter–sound strategy. I did not check *Keeps Meaning*, because I believe there is a semantic difference between *went* and *wanted*—between going somewhere and wanting something.
- *animals/aminals*: The substitution and the text word were similar in the beginning and ending sounds, so I checked both *Same Beginning* and *Same Ending*. I marked Jamael as using a letter–sound strategy because of this. I also marked him as using a meaning strategy, because he self-corrected an error that distorted meaning.

Miscue Analysis Worksheet

Student name ___Jamael___

Date _____

Selection ___The Trip___

Text Word	Miscue (Substitution or Mispronunciation)	Same Beginning	Same Ending	Keeps Meaning	Self-Corrected	Strategy M	LS
spring	summer	✓		✓		M	LS
going	gone	✓		✓		M	LS
wanted	went	✓					LS
animals	aminals	✓	✓		✓	M	LS
wanted	wasn't	✓					LS
saw	was						
going	gone	✓					LS
class	kalass	✓	✓				LS
thought	thogut	✓	✓				LS
stopped	stops	✓		✓		M	LS
helped	here	✓			✓	M	LS
fix	fox	✓	✓		✓	M	LS
the	he		✓		✓	M	LS
yea	yes	✓		✓		M	LS
pig	pigs	✓		✓		M	LS
petting	pigs	✓			✓	M	LS
learned	liked	✓	✓				LS
milking	making	✓	✓				LS

- *wanted/wasn't*: I checked *Same Beginning* and marked Jamael as using a letter–sound strategy. I did not mark him as using a meaning strategy, because his substitution actually distorted the meaning of the text.
- *was/saw*: I was unable to place any checkmarks. The error was not similar to the text word in either beginning or ending sounds. It did not keep meaning, and Jamael did not correct it. As a result, I was unable to determine what strategy (if any) he used.
- *going/gone*: This error is identical to the one made earlier by Jamael. The error is similar to the text word in the beginning sound, so I marked this and indicated a letter–sound strategy. I did not mark it as *Keeps Meaning*, as I did the previous substitution of *gone* for *going*. I felt there was a subtle shift in meaning between *gone on a trip* and *gone to make a book*. (You may disagree. This happens with miscue analysis; two individuals can score the same miscue slightly differently. Don't worry about this. You are looking for patterns and one miscue will not destroy a pattern.)
- *class/kalass*: Jamael substituted a nonword for *class*, but it retained the same beginning and ending sounds. Because it was meaningless, I only marked Jamael's strategy as using letters and sounds.
- *thought/thogut*: Again Jamael substituted a nonword that was similar to the text word in beginning and ending sounds. No meaning was retained, so I marked Jamael as only using a letter–sound strategy.
- *stopped/stops*: This miscue involved a change in tense. It was similar to the text word in the beginning. It did not really change meaning. I marked Jamael as using both a letter–sound and a meaning strategy.
- *helped/here*: The miscue was similar in the beginning, and Jamael corrected it. I marked him as using both a meaning and a letter–sound strategy.
- *fix/fox*: The miscue was similar in both beginning and ending sounds, so I marked him as using a letter–sound strategy. Because Jamael corrected a substitution that distorted meaning, I marked him as also using a meaning strategy.
- *the/he*: The miscue retained the same ending as the text word. For this reason, I marked Jamael as using a letter–sound strategy. Because he corrected a meaningless substitution, I marked him as also using a meaning strategy.
- *yea/yes*: Both were similar in beginning sounds. I did not believe that meaning was changed by the substitution. I gave Jamael credit for using both strategies, letter–sound and meaning.
- *pig/pigs*: The miscue and the text were similar in the beginning sounds. Because Jamael omitted *a* before *pig*, the substitution of *pigs* did not change meaning. Jamael was using both strategies.

- *petting/pigs*: The substitution of *petting* for *pigs* was similar in the be-ginning sound to the text word, but it changed meaning. Because Jamael cor-rected it, I marked him as using both strategies.
- *learned/liked*: The substitution was similar to the text word in the be-ginning and ending sounds. However, it changed meaning. Jamael was marked as only using a letter–sound strategy.
- *milking/making*: The same coding was applied to this substitution. It was similar in beginning and ending sounds to the text word, but it changed meaning. Jamael was marked as using a letter–sound strategy.

What patterns do you see? Out of 18 miscues, Jamael used both a letter–sound strategy and a meaning strategy to identify 10 words. He used a letter–sound strategy only for 8 words. We could say that Jamael favored the letter–sound strategy, but that he was still focused on meaning.

What do such patterns this mean for instruction? Assessment should al-ways inform instruction. Jamael seemed to have achieved a balance in the strategies he used. Not all readers do this. A reader who focuses primarily on letter–sound matching may need to pay more attention to meaning. Ausha-bell, for example, would benefit from activities to draw her attention to the meaning of the words and sentences she pronounced so accurately. But what about the opposite pattern? Is it possible to overemphasize meaning? Yes, meaning *as a word identification strategy* can be overemphasized. Such a strategy may work very effectively in text on familiar topics and in text with supportive context. But it tends to break down when the reader faces more complex selections containing unfamiliar words and concepts. When a reader encounters a new word, letter–sound matching provides the first clue. Re-member your strategies with *tergiversation* and *twisdorsercleck*! A reader who avoids matching letters and sounds, or is unable to do so quickly and ef-fectively, will soon encounter difficulties in higher-level text.

Word Sorts

As I have mentioned in Chapter Two, it is difficult to separate assessment and instruction. Very often, the instructional activity that a teacher or tutor em-ploys is also the evidence that he or she collects. Engaging in word sorts is a perfect example of this blend of assessment and instruction (Bear, Invernizzi, Templeton, & Johnston, 2000). The teacher or tutor writes words on separate cards, and the student separates these into categories. Depending upon the words that are included in the sort, the teacher or tutor can evaluate the stu-dent's understanding of basic principles of letter–sound matching. Word sorts can shed light on a student's recognition of consonant sounds; they can also indicate whether the student can differentiate rime or vowel patterns.

Word sorts are of two kinds: *closed* sorts and *open* sorts. In a closed sort, you, the teacher or tutor, provide the categories. In an open sort, the students devise the categories themselves and sort accordingly. When you first begin using word sorts, it is less confusing for both you and the students if you give the categories. Later, when the students have experience with word sorts, you can move into closed sorts.

Consider the following words: *hat, nut, top, hate, rat, bite, rate, bit, cute,* and *rope.* What categories could you give? You could ask students to sort these words according to the initial consonant in order to determine whether they recognize the difference between the letters. The resulting sort might look like this.

hat	*nut*	*top*	*rat*	*bite*	*cute*
hate			*rate*	*bit*	
			rope		

You could also assess their recognition of short and long vowel patterns by asking them to separate them into words where the vowel says its own name (long vowels) and words where the vowel makes a different sound (short vowels).

hat	*hate*
nut	*bite*
top	*cute*
rat	*rate*
bit	*rope*

There are some guidelines for choosing words for a word sort. First, choose words to illustrate what you are teaching. If you are emphasizing rhyming word families or *phonograms* (like *-at, -an,* and *-ap*), make words containing these phonograms the focus of your word sort. If you are calling your students' attention to consonant–vowel–consonant patterns that do not rhyme (like *lap, lip,* and *stop*), choose words to illustrate these. As you use a word sort to teach a word identification concept, you simultaneously assess your students' skill. Bear et al. (2000) offer many suggestions for word sorts.

You do not want too many words in a single sort. From 10 to 12 is an adequate number. The sort should involve only two or three categories. More than three can be somewhat confusing for the students as well as for you (since you need to keep track of what is going on!).

Nonsense Words

What are nonsense words? Often called *pseudowords*, they are pronounce-able combinations of letters such as *pleck* and *glomb*. They do not stand for meaning. *Tergiversation* is a real word with a meaning that can be found in the dictionary. In contrast, *twisdorsercleck* is a pseudoword, a nonsense word that I have made up. Individuals who regard the use of word cards as nonauthentic will probably be even more opposed to nonsense words. How-ever, nonsense words do have a place in assessing students' ability to engage in letter–sound matching. They can be quite effective in pointing out which letter and sound elements the students know and which ones they do not know.

Consider the following scenario. A teacher or tutor asks a student to read a list of real words. The student is successful with some words. Does this mean that the student is adept at letter–sound matching? Possibly not. These words may be sight words that the student is pronouncing from memory. In other words, the student's successful pronunciation may not be the result of matching letters and sounds.

Nonsense words allow a teacher or tutor to present a student with word units the student has never seen before. In order to pronounce a nonsense word, the student must apply letter–sound matching. There is just no other way. Some published assessment instruments use nonsense words; however, it is easy for the teacher or tutor to construct nonsense words that parallel in-struction. Suppose a teacher or tutor has been focusing instruction on the fol-lowing vowel patterns: *-eat*, *-ight*, and *-ock*. The teacher or tutor could con-struct a short list like the following: *pight*, *dreat*, *trock*, *weat*, *cright*, *brock*, *keat*, *gight*, and *vock*. When a student is asked to read these words, this can provide a brief assessment of which vowel patterns and which consonant and consonant blends are known or unknown.

Doesn't the use of nonsense words confuse the student? Doesn't it ask the student to do something that is alien to the reading process—that is, to making meaning? These concerns can be alleviated by a careful explanation to the student. Tell the student that you are asking him or her to read "pretend" words, word that do not really exist. Explain that you just want to see whether he or she can pronounce these words. Most students accept this quite readily and even enjoy the process. They often delight in making up meanings to fit certain psuedowords. I remember one little fellow who, after successfully pro-nouncing *blash*, announced that if *blash* were a word, it would probably mean a splash of black mud!

Asking Students How They Identify Words

Asking a student what he or she does when faced with an unknown word can often provide valuable insights into the student's word identification strategies. Some students find it very difficult to talk about their word identification strategies, and this can suggest a need to bring such strategies to a more conscious level. Other students are very aware of their strategies and of their success or lack of effectiveness.

Toby was a second grader who was not doing well in reading. I asked Toby this question: "What do you do when you come to a word that you can't pronounce?" Toby promptly replied, "I ask my teacher." "But what if your teacher is busy?" I asked. Toby thought for a minute and responded, "I would wait for her or ask Megan, who knows all the words." Probing a bit deeper, I asked Toby to pretend that he was all by himself reading and he came to an unfamiliar word. What would he do? Toby replied, "I would put the book down and wait till someone came." Clearly, Toby had no strategies for pronouncing words. He was totally dependent upon adults or peers to help him out.

When I asked Twinda what she would do if faced with an unfamiliar word, she stated, "Sound it out." "How do you sound the word out?" I asked her. Twinda was clearly puzzled, and it was evident that she had never considered the matter. Finally she responded, "I don't know how I do it. I just do." When I asked her whether sounding out worked for her, she admitted, "Not really. Most of the time, I have to ask someone."

Contrast Toby's and Twinda's strategies with that of Alton, a third grader. Alton first said he would sound out the unknown word, but he then expanded upon this strategy. "I would take each letter and try to give it a sound, and then try to kinda run the sounds together to make a word. Sometimes this works and sometimes it doesn't." Alton had a measure of strategy awareness, and he had grasped the basics of letter–sound matching. However, his strategy of matching individual letters and sounds might be unworkable when he encountered longer words.

Consider Damon, who also said he sounded out words. When I asked him how he did this, he offered the following explanation. "I look for parts in words that I know, like maybe letters and maybe a bunch of letters. Like in this one [pointing to *celebrate*], I know *rate* and I know *cell*. [He then pointed to *boundaries*.] I wasn't sure of *boundaries* right away, but I knew *bound*, and I tried the last part in a couple of different ways and then I got it." Damon's strategy was certainly more advanced than any of the other children's. He was clearly focusing on larger units than single letters; he was aware of his mental processes; and he was not dependent upon others for word identification. Sometimes the simplest form of assessment is to ask the students what they do or how they do it!

ASSESSING STUDENT PROGRESS IN WORD IDENTIFICATION

A teacher or tutor can assess individual progress in word identification by using the IRI process and graded word lists to compare performance on the same passage or list at different points in time.

At the beginning of the school year, Nancy asked each of her first graders to read a preprimer word list. Many were only able to read one or two words. She repeated this each month and recorded individual scores. When a student reached an independent level on the preprimer list, Nancy moved to the primer list. In this way, she maintained an ongoing record of each student's progress throughout the year. Nancy placed the word list record in each student's portfolio.

Jeremy employed the same technique with his second graders, but he asked each student to orally read a passage as opposed to a word list. One he had determined a student's highest instructional level for word identification, he asked that student to read the same passage approximately six weeks later. If the student scored at an independent level for word identification, Jeremy moved to the next highest passage. Jeremy placed the first administration and last administration of a passage in the student's portfolio. Documenting progress can be rewarding for the teacher or tutor, and it can also be very motivating for the student. Lack of progress can be disturbing and frustrating to the teacher or tutor, but it can also signal the need for changes in instruction. Perhaps the teacher or tutor needs to provide additional instructional support for a student or reexamine how students are grouped for instruction. It is important to remember that assessment that does not influence instruction is questionable at best.

PUBLISHED TESTS OF WORD IDENTIFICATION

Formal Instruments

Several formal tests of word identification have been published. Most are subtests of large diagnostic batteries. These tests are generally norm-referenced; that is, the student's score is compared to the score of students who acted as the norm group. A student's score is expressed as a grade equivalent, a percentile, or a standard score (see Chapter Nine). These tests are administered the same way to all students, and the examiner is not allowed to deviate from the published directions in any way. Diagnostic specialists generally use these tests. Teachers and tutors are rarely given the time or opportunity to administer them; however, they should have some awareness of their existence and format.

The Woodcock Reading Mastery Test—Revised (Woodcock, 1987) is used quite frequently by diagnostic specialists. It is administered to individual students and is made up of four reading subtests. Two of these deal with a student's ability to pronounce words. The Word Attack subtest is a list of nonsense words that correspond to common elements in letter–sound matching. The Word Identification subtest is a list of real words of increasing difficulty.

The Reading Diagnostic Tests (Gates, McKillop, & Horowitz, 1981) constitute another individually administered battery that includes Word Attack and Word Identification subtests. For Word Identification, students read isolated words in a timed as well as an untimed format. The Word Attack subtest includes measures of syllabication, recognizing and blending word parts, giving letter sounds, and naming upper- and lower-case letters.

The Brigance Diagnostic Inventories (Brigance, 1976) contain numerous subtests of letter–sound matching, such as Consonant Sounds, Vowel Sounds, and Irregular Sounds. This battery is administered to individuals.

The Wide Range Achievement Test 3 (1993) is an individually administered battery that consists of Reading, Spelling, and Math Measures. The Reading measure focuses on word identification and is a list of isolated words arranged in order of increasing difficulty.

Informal Instruments

A short and easily administered test of word pronunciation is the Names Test (Cunningham, 1990; Duffelmeyer, Kruse, Merkeley, & Fyfe, 1999). This measure provides words that students probably have never seen before, but avoids the use of nonsense words. The test consists of pairs of first and last names, such as *Fred Sherwood, Dee Skidmore,* and *Bernard Pendergraph.* Although students may be acquainted with some of the first names, the last names generally represent unfamiliar words. The names sound like their spellings, and they represent multiple instances of the following common phonics elements: initial consonants, initial consonant blends (*sp-, cr-, fl-, dr-, st-, gr-, pl-*), consonant digraphs (*sh, ch, th, ph, wh*), short vowel sounds, long vowel sounds (*-ate, -ake, -y, -ale, -o, -ene, -ace, -oke, -ine, -ane, -ade, -ale, -ane*), vowel digraphs (*au, oo, ay, ea, ee, oy, ay, oa, ey, ai*), controlled vowels (*er, ar, ew, or, ur, aw*), and the schwa sound. The student reads the names, and the teacher or tutor records the student's performance. Then the teacher or tutor analyzes performance in terms of which letter–sound elements were known and which were unknown.

SUMMARY

- Word identification is a necessary part of the reading process, but it is not sufficient. Reading is constructing meaning. Word identification is the key to comprehension, but skill in identifying words does not ensure comprehension.
- There are basically four ways to identify words. One way is to pronounce the word from memory; words that are identified in this way are called *sight words*. Words can also be identified by matching individual letters and sounds or by predicting the pronunciation from context. Finally, good readers identify unknown words by analogy to known words.
- Younger and beginning readers use context as an aid to word identification, but they soon move beyond this. Good readers rarely use context to identify words, because they have large sight vocabularies. Poor readers often overuse context as a word identification aid.
- The teacher or tutor can assess word identification levels by listening to students orally read grade-level passages and by asking students to read graded word lists.
- The teacher or tutor can assess good reader behaviors in word identification by using miscue analysis. The teacher or tutor evaluates word substitutions and mispronunciations to determine whether the reader is paying attention to letter–sound matching, to meaning, or to both.
- Word sorts allow the teacher or tutor to examine how well the student understands principles of letter–sound matching.
- Using nonsense words as an assessment tool can indicate how well the student can analyze completely unfamiliar words.
- Asking a student how he or she pronounces unfamiliar words can reveal which strategies the student uses or does not use.
- A student's progress in word identification can be indicated by comparing oral reading performance on the same graded passage and by comparing performance on the same graded word list.

ACTIVITIES FOR DEVELOPING UNDERSTANDING

- Here is a list of words that you may not have seen in print before. Attempt to pronounce them. What analogues did you use? Compare your analogues with those of a peer.

contumacious
dreadnaught
mephitic
exacerbate
misogynist

- Here are three of these words placed within the context of sentences. Notice how the context helps you with word meaning, not pronunciation. What do you think these words mean?

April was such a *contumacious* child that her parents had extreme difficulty finding a babysitter.

He wrapped his *dreadnaught* tightly around him and stepped into the raging blizzard.

Jon's yard was so *mephitic* that his neighbors chipped in to buy him a pooper-scooper.

- Choose a short selection with pictures, and type it on a plain sheet of paper. Contrast a student's word identification in the text with pictures and without pictures.
- Using a published IRI, contrast a student's word identification performance on a graded word list with performance on the passages.
- Fill out a Miscue Analysis Worksheet and analyze a student's focus on letter–sound matching and on meaning. (Appendix 5.1 provides practice with this.)
- Construct a word sort to illustrate components of letter–sound matching. Ask students to sort according to the categories you chose and evaluate their performance.
- Construct nonsense words for the following phonograms: *-ash*, *-ump*, *-ore*, *-ame*, and *-unk*. Administer these words to a student and evaluate his or her performance.
- Complete the self-evaluation form provided at the end of this chapter (following Appendix 5.1).

APPENDIX 5.1

Practice Using Miscue Analysis

In Chapter Three, I have described Billy's reading of a second-grade selection. Billy's substitutions and mispronunciations (not his insertions and omissions) have been recorded on a Miscue Analysis Worksheet. Code Billy's errors and determine what strategy he used. Afterward, compare your coding to mine and to my reasons for coding Billy's errors as I did.

YOUR CODING OF BILLY

Miscue Analysis Worksheet

Student name   _Billy_____

Date   _____

Selection   _"One, Two, Three—Ah-Choo!"_____

Text Word	Miscue (Substitution or Mispronunciation)	Same Beginning	Same Ending	Keeps Meaning	Self-Corrected	Strategy M	LS
fur	fun						
Springer	Spriger						
sneeze	snooze						
allergic	algic						
groaned	grumbled						
allergic	allegic						
wiggled	wigged						
swam	swimmed						
least	lease						
sprout	sprut						
singing	stinging						
sing	sting						
banded	banding						
creamy	cremmy						
wrapped	wound						
Sheila	She-eye-la						
terrarium	terrium						
cloth	clothes						
refrigerator	referator						
refrigerator	refregator						

MY CODING OF BILLY

Miscue Analysis Worksheet

Student name   *Billy*

Date _____

Selection   *"One, Two, Three—Ah-Choo!"*

Text Word	Miscue (Substitution or Mispronunciation)	Same Beginning	Same Ending	Keeps Meaning	Self-Corrected	M	LS
fur	fun	✓					LS
Springer	Spriger	✓	✓	✓		M	LS
sneeze	snooze	✓	✓		✓	M	LS
allergic	algic	✓	✓				LS
groaned	grumbled	✓	✓	✓		M	LS
allergic	allegic	✓	✓				LS
wiggled	wigged	✓	✓				LS
swam	swimmed	✓			✓	M	LS
least	lease	✓					LS
sprout	sprut	✓	✓				LS
singing	stinging	✓	✓				LS
sing	sting	✓	✓				LS
banded	banding	✓					LS
creamy	cremmy	✓	✓				LS
wrapped	wound	✓		✓		M	LS
Sheila	She-eye-la	✓	✓	✓		M	LS
terrarium	terrium	✓	✓				LS
cloth	clothes	✓					LS
refrigerator	referator	✓	✓				LS
refrigerator	refregator	✓	✓				LS

MY REASONS FOR CODING

- *fur/fun*: Because both the error and the text word began with the same letter and sound, I marked Billy as using a letter–sound strategy. His error occurred on the first word of a heading within the story. I did not feel that there was enough information for Billy to use a meaning strategy, so I did not code it.
- *Springer/Spriger*: The error and test word had the same beginning and ending. I marked Billy as using a letter–sound strategy. I also did not think that the mispronunciation of a proper name seriously distorted meaning. I reasoned that it would have sounded fine to Billy, given the many different kinds of surnames he had probably been exposed to. I marked him as using a meaning strategy.
- *sneeze/snooze*: Both were similar in the beginning and the ending, so Billy received credit for using a letter–sound strategy. Because he corrected his error, I marked him as also using a meaning strategy.
- *allergic/algic*: Again we see similarity in the beginning and ending of the two words. Billy was obviously trying to match letters and sounds to pronounce an unfamiliar word. However, because his pronunciation was a nonsense word, it distorted meaning.
- *groaned/grumbled*: Billy was clearly using meaning when he substituted *groaned* for *grumbled*. He was clearly aware of Wally's feelings at this point in the story. In addition, both words were similar in the beginning and ending. I marked Billy as using both a meaning strategy and a letter–sound strategy.
- *allergic/allegic*: This was another attempt on Billy's part to pronounce *allergic*. The attempt looked and sounded like the word in the beginning and ending. Because it distorted meaning, I marked Billy as only using a letter–sound strategy. His mispronunciation was so close to the actual word that one wonders why he did not recognize *allergic*. Perhaps Billy had never had an allergy. Perhaps he had never even heard the word. Unless a student has heard a word before, approximate attempts at pronunciation will not lead him or her to the correct word.
- *wiggled/wigged*: Billy's mispronunciation was similar to the text word in the beginning and ending. However, as a nonsense word, it distorted meaning. Billy received credit for usage of a letter–sound strategy.
- *swam/swimmed*: The mispronunciation was similar in the beginning, and Billy quickly corrected it probably because it just did not sound right. I marked him as using both strategies.
- *least/lease*: This was another miscue that distorted meaning because it was a nonsense word and was not corrected. Billy received credit for using a letter–sound strategy.
- *sprout/sprut*: We see another attempt to pronounce an unfamiliar word by matching letters and sounds. However, the resulting nonsense word was not cor-

rected. Billy was not using or was unable to use a meaning strategy to help him with *sprout*.

• *stinging/singing*: The two words are almost identical, so Billy was clearly paying attention to letters and sounds. However, his miscue changed the meaning of the passage quite a bit. I wonder if Billy did not correct his error because stinging frogs made more sense to him than singing ones. I personally have never heard of a singing frog.

• *sting/sing*: The same comments apply to this miscue.

• *banded/banding*: Billy's mispronunciation only differed in the ending. I do believe it changed meaning, because the *-ing* suffix does not sound right when applied to a description of an animal. For example, we say *a spotted pony*, not *a spotting pony*.

• *creamy/cremmy*: This was another nonsense word that was similar to the text word in the beginning and ending. Billy was using a letter–sound strategy, not a meaning one.

• *wrapped/wound*: This was a miscue just like the substitution of *groaned* for *grumbled*. Billy clearly knew that he was reading about a snake. I gave him credit for using both strategies.

• *Sheila/She-eye-la*: Billy used a letter–sound strategy to deal with the snake's name. I did not think that it changed meaning, because we often give strange names to our animals. I have one cat named Nelix and another called Mops!

• *terrarium/terrium*: Again we see Billy matching letters and sounds, but not correcting a miscue that changes meaning.

• *cloth/clothes*: Billy's mispronunciation was similar in the beginning. However, there is a difference between a cloth bag and a clothes bag. I only gave Billy credit for using a letter–sound strategy.

• *refrigerator/referator, refrigerator/refregator*: Both these errors again showed Billy only using a letter–sound strategy. Don't you wonder why Billy had so much difficulty with the name of a common household item? Perhaps, in Billy's world, the refrigerator was called a *fridge*!

Every one of Billy's mispronunciations showed attention to letter–sound matching. Billy knew that letters and sounds are the key to pronouncing unfamiliar words, but he clearly needed more skill in doing this. Six miscues also showed attention to meaning. Those six miscues demonstrated that Billy understood what he read. They suggested that Billy was aware that what he read should make sense. He was not so focused on pronouncing words that he lost the meaning of the story.

Teacher or Tutor Self-Evaluation

I use the IRI process to assess word identification.

       Regularly   Occasionally   A future goal

I use graded word lists to assess word identification.

       Regularly   Occasionally   A future goal

I compare my students' word identification with and without supportive context.

       Regularly   Occasionally   A future goal

I use miscue analysis to determine good reader behaviors in word identification.

       Regularly   Occasionally   A future goal

I use word sorts to assess word identification.

       Regularly   Occasionally   A future goal

I use nonsense words to assess word identification.

       Regularly   Occasionally   A future goal

I ask my students how they pronounce unfamiliar words.

       Regularly   Occasionally   A future goal

I assess individual student progress using the IRI process and/or graded word lists at different points in time.

       Regularly   Occasionally   A future goal

SIX

Reading Fluency

How Can We Assess Reading Fluency?

CHAPTER TOPICS

The Role of Fluency in the Reading Process
Purposes of Fluency Assessment
Assessing Fluency Levels
Assessing Components of Fluency
Assessing Student Progress in Fluency
Summary
Activities for Developing Understanding

THE ROLE OF FLUENCY IN THE READING PROCESS

Fluency involves three components: accuracy, speed, and intonation (Wilson, 1988). Fluent readers identify words accurately. Moreover, they do this automatically and instantaneously, without pausing to analyze letters and sounds. As noted in Chapter Five, words that are recognized immediately and without analysis are called *sight words*. Good readers have large sight word vocabularies that include most of the words they meet (Samuels, 1988). These are words they have seen before. When they first encountered them, good readers may have analyzed the words by matching letters and sounds; now, however, having met them over and over again, they can identify them from memory. Even if good readers come across an unfamiliar word, they are so skilled at matching letters and sounds that they hardly pause. (Remember how quickly you pronounced *tergiversation?*)

Because good readers do not have to think about word identification, and can read at an appropriate rate of speed, they can direct their attention to meaning. This focus on meaning, in turn, allows them to read with proper intonation. Intonation involves reading at a rhythm that approximates natural speech (i.e., quickly, but not so fast that meaning is lost), paying attention to punctuation signals, and using the rise and fall of the voice to make the text sound meaningful. This combination of qualities is often called *prosody*— projecting "the natural intonation and phrasing of the spoken word upon the written text" (Richards, 2000, p. 535). The fluent reader is a smooth and expressive reader and is enjoyable to listen to. Have you ever listened to taped books? These represent wonderful examples of oral reading fluency. Achieving fluency is one of the stages that students move toward in their journey toward good reading. Ehri (1991) refers to this stage as *sight word reading*, and Spear-Swerling and Sternberg (1996) call it the stage of *automatic word recognition*. Nathan and Stanovich (1991) state that fluency "may be almost a necessary condition for good comprehension and enjoyable reading experiences" (p. 176).

In contrast to good readers, many students with reading problems lack fluency. They do not have adequate sight word vocabularies and are forced to analyze almost every word. Unfortunately, they often lack effective strategies for matching letters and sounds as well, so word identification becomes a laborious process. Because poor readers direct most of their attention to identifying words, they have few resources left for meaning. Their oral reading is slow and halting. They pause often and repeat words. Because they do not comprehend what they are reading, their voices lack expression, and they ignore punctuation signals. After reading, they have little comprehension of the meaning of the passage.

There are three requirements for developing and maintaining reading fluency. First, a reader must have a large store of sight words. Second, the reader needs efficient strategies for analyzing new and unfamiliar words. Third, the reader must focus on meaning. The interaction of these three elements forms the basis of reading fluency.

How does fluency develop? It seems simplistic to say this, but you learn to read fluently by reading. In other words, the more you read, the more your sight word vocabulary grows. You meet some new words and efficiently analyze them by matching letters and sounds. As you meet them again, their identification becomes fixed in your memory, and your sight word vocabulary expands. This is certainly an argument for providing students with many opportunities to read. Unfortunately, many students who are experiencing reading difficulties tend to avoid reading. As a result, they do not develop large sight word vocabularies. This in turn makes reading more difficult, and a vicious cycle develops (Stanovich, 1986).

Other factors influence the development of fluency (Allington, 1983). Students need models of fluent oral reading in the home and in the classroom. In too many classrooms, students of similar ability are grouped together for oral reading. This practice ensures that fluent readers listen to fluent readers. On the other hand, nonfluent readers, who are in most need of fluent reading models, are forced to listen to their peers stumble and hesitate their way through the text.

Students need to be aware of the importance of fluency. Many think that the most important aspect of oral reading is accuracy, and they therefore emphasize avoiding pronunciation errors. Teachers and tutors should encourage students to focus on expression and on making the oral reading meaningful and enjoyable for their audience.

Fluency development is also influenced by the kind of reading that students do. Fluency is best fostered if a student reads independent- or instructional-level text and text that is on familiar topics (Allington, 2001). Frustration-level text contains too many unfamiliar words and concepts to allow for fluency development. Perhaps an analogy will clarify this. Do you consider yourself a fluent driver—that is, a skilled driver who steers, brakes, and accelerates almost automatically in a variety of situations? I imagine you do. Think back to when you first learned to drive. Where did you practice? You probably began in a large parking lot and on relatively familiar and traffic-free roads in the country or a suburb. As you gained confidence and competence, you moved to city streets with more traffic and more signals to attend to. As you became more fluent in this arena, you ventured onto the expressway, possibly during the midmorning or early afternoon. Finally you tackled rush-hour traffic. Now think what would have happened if you had begun your driving practice on the expressway during rush hour! This may help you to understand why it is difficult to develop fluency in a frustrating and anxiety-fraught situation.

PURPOSES OF FLUENCY ASSESSMENT

The teacher or tutor needs to know at what level a student demonstrates fluency and in what kind of text. A student may be at an instructional level for word identification and comprehension, but may still lack fluency. The informal reading inventory (IRI) process uses accuracy in word identification as one measure of determining reading level. Accuracy is only one component of fluency, however; the other two components, as noted above, are speed and intonation. A student may be accurate but slow, or the student may be accurate but expressionless. Because of the importance of fluency as a good reader behavior, the teacher or tutor needs to determine whether word identification accuracy at any level is tied to speed and intonation. Therefore, these components of fluent reading may need to be assessed separately. Finally, the teacher or tutor must note student progress in fluency.

ASSESSING FLUENCY LEVELS

A teacher or tutor can assess a student's general level of reading fluency simply by listening to the student read orally. It is easy to recognize lack of fluency. Wilson (1988) describes three types of nonfluent readers: the *choppy* reader, the *monotonous* reader, and the *hasty* reader. In choppy reading, the student hesitates often and repeats words and phrases. It almost sounds as if the student is reading a list of unconnected words. In monotonous reading, there is little variation in the student's tone of voice. This lack of expression suggests that the student is paying little attention to meaning. In hasty reading, the student races through the text, ignoring sentence breaks and punctuation. Finishing the reading as quickly as possible seems to be the hasty reader's goal. Most nonfluent readers demonstrate a combination of these three patterns. They are very easy to recognize!

To assess fluency, simply ask the student to read aloud a selection at his or her instructional or independent level, and use your judgment to decide whether the student demonstrates acceptable fluency. It is important that the selection be at an independent or instructional level, since all readers tend to be somewhat nonfluent in frustration-level text (Think about your reading of an insurance policy or directions for filling out income tax forms!)

When can you find time to assess fluency? If you are using the IRI process to determine reading level, make the observation of fluency a part of your procedure. You can also assess fluency during self-selected silent reading time. For pleasure reading, students tend to choose books that they can read (i.e., books at their independent and instructional reading levels). This makes silent reading time an appropriate opportunity to assess fluency. As you move around ask individual students to read a short segment of their book aloud, and make notes on their performance.

ASSESSING COMPONENTS OF FLUENCY

Various means of assessing the first component of fluency, accuracy, have been described in Chapters Four and Five. The IRI process, the running record, and miscue analysis can all be applied to a student's oral reading to determine the student's accuracy level. For that reason, accuracy is not discussed further here. The emphasis is on assessing the other two components of fluency—speed and intonation.

Assessing Speed

Determining Reading Rate

Reading rate indicates reading speed. It is one factor in fluency, but it is not the whole picture. Reading speed suggests automaticity of word identification. However, it says nothing about accuracy or intonation. Reading rate is measured in words per minute (WPM). As the student reads (either orally or silently), the teacher or tutor times how long this takes. A stopwatch is the most accurate measure of reading time, but a watch with a second hand will also suffice. Multiply the numbers of words in the passage by 60, and divide this by the number of seconds it took to read the passage. This results in a words-per-minute score. For example, Sandie read a 288-word passage in two minutes and 40 seconds, for a total of 160 seconds. The number of words in the passage, 288, multiplied by 60, equals 17,280. This, divided by Sandie's 160 seconds, equals 108 words per minute. Both oral and silent reading rate can be measured. If you are measuring silent reading rate, you need to ask the student to look up the minute he or she has finished reading so you can note the time.

Once you have a words-per-minute score, what does it mean? As a teacher or tutor, you must realize that reading rate is extremely variable. Reading rate varies according to the passage read. More difficult and unfamiliar passages tend to be read more slowly than narratives. Rate also varies according to readers' purposes. Think about how your rate varies when you read a textbook or an editorial versus an adventure novel or some other form of escape reading. Readers' interests can affect reading rate as well. Moreover, reading rate varies across individuals; students at the same instructional level often display very different reading rates. Carver (1990) suggests that some readers are just naturally faster than others, and this may be related to individual cognitive processing speed.

Silent reading is generally faster than oral reading. Huey (1908/1968) suggested many years ago that good readers read one and a half to two times faster silently than they do orally. This just makes good sense. In oral reading, people have to pronounce the words. In silent reading, they do not, and good readers can process words much faster than they can say them

Because of this natural variability in reading rates, a teacher or tutor should never compare the reading rates of two individual students. Also, it would be unwise to choose a specific reading rate as a goal for students at a certain grade level.

Once you have a measure of rate for a grade-level passage, do not assume that this rate will carry over to other passages at that same grade level. It may or it may not. A student may read an expository passage more slowly than a narrative passage. If a student is interested in the topic of the selection, the student may read more quickly. It is best to compare the reading rate of an individual student in oral and silent reading of passages that are as similar as possible. This is most important at the end of second grade or the beginning of third grade, when students normally make the transition to efficient silent reading strategies. A student whose oral and silent reading rates are the same may not be actually reading silently, but may be mentally pronouncing each word—something that good readers do not do.

Reading rate is perhaps most valuable in identifying students who are extremely slow readers at their independent or instructional levels. Several things can cause such slow reading. The student may be mentally analyzing each word in the absence of an adequate sight word vocabulary. Or the student may be overly deliberate; slow reading can signal an undue focus upon word identification accuracy.

Should teachers or tutors be concerned about slow reading? What about a student who reads slowly but understands what he or she is reading? Should this worry a teacher or tutor? I think it should. Think about the result of slow reading. A slow reader takes much longer to read assignments than his or her peers, and this affects homework as well as class activities. If the teacher or tutor asks students to read something in class, the slow reader seldom finishes and is generally aware that classmates have all completed the selection while he or she may be only halfway through it. This easily leads to frustration. It is natural to avoid a frustrating situation, so the slow reader avoids reading whenever possible. Then what happens? Because fluency is fostered by reading, and because the slow reader chooses not to read, the problem not only continues but probably worsens. For these reasons, teachers and tutors must evaluate reading speed even if understanding is in place.

If reading rate is so variable, how do we interpret it? A colleague and I (Leslie & Caldwell, 2001) examined the oral and silent reading rates of normal readers reading at their instructional level. We found a steady rise in oral and silent reading rate as reading level increased, and a drop in silent reading rate in upper middle school and high school passages, due no doubt to the increased difficulty of the passages. Harris and Sipay (1990) reviewed information on reading rates derived from standardized assessments of reading speed. They did not differentiate between oral and silent reading rate. The following chart summarizes our findings (Leslie & Caldwell, 2001) and those of Harris and Sipay (1990). It is important to understand that these rates simply suggest typical reading rates and should only be used as rough estimates or general guidelines of acceptable reading speed.

Reading Rates (Words per Minute)

Level	Leslie & Caldwell (2001) (oral)	Leslie & Caldwell (2001) (silent)	Harris & Sipay (1990)
Preprimer	13–35		
Primer	28–68		
First	31–67		60–90
Second	52–102	58–122	85–120
Third	85–139	96–168	115–140
Fourth	78–124	107–175	140–170
Fifth			170–195
Sixth	113–165	135–241	195–220
Upper middle school		73–370	215–270
High school		65–334	250–300

Timed Administration of Word Lists

A student's ability to identify single words automatically can be assessed through timed administration of a word list. Does the student identify each word immediately, or does the student pause? A pause may indicate that a word is not a sight word, but a word the student must analyze in order to identify.

Take a graded word list and ask the student to pronounce the words. If the student correctly pronounces a word within one second, mark it A to indicate automatic identification. How can you time one second? Simply say to yourself "one thousand." If the student pronounces the word before you have finished, it is probably within one second. If the student takes longer, mark the word as C if correctly identified. Of course, mark all incorrect responses. Count the total number of correct words. Compare this to the number of words that were identified automatically. If a student's total number of words is greater than the number of words recognized automatically, the student may lack a sight word vocabulary appropriate to that level.

Donika read a list of second-grade words from a published informal reading inventory (IRI) and scored at an instructional level for the total number of words that she recognized correctly. Of the 17 correct words, only 3 were identified automatically which suggested that Donika was primarily analyzing words in instructional-level text. When Donika read a second-grade selection, her oral reading was very accurate, but her reading rate was only 35 words per minute. It was not surprising that she remembered very little of what she read. All of Donika's energies were taken up with analyzing words, and she did this quite efficiently. However, she needed to develop and expand her sight word vocabulary.

A different picture emerged with Jeffrey. His performance on a word list from a published IRI placed him at an instructional level for preprimer text. Jeffrey identified 14 words correctly, and all of them were identified automatically. However, he was not able to analyze words such as *make, place, write,* and *other.* Jeffrey either knew the word or he didn't. If he didn't, he had no word analysis skills to help him with unfamiliar words. Unlike Donika, Jeffrey needed help with word analysis.

Remember that use of a word list is a "quick and dirty" way of estimating automaticity. Listening to a student read orally offers a far richer opportunity for fluency assessment.

Assessing Intonation

Good readers are accurate and they are automatic in their identification of words. Marking oral reading errors (as described in other chapters) indicates reading accuracy; determining reading rate and the timed administration of word lists suggest reading speed. But what about the third component of fluency, intonation? Good oral readers are expressive. Their performance pleases and delights their audience. Teachers and tutors can use a simple checklist (such as the one provided here) to assess intonation whenever students read orally during classroom instruction. Using a simple coding system such as "Yes," "No," and "Sometimes" on this checklist may be more informative than simply checking off the items.

Intonation Checklist

_____ Read at a rhythm resembling natural speech (quickly, but not too fast to be understood).

_____ Read smoothly without hesitations and repetitions.

_____ Used vocal expression.

_____ Noted punctuation signals.

_____ Grouped words into meaningful phrases.

From _Reading Assessment: A Primer for Teachers and Tutors_ by JoAnne Schudt Caldwell. Copyright 2002 by The Guilford Press. Permission to photocopy this form is granted to purchasers of this book for personal use only (see copyright page for details).

ASSESSING STUDENT PROGRESS IN FLUENCY

A teacher or tutor can assess an individual's fluency at different points in time. For example, the teacher or tutor can compare reading rate before and after oral reading practice or after several months of instruction. Some students enjoy recording their reading rate and watching it increase as they become more fluent. Administering a simple checklist of intonation behaviors (as described above) at different points may be the most effective means of assessing this component of fluency over time.

Given the importance of fluency, it is a good idea to schedule regular oral reading practice. Asking students to engage in repeated reading of a selection has been found to increase fluency (Allington, 1977, 2001; Samuels, 1979; Rasinski, 1986; Stahl, Heubach, & Cramond, 1997). Students can practice part of a selection alone or with peers. They can tape their first reading and their last reading to note progress. They can use a checklist to evaluate their own and their peers' intonation during oral reading. In fact, they can evaluate their intonation using the same checklist as the teacher or tutor. This provides a wonderful opportunity to assess the progress of each student. It is a time when instruction and assessment truly merge.

Should a teacher or tutor group students according to their fluency? Probably not. First, it would be very difficult to do given the variability among readers' fluency in different kinds of text. Second, students profit from the modeling of their more fluent peers. Consider what often happens when students of like reading ability are grouped together for oral reading practice.

The good readers and the more fluent ones listen to peers who are as skilled as they are. On the other hand, the poorer readers are subjected to repeated examples of slow, halting, choppy, or inexpressive reading. It makes more sense to group students of mixed fluency levels. If the practice activity is motivating enough, students will learn from each other and eagerly work together to improve their performance.

There are various instructional activities for practicing oral reading and for assessing student progress in developing fluency (Koskinen & Blum, 1984; Maccinati, 1985; Rasinski, 1988; Dowhower, 1991; Hoffman & Isaacs, 1991; Zutell & Rasinski, 1991; Allington, 2001). Students enjoy performing. Teachers or tutors can foster repeated reading by assigning character and narrator roles to stories and having the students practice for the final performance. They can put on plays. Class choral reading can also promote fluency development. Older students can practice reading stories in order to read to younger students. All of these activities provide the teacher or tutor with opportunities to evaluate their students' developing fluency.

SUMMARY

- Fluency involves accuracy, speed, and intonation. Fluency allows the reader to pay attention to meaning.
- A reader's sight vocabulary develops and expands through wide reading of independent- and instructional-level text. It also develops through good modeling and the realization that reading is more than accurate word pronunciation.
- A teacher or tutor can assess general fluency level by listening to students read orally in instructional-level text.
- The teacher or tutor can assess accuracy by recording oral reading errors (as described in other chapters). The teacher or tutor can assess intonation by using a checklist.
- The teacher or tutor can assess speed by determining reading rate and by timed administration of graded word lists. Reading rate is measured as words per minute. Reading rate varies across individuals and texts; it also varies according to readers' purposes. Compare a student's reading rate in oral and silent reading or at different points in time. Do not assume that reading rate on one graded passage will be the same on other passages at that grade level. Do not compare the rates of different students.
- Regularly schedule oral reading practice in the classroom or tutoring session, and use this as an opportunity for assessment.

ACTIVITIES FOR DEVELOPING UNDERSTANDING

• Choose an unfamiliar and difficult selection. Read it orally and tape-record your reading. Then practice the selection by repeatedly reading it. Tape yourself a second time. Listen to the two tapes. What differences do you note?

• Listen to several students read orally and tape-record their reading. Listen to the tapes and determine accuracy and speed. Use a checklist to assess intonation.

• Time someone silently reading a difficult selection, such as a newspaper editorial. Then time the person reading an easy selection, such as a movie review. Determine the reading rate in each selection. What differences do you notice?

• Ask a student to read a graded word list and tape-record his or her performance. Listen to the tape and differentiate between words that were identified automatically and those that were analyzed.

• Complete the self-evaluation form provided on the next page.

Teacher or Tutor Self-Evaluation

I assess reading fluency when I use the IRI process.

   Regularly   Occasionally   A future goal

I assess reading speed through reading rate.

   Regularly   Occasionally   A future goal

I use timed administration of graded word lists to assess word identification speed or automaticity.

   Regularly   Occasionally   A future goal

I assess students' intonation using a checklist.

   Regularly   Occasionally   A future goal

I record students' individual progress in fluency.

   Regularly   Occasionally   A future goal

I use repeated reading and oral reading practice as opportunities for assessment.

   Regularly   Occasionally   A future goal

SEVEN

Comprehension of Narrative and Expository Text

How Can We Assess Understanding of Stories and Textbooks?

THE ROLE OF COMPREHENSION IN THE READING PROCESS

To state it simply, comprehension is reading. Without comprehension, there would be no purpose to reading words. Comprehension is what entices the reader to continue reading. Let's consider a familiar scenario. Picture yourself at two in the morning. You know you should be in bed, but you can't put down the novel you are reading. You only have 50 pages left, and you have to discover how it turns out. You know you will not get enough sleep and will probably wake up crabby, but you have to finish the book. This illustrates the power of comprehension. If you did not understand what you are reading, you would find it very easy to set the book aside and go to bed.

Comprehension is an active process. Good readers use the words of the author to construct a personal version of the text in their minds. This text is similar to what the author has written, but good readers supply additional details and make inferences that are not stated in the text. Remember the story of Peter and Bridget in Chapter One, and all the things you did in your mind as you read? You understood information that was stated directly, such as the names of the characters and some of their actions. This is called *literal comprehension*. But you did much more. You created visual images. You made predictions and confirmed their accuracy. You asked questions and synthesized information. You drew on your knowledge of waiting rooms and doctors' offices to make inferences. You became emotionally involved in the fate of the characters. All of these actions are among the good reader behaviors involved in comprehension. Good readers sometimes take comprehension for granted because it seems to happen so effortlessly.

Good readers are also *metacognitive*; that is, they are aware of their own comprehension, and if their comprehension fails, they know what strategies

---

Good Reader Behaviors Involved in Comprehension

Before, during, and after reading, good readers . . .

Learn new words and refine the meanings of known ones.
Connect what they know with the information in the text.
Determine what is important in the text.
Recognize the structure of the text.
Summarize and reorganize ideas in the text.
Make inferences and predictions.
Construct visual images.
Ask questions of themselves and the author, and read to find answers.
Synthesize information from different sources.
Form and support opinions on ideas in the text.
Recognize the author's purpose/point of view/style.
Monitor comprehension and repair comprehension breakdowns.

to employ. In other words, they know when they comprehend, they know when they don't comprehend, and they know what to do about it when they don't. They possess two kinds of knowledge: "(a) the awareness of whether or not comprehension is occurring, and (b) the conscious application of one or more strategies to correct comprehension difficulties" (Baumann, Jones, & Siefert-Kessell, 1993, p. 185). These strategies may include self-questioning, rereading, predicting and verifying, retelling, reading out loud, and others.

I remember working with Kellie, a middle school student who had few strategies for effectively analyzing unfamiliar words. As her skill in word identification improved, she was able to pay more attention to meaning, and for the first time she actually began to understand what she read. After reading a short article on her favorite singer, she commented, "You know, there was a lot of good stuff in here." Comprehension is the good stuff! Teachers and tutors need to know whether that good stuff is accessible to their students.

A variety of elements can positively or negatively affect comprehension. Some examples are fatigue, the reader's purpose for reading, the difficulty level of the text, and the reader's interest in the topic. Two other components that play a large role in the comprehension process are the reader's background knowledge and the structure of the text. If the topic is familiar, we comprehend more easily and more completely. The structure of narrative text makes it easier to comprehend than expository text. Let's examine each of these components.

THE ROLE OF BACKGROUND KNOWLEDGE

Our ability to understand what we read is highly dependent upon the background knowledge that we bring to the act of reading. If we know a lot about a topic, we use this knowledge to interpret the text, to make inferences, to create visual images, and to evaluate the author's point of view. Let me demonstrate the power of prior knowledge. Read the following short selection.

> **He opened his eyes. His family was all in the room. "Strike the tent," he murmured softly. His wife began to cry and his son buried his face in his hands.**

What was going on? What was happening to this man? Given the fact that members of his family were with him, and given their obvious distress, you probably inferred that he was gravely ill and perhaps dying. You could do that because you took the clues surrounding his family's reactions, matched these to what you know about the death of loved ones, and concluded that he was probably on his deathbed. Your prior knowledge played a large part in your ability to comprehend.

Now consider a very different question. What was this man's profession? There is a clue in the passage, but were you able to pick it up and match it to your knowledge base? Perhaps you made some great guesses, but unless you are a Civil War historian, you probably were not sure. However, if you knew that the last words of the Confederate general Robert E. Lee were "Strike the tent," you might have figured it out. In order for comprehension to occur, we need to bring some background knowledge to the act of reading. Lack of prior knowledge is what makes some textbooks so difficult to understand. Until we develop knowledge of the topic (and this usually occurs as we continue to read about the subject), our comprehension is often limited to literal understanding.

It is important for a teacher or tutor to evaluate comprehension in light of a student's background knowledge. A student may comprehend a short story very well and demonstrate evidence of higher-level thinking. However, it may be unrealistic to expect this same level of comprehension in a textbook chapter on an unfamiliar topic.

THE STRUCTURE OF NARRATIVE AND EXPOSITORY TEXT

Narratives embrace a variety of literary genres. These include fairy and folk tales, fables, fantasy stories such as science fiction and horror stories, realistic fiction, historical fiction, mysteries, plays, biographies, and autobiographies. Narratives share a common structure or form. Each narrative is written about characters. These characters live in a setting—that is, a certain time and place. They experience problems and seek to solve them. The narrative involves a series of steps or events that eventually lead to a solution or resolution of some sort. Good readers instinctively recognize this format and use it as a guide for comprehension and memory. For example, if asked to summarize a story, good readers generally include the components of character, setting, problem, and solution in their summary (Stein, 1979; Stein & Glenn, 1979).

Expository text is not as user-friendly as narrative text. Expository text is nonfiction. It is what we read in newspapers and textbooks. Authors write expository text to convey information, such as a news account of an earthquake or a textbook explanation of the process of cell division. Authors also use expository text to explain an idea or a point of view. When you read a newspaper column or an editorial, you are reading expository text.

Expository text is usually organized in one of five ways (Englert & Hiebert, 1984; Horowitz, 1985; Meyer & Freedle, 1984; Taylor, 1992). One organizational pattern is *sequence* or *time order*. For example, an account of the battle of Gettysburg would probably involve a sequential presentation of events. Authors may also use *listing* or *description* to explain the features of an object or event. A science textbook might list the features of viruses (their characteristics, the different kinds, how they reproduce, etc.). A third pattern is *comparison and contrast*, in which the author explains how two things are alike and how they are different. For example, how do two candidates differ in their policies on education, and how are they alike? The fourth pattern, known as *cause and effect*, gives reasons for events. The author describes an event such as a riot and gives reasons why it occurred. A final pattern is *problem and solution*. Using this pattern, an author might describe a problem facing the federal government and suggest various solutions.

Good readers recognize these patterns just as they recognize the pattern of narrative text, and they use them to aid their comprehension and their memory (van Dijk & Kintsch, 1983). Poor readers do not recognize the patterns as naturally, often because they are focused on recognizing words. However, expository text presents challenges that narrative text does not. The patterns are not as clearly differentiated. One reader may see a cause-and-effect pattern, while another may identify it as time order. Expository text often involves far more complex topics than narratives, and it tends to contain more difficult vocabulary and more technical terms. Moreover, it is not as personal as narrative text: We can become emotionally involved with a character, but it is difficult to feel allegiance to a virus or to the laws of leverage. In addition, much expository text is written on unfamiliar topics, and dealing with these is always more difficult than dealing with familiar concepts. Think about the differences involved in reading about the economics of the stock market versus reading about the latest trials and tribulations of a movie star or sports hero.

PURPOSES OF COMPREHENSION ASSESSMENT

The teacher or tutor needs to know a student's level of comprehension and in what kind of text in order to plan instruction and group students effectively. Can the student understand familiar narratives? Can the student make sense out of expository selections? How does the student perform when faced with material on unfamiliar topics? The teacher or tutor also needs to know which of the good reader behaviors involved in comprehension a student does or does not display. Comprehension occurs in the mind; what mental strategies does the student use to make sense out of his or her reading? Finally, the teacher or tutor must recognize and record student progress in developing successful comprehension strategies.

ASSESSING COMPREHENSION LEVELS

The teacher or tutor can determine comprehension levels by using the informal reading inventory (IRI) process with a published informal reading inventory (IRI) or with classroom texts. However, some caution must be exercised. The IRI process provides two scores: a level for word identification accuracy and a level for comprehension. As noted in Chapter Three, the teacher or tutor cannot assume that these will be identical for the same passage. Sometimes a student will demonstrate poor word identification accuracy but acceptable comprehension. This usually occurs with very familiar narrative text, where the student can follow the story line and successfully guess at answers despite difficulties with word identification. Some students display the opposite pattern of acceptable word identification accuracy and poor comprehension. This often occurs if a student focuses upon saying the words as opposed to making sense out of the selection, or if the student reads extremely unfamiliar text. Because word identification does not always suggest comprehension, the teacher or tutor must not confuse the two.

Because prior knowledge and text structure greatly affect comprehension, the teacher or tutor cannot assume that comprehension of familiar and/ or narrative text will be the same as comprehension of unfamiliar and/or expository text. It is not expected that a busy teacher or tutor will be able to use the IRI process to determine comprehension levels for all students in familiar, unfamiliar, narrative, and expository text. However, the teacher or tutor must understand that comprehension varies across different kinds of selections and not infer comprehension of other kinds of text from comprehension of one selection. For example, assessment of classroom activities and assignments may indicate that a student demonstrates fine comprehension when reading narratives. The teacher or tutor cannot assume that the student will perform similarly in a science or social studies textbook. When one is talking with parents or writing reports, it is always wise to qualify statements about a student's comprehension by differentiating comprehension of narratives from comprehension of expository textbooks, and by separating comprehension of familiar from unfamiliar text.

Assessing comprehension levels with the IRI process moves more quickly in the lower grades, where the passages are relatively short. Some published IRIs provide short passages for the upper grades, but these are not typical of what older students read. Administering the IRI process with longer passages is probably more authentic; however, it does take longer. Because of this, many teachers and tutors of older students reserve the IRI process for students who are obviously struggling with class materials. For the majority of older students, a teacher or tutor can use class activities and assignments to assess comprehension levels. In other words, if the student comprehends classroom texts, the teacher or tutor can assume the student is comfortable reading material at that grade level. This is obviously not the same as a formal evaluation of whether the student is reading at an independent, instructional, or frustration level, but it does indicate that the student can comprehend materials chosen for his or her grade level.

ASSESSING GOOD READER BEHAVIORS IN COMPREHENSION

Comprehension is an extremely complex process, and a host of factors interact to facilitate it or to obstruct it. Although we know more about comprehension than we did in the past, we are still very far from effectively describing or even understanding exactly what goes on in the minds of readers as they interpret text. We know some of the things that good readers do during the act of comprehension, but we do not know all of them. Neither do we fully understand how these interact with one another, or which (if any) are more important to the comprehension process.

We educators have attempted to explain comprehension by breaking it into parts. We have listed possible mental activities that readers perform when they comprehend. At one time, we arranged these activities into scope and sequence charts. Unfortunately, we went a bit too far by collecting more comprehension skills than any teacher or tutor could realistically keep track of. Now we are turning the scope and sequence charts into pupil performance expectations, and we continue to make the same mistake. The 12 good reader behaviors listed at the beginning of this chapter are also an attempt to explain the comprehension process. However, 12 behaviors are more manageable than the number contained in most scope and sequence charts or lists of pupil performance expectations!

Assessing comprehension involves knowing what good reader behaviors are being taught and evaluated. A teacher or tutor can concentrate on a single behavior. For example, he or she may direct students' attention to determining importance, teach students how to decide what are the most significant parts of a selection, and assess their ability to do this. Many classroom activities, however, actually involve a blend of good reader behaviors. Should the teacher or tutor attempt to identify all of the underlying behaviors? This could be a very time-consuming procedure. Instead, the teacher or tutor should choose two or three good reader behaviors at a time and focus on these.

In the past, teachers or tutors attempted to group children according to their comprehension levels in order to offer differentiated instruction. Sometimes this did not work very well. If the teacher or tutor assessed comprehension in a general way and did not pay attention to the role of prior knowledge and text structure, the groups were often more different than alike! If you intend to group children of like comprehension ability, use the good reader behaviors as your focus and pay attention to the role of text structure. Do not assume that a student who displays one of these behaviors while reading a story will necessarily do the same thing in a textbook. If you group according to the specific guidelines of good reader behavior and text type, you will probably have groups that are relatively alike.

Many teachers and tutors feel comfortable with a focus on a few behaviors at one time. It is more manageable and allows them to keep track of individual students. It also allows them to be more precise in their comments to parents as well as to students. However, teachers and tutors often worry about effectively covering all the good reader behaviors; they become concerned that they are not spending enough time on each one. Teachers and tutors must realize that the good reader behaviors are not really separate entities. For example, it is difficult to imagine that a student who recognizes important parts of a text is not using text structure to do so. In noting importance, the student may have also connected what he or she knew to the text. The student possibly self-questioned during the process and synthesized information as well. In fact, deciding that a segment of text was or was not important probably represented an inference on the student's part. The good reader behaviors blend together. They are more devices for our convenience in designing instruction and assessing learning than actual separate realities. If we focus on one good reader behavior, we are probably developing others

Ramya divided her fourth graders into groups. She then asked the members of each group to choose an animal that they did not know much about, and to learn all they could about it. After researching their choice, the group members presented the animal to the rest of the class in the form of a sales promotion. The class took the role of a prospective buyer, and the group had to talk the class into buying the animal. The presentation described the benefits of owning the animal, the cost of the initial purchase, and the expense of maintaining or using the animal after the sale was completed. Groups employed various devices to convince their classmates to buy their animal (illustrations, posters, jingles, skits, sales guarantees, etc.). The class then voted on whether or not they would purchase the animal. Ramya used a rubric that focused on two good reader behaviors: noting importance and synthesizing information from different sources. But it was evident that much more went on as the students researched and prepared their presentations. How could Ramya have identified, separated, and kept track of all the good reader behaviors that each fourth grader engaged in? Concentrating on two made it a manageable task. If a complex classroom activity is successful as Ramya's certainly was, the teacher or tutor who focuses on one or two good reader behaviors can assume that the rest are probably alive and well, at least for that task and that selection.

Some might argue that by reducing the comprehension process to a few good reader behaviors, we are losing our sense of the wonderful complexity that characterizes comprehension. Unfortunately, our brains have limitations. In everyday life, we deal effectively with many complex situations by simplifying them in some way. We often break them into parts and address each part separately.

Several years ago, my family and I bought a house in the country. It had a beautiful view, but it lay in the middle of a farmer's field, and nothing had been done about landscaping that field. The land had not been graded, and the driveway was full of ruts. The five-acre lot contained a few scraggly and sick trees, a lot of hidden barbed wire, and an abundance of weeds that had gained a strong foothold. Where should we begin? We focused on one small part at a time and started with tearing out the barbed wire, always keeping in mind the big picture of what our lot would eventually look like. In truth, we were not really sure what it would look like. We were too overwhelmed by the enormity of our task and our own inexperience as gardeners even to have a sense of that big picture. But we persevered, bit by bit, and gradually things came together.

Instructing and assessing comprehension are much more complex than landscaping, but there are similarities. Comprehension is the big picture, and it is a picture that we do not fully understand. We make it manageable by simplifying it into 12 good reader behaviors and focusing on a few of these at a time. The analogy of the garden, like most analogies, tends to break down eventually. Teaching and assessing the good reader behaviors are certainly more rewarding and enjoyable than tearing out barbed wire, dealing with pockets of poison ivy, and routing a nest of aggressive garter snakes!

A teacher or tutor can use several activities to effectively assess comprehension and suggest the presence or absence of good reader behaviors. Some of these focus on a single good reader behavior; some evaluate several good reader behaviors at the same time. These measures can be used with a whole class, a small group, or individual students. They include vocabulary application activities; teacher and student questions; questioning with look-backs; oral or written retellings; think-alouds; focused discussion; and good reader response logs.

Vocabulary Application Activities

Before, during, and after reading, good readers learn new words and refine the meanings of known ones. How can the teacher or tutor assess this important good reader behavior? In the past (and, I suspect, even now), our assessment of students' vocabulary knowledge left much to be desired. A typical method was some form of paper-and-pencil vocabulary test. Students chose a word's definition from four possible choices or matched a column of words to a second column of definitions. I imagine that many students received acceptable grades because they were lucky guessers, not because they had a profound understanding of word meanings.

A second common method of assessing vocabulary knowledge was to ask a student to use a word in a sentence. If the student used the word correctly, it was assumed that he or she understood it. This was probably true for those students who demonstrated correct usage, but what about those who offered an incorrect, incomplete, or ambiguous usage? Did this mean they did not understand the word? Perhaps they knew the meaning, but failed to construct a sentence that adequately demonstrated their understanding. I remember assigning the word *extrovert* as part of a vocabulary exercise. One student wrote, "I extroverted down the hall on my birthday." The student obviously had some sense of the word's meaning, but did not understand that *extrovert* was a noun rather than a verb. And then there were the students who knew how to play the vocabulary game and offered correct but ambiguous sentences, such as "I saw an extrovert," or "There goes an extrovert!" What did they understand about the meaning of *extrovert* beyond recognizing it as a noun? Perhaps these students' performance was a function of disliking the sentence construction task as opposed to knowing the word meanings. I cannot recall any students who approached the sentence-writing assignment with enthusiasm. Most picked up their pencils with glum resignation, and some with downright antipathy.

There are better alternatives for vocabulary assessment that fit under the general category of application activities. These activities can entice students to talk about words and expand their understanding of word meaning. It is really difficult to separate assessment and instruction. Many activities that suggest the presence or absence of good reader behaviors actually provide opportunities for developing and expanding the behaviors.

One application activity is to have students sort a group of words on the basis of their meaning. Chapter Five has talked about word sorts as a way of assessing knowledge of letter–sound patterns. The activity of meaning sorts can develop vocabulary knowledge as well as reveal it. Students can work in pairs or groups to sort the words. You can also use sorting as a whole-class or large-group activity. Simply give each individual several word cards. Then state a category, such as "something you can buy," and ask individuals to hold up a word card that matches that category. Each student then provides a rationale for holding up that specific word.

A teacher or tutor can provide the categories for sorting or can allow students to choose their own categories. The categories for meaning sorts must be rather general in order to allow students to realistically group words that have very different meanings. Of course, the key to an effective meaning sort is a student's reason why a word fits a certain category. The teacher or tutor can assess whether a student is learning new words and refining the meaning of old ones by observing the student's participation in a meaning sort. The teacher or tutor can also ask the student to sort several words in writing and provide reasons for the chosen grouping.

Consider the following words from a fifth-grade classroom: *mosaic, significant, nourishment, reluctant, asylum, mirage, preen, crest, blunt, glaze, strut*, and *fluster*. Can any of these very different words be tied together into a single category? Examine the list of possible meaning sort categories in the accompanying box. How would you sort and re-sort these vocabulary words?

A second vocabulary application activity that reveals whether students understand a word is to ask them to put this word in their own lives. That is, instead of composing a dull sentence using the word, they must describe how the word could fit into their world. They can do this either orally or in writing. Does the word describe someone in their family, neighborhood, or favorite television program? Does the word depict an event, an action, or an emotion that they have experienced or observed in others? What are the circumstances surrounding this word? As an example, can you place *extrovert* in your own life? I could easily describe a colleague of mine who is a perfect example of a cheerful extrovert. What about *nourishment, strut*, or *reluctant*? Elena chose to place *strut* in her life. She described the proud antics of her dog when he returned from the groomer. Tomas selected *nourishment*. He

---

Categories for Meaning Sorts

- Words that stand for something you can touch, see, hear, taste, or smell.
- Words that stand for something you can buy, sell, own, trade, learn, or make.
- Words that stand for something that is in your house, locker, book bag, kitchen, bedroom, or classroom.
- Words that stand for something your mother will/will not let you bring home.
- Words that stand for something you can do or be.
- Words that stand for something you saw someone do on TV, in the movies, or in your neighborhood.
- Words that stand for something an animal, plant, or machine can be or do.
- Words that can describe a person, an animal, a plant, a food, a sport, and so on.
- Words that make you feel happy, sad, angry, resentful, or some other way.
- "Glue" words (articles, prepositions, helping verbs, conjunctions, etc.).

---

listed all the nutritional items that he had eaten at dinner the previous night and staunchly defended his choice of chocolate cake as nourishing. Wayne described his parents as *reluctant* to let his older sister drive the new car to school. His description of the ensuing argument suggested, however, a much stronger emotion than reluctance!

Vocabulary words are also parts of speech. They are nouns, verb, adjectives, and adverbs. Only in a word list do parts of speech stand alone. In sentences, nouns join with verbs and adjectives. Adverbs join with verbs. Ask students to match each vocabulary word with another part of speech. If the vocabulary word is a noun, match it to a verb. What would this noun do or what might it look like? What would an *asylum* do? What would a *mosaic* look like? An *asylum* might *comfort* or it might *threaten*. A *mosaic* might *sparkle* or *impress*. In order to make a reasonable match, the student has to understand the word's meaning. If the word is a verb, have students tell who or what would perform this action, and why they would do so. What nouns would match with *preen* or *fluster*? If the word is an adjective, whom or what would it describe? What nouns could be joined with the adjectives *significant* and *blunt*? Some words, like *crest*, can be either nouns or verbs. Students can choose either or both parts of speech to match with another word. What verb would you match with the noun *crest*? What noun would you match with *crest* used as a verb? As I write this, floods are threatening in the western part of my state, and *river* would certainly be a good match for the verb *crest*!

Vocabulary application activities like these stimulate student discussion about word meanings. They help students expand their word knowledge. They also offer a teacher or tutor opportunities to assess the good reader behavior of learning new words and refining the meanings of old ones. If the activity is oral, the teacher or tutor must take care to record student behavior on a checklist. Such a checklist may be quite simple and involve only two items: "Applies word correctly" and "Does not apply word correctly." If the vocabulary application activity is written, the teacher or tutor will need a simple rubric to assess the effectiveness and accuracy of the student's vocabulary application. If the teacher or tutor has a page in his or her grade book that is labeled for the good reader behavior of learning and refining word meanings, student performance on this behavior can be recorded and evaluated over each grading period.

Don't attempt to assess whether or not a student knows individual words. This is impossible to keep track of. Your interest as a teacher or tutor is in the *process* of learning new words and expanding the meanings of old ones. The good reader behavior is the focus of assessment, not the meanings of individual words. Word knowledge is very personal. Students may understand a word in one context and not in another. They may remember a word because they are interested in a specific topic. They may forget a word because the topic bores them. It is unrealistic to expect that all students at a certain grade level should know the meanings of the same body of words. Learning word meanings and expanding upon them go on throughout life. Teaching students to apply word meanings fosters the development of this good reader behavior. Assessing their ability to apply word meanings indicates that it is in place even if some words are still unknown.

Teacher and Student Questions

Teacher Questions

The typical method of assessing comprehension has been for teachers and tutors to ask questions, questions, and more questions. However, this has serious limitations. First, good readers ask questions of themselves and of the author as they read. It is those questions that keep them up late to finish a book or chapter. Unfortunately, the heavy emphasis in our schools upon teacher questions tends to overshadow this role of the good reader. Students soon learn that teachers and tutors ask the questions, and that their job is to provide the answers. Teachers and tutors need to decrease the number of questions they ask and increase the opportunities for students to construct questions and discuss possible answers.

A second limitation rests in the kind of questions we ask. Many teachers and tutors, as well as authors of textbook manuals, ask questions that primarily assess literal comprehension. They seldom evaluate higher-level comprehension processes, such as the good reader behaviors of making inferences, synthesizing information, and summarizing. In addition, literal questions can test memory more than they test actual understanding. Did a student fail to answer because he or she did not understand the text? Or did the student understand the text during reading, but then forget certain pieces of information? Literal questions do not clearly differentiate between the processes of understanding and memory.

Asking students questions about their reading can offer insights into the presence or absence of good reader behaviors. However, this is only possible if the teacher or tutor is aware that all questions are not the same. Questions focus on different reader behaviors. Answering some questions requires the reader to recall literal meaning, such as definitions and facts; answering other questions demands higher-level skills, such as generating hypotheses and justifying opinions. The teacher or tutor can use questions to assess good reader behaviors only if the questions are constructed and/or grouped into categories and if these categories are made evident to the students.

Questions can be categorized in a variety of ways. One simple and workable system is to classify questions as *memory* questions, *convergent thinking* questions, *divergent thinking* questions, and *evaluative thinking* questions (Ciardiello, 1998). The last three categories parallel good reader behaviors.

Memory questions usually begin with *who, what, where,* and *when* (Ciardiello, 1998). Students answer a memory question by offering definitions (*What is a virus?*), by identifying facts ("Who was Woodrow Wilson?"), by designating a time or place ("Where was the armistice signed?"), or by offering a yes–no response ("Are viruses the same as cells?"). Memory questions assess recall of content. They may not indicate understanding of that content. In fact, a student may be simply parroting the words of the text. Have you ever had a student complain that he or she cannot find the answer to a question because "it isn't in the book?" In most such cases, the answer actually is there, but it is framed in different words than the question. For example, the question is "What are the principal products of Denmark?", and the text read, "The primary exports of Denmark are . . . " The student can't find the answer because he or she is simply matching question words to text words, and "principal products" does not match "primary exports." No true comprehension is occurring. Because memory questions can usually be answered by matching question words and text words, they actually tell the teacher or tutor little about the presence or absence of good reader behaviors.

Convergent thinking questions begin with *why, how,* and *in what ways* (Ciardiello, 1998). Students answer convergent thinking questions by explaining ("Why did the United States enter World War I?"), by describing relationships ("How did the Big Three compromise during the Paris Peace Conference?"), and by comparing and contrasting ("How are viruses and cells different?"). In order to answer convergent thinking questions, a reader must engage in several good reader behaviors: determining what is important in the text; summarizing and reorganizing ideas in the text; and synthesizing information.

Divergent thinking questions begin with such signal words as *imagine, predict, suppose, if . . . then, how might, can you create, and what might happen if* (Ciardiello, 1998). In order to answer a divergent thinking question, a student must infer ("Why do you think the Big Three refused to let Germany attend the Paris Peace Conference?"), predict ("Predict how the terms of the Versailles Treaty paved the way for the rise of Hitler"), hypothesize ("What differences in U.S. foreign policy might have occurred if the Russian czar had maintained power?"), or reconstruct ("Draw up new terms for the Versailles Treaty that might have prevented the rise of Hitler"). A student who successfully answers divergent thinking questions is also noting importance, summarizing/reorganizing, and synthesizing. In addition, the student is using existing knowledge to make predictions and inferences.

Evaluative thinking questions begin with *defend, judge, justify, what do you think,* and *what is your opinion* (Ciardiello, 1998). To answer these questions successfully, a student must value ("How do you feel about Wilson's Fourteen Points?"), judge ("What do you think of the terms of the Versailles Treaty?"), and defend or justify ("Were the Allies shortsighted in their demands, and why do you think so?"). Answering evaluative thinking questions requires an integration of almost all the good reader behaviors!

In order to evaluate the presence or absence of good reader behaviors, you must focus on convergent, divergent, and evaluative thinking questions. It is probably a good idea to place the question stems in your lesson plan book, so you will have easy access to them as you prepare lessons. It is not necessary to differentiate among these three question types and assess each

---

Signal Words for Question Types

Memory questions: *who, what, where,* and *when*
Convergent thinking questions: *why, how,* and *in what ways*
Divergent thinking questions: *imagine, predict, suppose, if . . .
then, how might, can you create,* and *what might happen if*
Evaluative thinking: *defend, judge, justify, what do you think,* and
what is your opinion

---

separately. This is too time-consuming. You do not want to waste time deciding whether a question is convergent or divergent. You do not want to match
a good reader behavior to a question type. You just want to separate memory
questions from the three higher-level types. If students are successful in answering questions in any one of these three categories, you can assume that
good reader behaviors are in place. If students are unsuccessful, you may
need to model and teach specific good reader behaviors, such as determining
importance, synthesizing information, or making inferences.

You do not necessarily have to construct questions using convergent, divergent, and evaluative question stems, although these are very helpful. You
can also construct questions that focus directly upon the good reader behaviors. For example, if you are teaching students to make an inference by matching what they know to a clue in the text, ask them to describe an inference
they made while they were reading and to explain the clues they used. In
other words, construct questions that focus on the process of comprehension
as opposed to the content of the text (Harvey & Goudvis, 2000). Use the good
reader behaviors to do this. Ask students how a sentence or text episode is
connected to their lives, to another selection, or to the world at large. Highlight a part of the text, and ask students to describe the visual image it brings
to their mind. Ask students to identify important parts of the text and explain
why they were important. Ask students to describe the questions that formed
in their minds as they read. Ask students to offer their opinions and give reasons for them. Ask student to indicate what parts of the text were confusing to
them and tell how they resolved their difficulties.

Student Questions

Good readers ask questions of themselves and the author, and read to find answers. As mentioned earlier, many students believe that it is the teacher's or

tutor's role to ask questions. They do not really see themselves as question-ers. In fact, some students avoid asking questions because they are afraid of looking dumb. Blend instruction and assessment by teaching students the different types of questions, the question stem signals to these types, and how they are answered differently. Teach students that some questions can be answered from the text and some from background knowledge. Other answers may have to be inferred or may be better answered through discussion or further research (Harvey & Goudvis, 2000). Have students generate questions. Applaud and dignify their attempts to do so. In order to construct convergent, divergent, or evaluative questions, a student uses the same good reader behaviors that are used in formulating answers. A student's ability to create questions is a powerful indicator that good reader behaviors are in place, but one that teachers and tutors often ignore

Questioning with Look-Backs

Looking back in a selection to find forgotten or unknown information is a common practice among good readers. Perhaps you are reading a novel that you have not picked up for several days. Before you begin reading again, you probably look back and skim the previous pages to refresh your memory about what happened. Perhaps you are reading a piece of nonfiction, and the author refers to a term or a process that you do not remember. What do you do? You look back in the text and locate where that term was defined or where the process was described. Do you remember when you were in college, and the instructor handed out a list of topics that just might be covered in an exam? Again, you looked back in the textbook to locate these topics and to reread the text sections that explained them. Because looking back and rereading for the purpose of comprehending are natural for good readers, you should encourage looking back to find answers to the convergent, divergent, and evaluative questions that have been explained in the preceding section.

Think about why a reader might fail to answer a question. Perhaps the reader did not comprehend the selection. On the other hand, perhaps the reader understood it quite well but just failed to remember certain portions. Assessing comprehension by questioning with look-backs allows you as a teacher or tutor to differentiate between comprehension failure and memory failure. If a student fails to answer a question but can locate the answer after looking back, you have learned two things. First, the student is effectively using a good reader behavior. Second, the initial failure to answer the question was due to memory lapse, not lack of understanding.

Unfortunately, many students do not spontaneously look back in the text to locate information. In fact, many think it is a form of cheating to do this, especially when they are taking standardized tests. Many students unrealistically believe that one reading of a selection should suffice for answering questions or completing any assignments. It is also unfortunate that many teachers and tutors assess comprehension without allowing students to look back in the text. Consider a typical classroom scenario. Having read a portion of the textbook, the teacher or tutor begins to ask questions. If a student does not know the answer, the teacher or tutor chooses another student and continues the process until a correct answer is given. Seldom does the teacher or tutor suggest that the first student look back in the text to find the answer that was missed. It is even more unusual to find a teacher or tutor who shows students how to do this by modeling the look-back procedure for them.

Good readers naturally employ the look-back strategy as a way of monitoring and increasing comprehension. We (Leslie & Caldwell, 2001) noted that students with instructional reading levels of third grade and above could successfully engage in look-backs. Students with reading levels below third grade, however, tended simply to reread the entire text, beginning with the first sentence. They did not skim or skip portions of the selection, as good readers do when engaging in look-backs.

The power of look-backs to mirror the comprehension process can be illustrated by contrasting a student's performance with and without look-backs. Using the IRI process, we (Leslie & Caldwell, 2001) found that students uniformly raised their comprehension level after looking back in the text. Students at a frustration level moved to an instructional or independent level. Students at an instructional level moved to an independent level. An assessment that does not allow for looking back in the text tends to underestimate a student's comprehension. For this reason, and because look-backs are a natural part of a good reader's repertoire of reading behaviors, it is important for teachers and tutors to model the look-back process as a form of instruction and to use it in assessment.

Questions with look-backs can take two forms, oral or written. A teacher or tutor can ask questions orally to an individual or to a group. However, when a student does not know an answer, the teacher or tutor should suggest that the student look back in the text to find the answer. If the question requires higher-level thinking, such as making an inference or constructing a personal reflection, the look-back procedure is still effective. The student can look for clues to making the inference or portions of the text with which he or she agrees or disagrees.

If the student has difficulty looking back, the teacher or tutor should model the process or ask questions that suggest look-back strategies.

"Where in the selection do you think you would find this information—the beginning, the middle, or the end?"

"What events in the story give you an idea where you might find the answer?"

"Does the question refer to a character or an event?"

"Do the pictures or headings help you to decide where to look back?"

"If you are skimming the selection, what key words are you looking for?"

As with all oral activities, the teacher or tutor should keep a checklist handy to record student responses. The teacher or tutor can check whether a student answered the question correctly, answered it after looking back in the text, or demonstrated difficulty with looking back.

Written questions with look-backs are more controversial. We are talking about an open-book scenario, in which students are allowed to look back in the text to locate answers to questions. Many content teachers and tutors frown upon this and require that students commit key concepts to memory. But reading teachers and tutors are not teaching content. They are teaching a process—the reading and comprehending process. Therefore, it makes good sense for reading teachers and tutors to determine whether their students can employ the look-back process efficiently.

One of the key components of the IRI process is asking comprehension questions in order to determine an instructional level for comprehension. Most published IRIs do not allow students to look back in the text if they have missed a question. We (Leslie & Caldwell, 2001) strongly recommend that look-backs be a regular part of the IRI process. We believe that a reading level based upon a combination of questions answered with and without look-backs is more representative of what good readers do when faced with concept-dense and unfamiliar text.

Oral and Written Retellings

Another assessment measure to gather evidence about a student's comprehension is asking the student to retell what was read, either orally or in writing. Actually, if this is done orally, we tend to call it *retelling*; if it is written, we generally refer to it as a *summary*. Retellings and summaries are often more difficult than answering questions. The question stem signals expectations for the answer; however, the reader who retells must reconstruct the text on his or her own. A question provides a clue to the student, but there are no clues given when a student is asked to retell or summarize. Have you ever asked someone to tell you about a movie or book? One of two scenarios probably occurred. If you were fortunate, your narrator gave you a brief and sequential account of important events. If you were unlucky, you listened to a disjointed account where the narrator jumped all around, offered explanations out of sequence, and added unimportant details. As a result, you gained little understanding of what the movie was about. Consider the following retelling:

> "There was a lot of shooting. This kid was in the middle of it. Oh, I forgot to say he and his parents were staying at a fancy house. It was by a river. His mother woke him up and they went downstairs. There were a lot of fireworks. They were visiting his grandparents. The father worked for someone, I don't remember who. And there were elephant tusks somewhere. And there were tanks and trucks. And he had two sisters. And a window broke."

What understanding, if any, did you gain from this retelling? Now consider a second one:

> "There were three kids and they were staying at a guesthouse and it was New Year's. There was a war going on because they saw all the trucks and tanks when they drove in. They were visiting their grandparents and the dad thought they would be more safe in the guesthouse. The mother woke them up because of the shooting. The mother made them go downstairs and they were almost hit by a bullet. No one knew when the shooting really started because of all the fireworks."

Can you see the difference between a well-organized retelling and a disorganized one? Both retellings are about the same length and contain approximately the same content. However, one suggests that the reader really understands the content and the sequence of events. The other only suggests that the reader remembers some events but cannot coherently tie them together. It is important for teachers and tutors to instruct students in crafting a coherent and complete retelling. Some students do not learn this on their own; they need teacher and tutor explanation and modeling, as well as the opportunity to look back in the text.

Good readers use the structure of both narrative and expository text to focus their retelling. Because they are able to determine what is important in a selection, they can center on important ideas as opposed to irrelevant details. However, when students retell, they seldom use the exact words of the text. They paraphrase the text and use synonyms. It is the role of the teacher or tutor to determine whether a student's recall matches the meaning in the text. Some published IRIs have retelling grids; the teacher or tutor simply checks which ideas the student remembered. If no grid is available, the easiest thing to do is to underline, highlight, or put parentheses around those segments that the student included in the retelling.

Recording and scoring retellings are easiest if the teacher or tutor is working with a single student. However, most of the time, the teacher or tutor is working with a group of students who have all read the same selection. In this case, the teacher or tutor has two options. The first option is to divide the selection into segments and, after each segment is read, ask a student to retell the contents. A second option is to read the entire section and then to divide the retelling among the students: One student begins the retelling, then another continues, and so on. Of course, a checklist is necessary to keep track of what each student contributes to the retelling.

In the case of a longer selection, students seldom remember all the content and all the details. Instead, they tend to retell in the form of a brief list of topics covered in the selection. For example, after reading a lengthy selection about viruses, Leesa succinctly stated, "It's about how viruses are different from cells. It told about the parts of a virus and how they don't reproduce but replicate. It explained about different cycles." Leesa's retelling was extremely brief, but it indicated her awareness of the main ideas present in the selection. If you are asking for a retelling of longer selections, expect gist statements of this kind and provide for them in your checklist.

If the selection is a narrative, the following questions can guide the construction of a simple checklist. Did the retellings focus on the important elements of character, setting, problem, events, and resolution? Were the retellings sequential? Were the retellings accurate? Were any inferences included? Did the students summarize key points? Did the students offer personal reactions? For an example of such a checklist, see the Retelling Checklist for Narrative Text provided in Chapter Three.

If the selection is an expository one, slightly different questions should guide the construction of a checklist. Did the retelling focus on main ideas and supporting details? Did the retellings contain important content? Were the retellings sequential? Were they accurate? Did the student offer a personal reaction? Again, for an example of such a checklist, see the Retelling Checklist for Expository Text provided in Chapter Three.

As a teacher or tutor, you also have the option to ask for summaries or written retellings. These are somewhat easier to score. You can use the same checklists as with oral retellings, but you can conveniently examine the retellings at your leisure. However, written retellings pose a different problem. The sad fact is that many students do not like to write, and a brief retelling may reflect unwillingness to write rather than not poor recall.

Think-Alouds

Think-alouds are a reader's verbalizations in reaction to reading a selection. They allow a teacher or tutor to gather information about a reader's thinking processes. During the reading process, the teacher or tutor stops at certain points and asks students to think out loud—to share their efforts to comprehend and monitor their comprehension. Think-alouds allow the teacher or tutor to examine what a reader does in order to comprehend and construct meaning from text (Wade, 1990). They are "overt, verbal expressions of the normally covert mental processes readers engage in when constructing meaning from texts" (Baumann et al., 1993, p. 185). Think-alouds can reveal the presence of just about every one of the good reader behaviors involved in comprehension.

Pressley and Afflerbach (1995) offer a comprehensive summary of studies that have examined think-alouds and the variety of activities that readers engaged in as they shared their thoughts during reading. Good reader behaviors were clearly evident as readers summarized and paraphrased, made inferences, noted important information, monitored their understanding or lack of it, reacted in a personal way, and integrated the text with their own prior knowledge. Primary, middle, and high school students all successfully engaged in think-alouds.

Think-alouds work well with individuals and with groups and with oral or silent reading. The teacher or tutor will have to model the process for the students, but once they get the idea, they participate eagerly. In fact, it has been my experience that students enjoy thinking aloud and find it far less threatening than answering questions and offering retellings. Think-alouds provide an alternative to the question-and-answer format that often follows reading. They are an exciting substitute for traditional discussion. Students enjoy hearing the thoughts of others, and they learn from their peers in the process. Think-alouds represent a wonderful blend of assessment and instruction. As teachers and tutors model the comprehension process through think-alouds, they assess the interaction and reaction of their students.

How should a teacher or tutor evaluate think-alouds? Researchers have used a variety of systems for defining types of think-aloud comments. A teacher or tutor needs a system that can be easily transferred to a checklist. It just makes good sense for the types of comments to parallel the good reader behaviors.

• *Retelling*. Good readers summarize and reorganize ideas in the text. The student retells the content of the selection. The student may use his or her own words, but basically preserves the language and sequence of the author: "The Germans came to sign the treaty, and they found very harsh terms."

• *Inferring*. Good readers make inferences and predictions. The student makes an inference, offers a prediction, or draws a conclusion: "The Allies wanted Germany to pay a lot of money, but they probably didn't have any because they lost the war, so there was no point in sending such a huge bill."

• *Questioning*. Good readers ask questions of themselves and the author and read to find answers. The student asks a question that is clearly based upon understanding of the selection. For example, the student may question the motivations of a character or ask a question that is not answered in the selection: "How long before the new countries they created would get their freedom?" The student may also ask a question that indicates lack of understanding about the content of the selection: "Why did they want Germany to pay all that money?" (This question indicates lack of understanding that Germany lost the war.)

• *Noting understanding or lack of understanding*. Good readers monitor comprehension and repair comprehension breakdowns. The student states that he or she understood the selection or part of it: "Well, this certainly makes sense. If you win a war, you get to really step on the losers." The student can also state that he or she does not understand and is confused: "I don't know what a mandate is. Is it a country or a law?"

• *Connecting prior knowledge*. Good readers connect what they know with the information in the text, and they synthesize information from different sources. The student matches the content to prior knowledge or indicates that prior knowledge was absent or in conflict with the text: "I saw something on television about the League of Nations, and I know it didn't work."

• *Reacting personally*. Good readers form and support opinions on

---

Types of Think-Aloud Comments

Retelling.
Inferring.
Questioning.
Noting understanding or lack of understanding.
Connecting prior knowledge.
Reacting personally.

ideas in the text. The student relates the text to personal experience and indicates agreement, disagreement, liking, or disliking: "This was boring, and I really don't care much for history."

Many students include several kinds of think-alouds in one comment. Some students tend to use the same kind of think-aloud comment while other students exhibit a variety. Does any one kind of comment, or any combination of kinds, indicate better comprehension? We (Leslie & Caldwell, 2001) found that think-aloud comments that indicated understanding, especially retelling and inferring, were significantly connected to comprehension. However, it is more important to ascertain that students can think aloud during the reading process, and less important to determine the specific type of think-aloud comment they make.

When you are setting up a think-aloud checklist, begin with two categories: "Can think aloud" and "Experiences difficulty thinking aloud." Some students find thinking aloud very difficult. They are used to answering questions that have one right answer. They are unsure as to what is expected of them. As the teacher or tutor, you will need to model different kinds of think-aloud comments, explain what you are doing, and guide students to produce their own. At this stage of the assessment process, you are only concerned with the students' willingness and ability to engage in the process of thinking aloud.

Once students understand the basic think-aloud process (and it has been my experience that this happens very quickly), you may want to focus on specific kinds of think-aloud comments and assess your students' understanding and production of these. Begin with two types of think-aloud comments, such as retelling and inferring. Divide your checklist into three columns: *Retelling*, *Inferring*, and *Other*. The *Other* column is for recording comments that are not examples of retelling or inferring. When you are comfortable noting these on a checklist, gradually add others.

Is it absolutely critical that you differentiate specific kinds of think-aloud comments on a checklist? Not really. The important issue is whether a student can effectively engage in thinking aloud. A student who can think aloud is demonstrating one or all of the good reader behaviors, and that is your assessment focus. Distinguishing among different kinds of think-aloud comments is difficult to do during an active discussion session. Ease into this process gradually, and don't feel guilty if it takes some time to arrive at the point where you are comfortable identifying and recording specific student comments. Because the good reader behaviors are not separate and discrete entities, you don't have to assess all of them at once. Be kind to yourself; focus on one or two.

A think-aloud dialogue between a teacher and three different students illustrates the sensitivity of the think-aloud process. The dialogue involved a selection on World War I. The teacher stopped at several places, modeled the think-aloud process, and invited the students to participate in the process. The think-aloud comments are labeled in brackets according to the types defined above, for your deeper understanding of the think-aloud process.

Text Segment 1

TEACHER: I was wondering if Germany knew they couldn't win because their allies were all quitting. [Questioning]

AMY: Me too, and I bet the allies were happy to be out of the war. [Inferring] I know I would be happy too. [Reacting personally]

TEACHER: It helps to put ourselves in the text like Amy did. It makes it more real.

WILL: I was thinking probably some of the Germans too were glad it was over. [Inferring]

TONY: So the war's all over. All the guns and stuff are quiet. [Retelling]

AMY: War is hard on everyone, all that killing and stuff. [Inferring]

TONY: Me too.

Text Segment 2

TEACHER: I'm thinking that the revolution was the German people's way of saying, "That's enough." The text doesn't say that, but it makes sense to me. [Inferring]

AMY: I wondered who formed the republic. I mean, not just anyone can form a government. [Questioning]

WILL: Could it be the sailors who mutinied first? [Questioning] That took a lot of guts, 'cause they might have been killed. [Inferring]

TEACHER: I am happy to hear all those questions. Good readers always ask questions as they read. Sometimes they find the answers in the text, and sometimes they have to figure it out on their own.

TONY: What is a *Kaiser*? [Questioning denoting lack of understanding]

AMY: I'm pretty sure it's the head guy in Germany, because they said he fled after the people rose up. [Inferring]

TEACHER: Good for you, Amy. You figured out the answer on your own.

TONY: I am thinking it's a real funny name. It doesn't make sense. It doesn't sound like a German name at all. [Noting lack of understanding that *Kaiser* is a title]

Text Segment 3

TEACHER: So they agreed to an armistice. [Retelling]

AMY: *Armistice*, that's a new word for me. [Noting lack of understanding] I guess it means to stop fighting. [Inferring]

WILL: Like a cease-fire? [Questioning]

TONY: Yep.

Text Segment 4

TEACHER: I remember learning about Wilson's Fourteen Points, and they seemed like good ideas. [Connecting prior knowledge] We could use them today! [Inferring]

AMY: But Germany is asking for these, and I think I know why. [Noting understanding] It will go a lot easier on them if the guys who won follow the points. [Inferring]

WILL: I'm wondering what kind of secret agreements were made. [Questioning] And I'm thinking if nationality groups can form their own nations, that might not be a good idea. If different groups decided to form their own nation, what would happen to our country? [Inferring and questioning]

AMY: Wow! I never thought of that.

TEACHER: Good thinking, Will. That did happen once! We called it the Civil War, only it wasn't based on nationalities. Tony, what are you thinking about now?

TONY: Not much. I guess, maybe, what are *armaments*? [Questioning noting lack of understanding]

TEACHER: Good readers try to figure out words on their own. Is there any part of the word that gives you a clue?

TONY: It sounds like *ornament*. But that doesn't fit. After we're finished, I could look it up, I guess.

Text Segment 5

WILL: Boy, a lot of people were killed! [Retelling]

TONY: That happens in war. I mean, it wouldn't be a war if people didn't die, would it? [Questioning]

AMY: I am really shocked about how many civilians died. You kind of expect soldiers to die, but not so many civilians. [Reacting personally]

TEACHER: I am thinking that nothing is worth all that destruction. If I had lost a family member, I would be very angry. [Reacting personally]

TONY: Me too.

AMY: But I am thinking that we still have wars. I guess we never learn from our mistakes. [Inferring]

TONY: How far are we going to read?

Text Segment 6

TEACHER: Tony, why don't you go first? What are you thinking about?

TONY: I am thinking that they called the three guys the Big Three. [Retelling]

AMY: I bet I know why. They had power, lots and lots of power. [Inferring]

WILL: The Germans weren't allowed to send people to the conference, and I bet the Big Three are really going to stick it to them. [Inferring]

AMY: Well, you can't really blame them after all the deaths and destruction. I certainly can understand why. [Reacting personally]

Text Segment 7

TEACHER: Tony, I am really interested in what you are thinking about.

TONY: I don't know what a *compromise* is and why he had to make one. [Noting lack of understanding]

TEACHER: How could you find out?

TONY: Look in the dictionary, but I really don't want to.

AMY: You could read on, and maybe it will say.

TONY: I suppose so.

The think-alouds clearly demonstrate which students comprehend the text and the good reader behaviors they use to do this. Amy and Will draw inferences, react personally to the text, and ask questions that signal their understanding. On the other hand, Tony's think-alouds either indicate lack of understanding and involvement or represent brief paraphrases.

Think-alouds represent a wonderful alternative to the typical question-and-answer dialogue that occurs in many classrooms. The beauty of think-alouds is that they are both an instructional and an assessment tool. All the teacher or tutor needs is a piece of text, a willingness to model the process, a checklist based on the good reader behaviors, a mouth, and some students!

Focused Discussions

A teacher or tutor can use focused classroom discussion to identify and assess good reader behaviors. Unfortunately, much classroom discussion tends to be rather unfocused. If a teacher or tutor has only a vague idea of the purpose of the discussion, it is difficult to assess the outcomes in terms of students' development as good readers. Some teachers or tutors interpret discussion as an "anything goes" scenario, where students are free to say whatever comes into their heads, whether or not it is relevant to the topic. Some discussion takes a rapid-fire question-and-answer format, with an emphasis upon literal-level comprehension or memory questions. The teacher or tutor asks a question, calls on students until the right answer is given, and then asks another question. Some teachers or tutors attempt to engage the students in higher-level thinking during discussion. Unfortunately, if the teacher or tutor does not specify what is meant by "higher-level," it often goes nowhere. Teachers and tutors need to have a clear goal for a discussion, and one or more of the good reader behaviors can provide that goal.

Discussion can serve as a tool for both instruction and assessment. Students need to be instructed in the art of discussion. They need to learn what to say and how to say it. Some comments are appropriate to discussion; others are not. What students say should be relevant to the topic. We have all seen students who violate this and attempt to interject comments that are totally unrelated. Students also need to learn what is acceptable discussion behavior. For example, if you disagree with a peer, what language and voice tone do you use to express your opposition?

Discussion can be a vehicle for instructing students in good reader behaviors through teacher and peer modeling and through student interaction. A variety of good reader behaviors can also be assessed during a literature discussion or a discussion about an expository selection. Do the students connect the text to their own lives or to other texts they have read? Do they connect the text to the world at large? Do the students make inferences? Can they offer a rationale for the inferences they make? Do they recognize narrative or expository structure? Can they recognize important elements of the text, such as the main ideas and supporting details? Can they retell or summarize the selection in their own words? Can they express agreement or disagreement with the author's point of view or a character's actions? Do they react personally? Do they recognize the author's purpose? Are they aware of writing style? Do they expand their knowledge of word meaning through use of context?

As a teacher or tutor, you need to state the purpose of the discussion in terms of good reader behaviors. Focus the discussion on two or three good reader behaviors and inform the students of your purpose. And because discussion often moves so fast that it can be difficult to keep track of, you should construct a simple checklist for recording student behavior. It is admittedly difficult to guide a discussion and record student behaviors at the same time, and a teacher's or tutor's first efforts may not be as satisfying as he or she might like (Paradis, Chatton, Boswell, Smith, & Yovich, 1991). Just as with think-alouds, it is wise to start small with one or two good reader behaviors as the targets and gradually build up to a more extensive checklist. In addition, no matter how you set the purpose for discussion, students still tend to offer irrelevant and unrelated comments. A discussion card device can help to keep the students focused on the intent of the discussion.

Write the good reader behaviors that are your focus on sets of index cards, and distribute a set to each student. Inform the students that these are the good reader behaviors that you want them to demonstrate. During the discussion, students are to hold up one of the cards as an indication of what they want to contribute to the discussion. What they say must be related to the card they hold up.

Elaine gave each fifth-grade student a set of four cards labeled *Character, Inference, Question*, and *Me*. After reading a segment of a story, students held up one of the cards to indicate what they wanted to say. If they held up the *Character* card, their comments had to center on a character, the character's problem, the character's action, or the character's motivation. If they held up the *Inference* card, they were expected to go beyond the words of the author and offer a prediction or a hypothesis as to future events. They could also describe a picture in their heads, inasmuch as creating a visual image is actually an inference on the part of the reader. Holding up the *Question* card allowed them to ask questions of the character, the author, the teacher, or any of their peers. The *Me* card was reserved for personal opinions and for relating the story to their own lives. Comments related to the *Me* card were often prefaced by "If it were me, I. . . . " The discussion cards focused the students' thoughts upon the good reader behaviors and made them more conscious of the content and quality of their responses. If a student offered an irrelevant comment, Elaine gently asked how the comment was related to the card that was held up, and suggested that the student rephrase his or her comment. Do you remember the cards Jayne used for her focused discussion activity, which was described in Chapter Two?

Discussion cards can focus on any good reader behavior that the teacher or tutor is instructing or assessing. Some possible choices of discussion card labels for narrative text are as follows: *Character, Setting, Time, Place, Problem, Solution, Motive, Question, My idea, Prediction, Inference, Author style,* and *Imagery*. Choices for expository text could include *Topic, Main idea, Detail, Text structure, Inference, Prediction, Vocabulary, My life, Question, monitoring,* and *Prior knowledge*. You can also use discussion cards to assess a reader's ability to make connections. A student who holds up *Text and me* would be expected to connect the contents of the text to his or her experiences or background knowledge. *Text and text* indicates a student's plan to connect the text to other pieces of writing. *Text and world* signals the student's intention to connect the text to a theme, problem, or issue. As with any new technique, start small. Begin with only two or three cards, and gradually expand your repertoire.

Discussion cards not only provide a focus for discussion, but they effectively foster good discussion skills. They help students understand what good readers talk about when they discuss their reading. They also make assessment manageable. A teacher or tutor needs only a simple checklist to record student behavior.

Discussion Card Labels for Narrative Text

Character	*Setting*	*Time*	*Place*	*Problem*
Solution	*Motive*	*Question*	*My idea*	*Prediction*
Author style	*Imagery*	*Vocabulary*	*Text and me*	*Text and text*
Text and world				

Discussion Card Labels for Expository Text

Topic	*Main idea*	*Details*	*Text structure*	*Inference*
Prediction	*Vocabulary*	*My life*	*Question*	*Monitoring*
Prior knowledge	*Text and me*	*Text and text*	*Text and world*	

Good Reader Response Logs

It is very easy for a teacher or tutor to confuse teaching the story or chapter with teaching the process. Teaching the story or chapter means emphasizing content. The teacher or tutor engages in activities to help the students understand and remember key content, such as which character stole the treasure or how viruses and cells differ. Teaching the process means focusing on what is going on in the minds of readers as they react to the selection and attempt to understand it. Unfortunately, in too many classrooms, there is no balance between the two. Remembering the content receives primary emphasis, even in reading classrooms, and teaching the process is often ignored.

Why is this so? Unfortunately, teachers and tutors sometimes tend to teach as they were taught. Past practice in reading classrooms did emphasize content of what was read, even of simple stories. Teachers and tutors assumed that if a student remembered content, the student understood the selection. Although this is probably true to some degree, it is not the whole picture, and it represents a very limited view. What about those students who did not remember the content? Perhaps they understood it but then forgot. Content emphasis does not differentiate between understanding and forgetting, as look-backs do. Perhaps the students did not understand. Content emphasis does not suggest reasons why this occurred, as think-alouds do.

Remembering content may be important, but having an awareness of what comprehension is and how to engage in it is equally important. Good reader response logs are another way to blend comprehension instruction and assessment. In these logs, students record two things. First, in their own words, they describe the good reader behaviors that have been modeled and emphasized in class. Second, they describe when they have demonstrated a good reader behavior and how it helped them.

Good reader response logs can follow a prescribed format, such as the one provided here. They can also be very open-ended. The teacher or tutor can ask specific questions ("What good reader behaviors did you use when you studied for the social studies test?") or allow the students to choose the good reader behavior they wish to focus on. When students first begin writing their response logs, they tend to focus on content, on what happened in the story, or on what they learned in their social studies lesson. The teacher or tutor will need to model the process by writing a response log of his or her own and sharing it with the students. Talking with students about their response logs will also help to focus their efforts on what good readers do.

Good Reader Response Log

Name _____

Good reader behavior:

I did this when I read:

It helped me to:

Kendall used good reader response logs with his first graders. After modeling and emphasizing prediction, Annabel wrote the following in her response log: *Perditing. Think of the picter. Think with your brane. Think of the tidel. Think of what could hapon.* Kendall also modeled and fostered what he called the "sound strategy." Kayla wrote: *Good readers use sounds. Look at the word. Think about the leters. Put the sounds toogeter. Think "Does this make sense?"*

Rachel taught a small group of struggling readers to use vowel patterns in known words to pronounce unfamiliar ones. Brittany wrote: *You think of a word you all redy now then you should get the word. Or tack the word in parts and think of words you now in it. Grump. Jump.*

Ellen used the theme of "star readers" to focus her third graders' attention on good reader behaviors. Therone's star reader log contained the following entry: *Star readers get a picture in my head of what is going on. The picture has to match the words in the book.* Daniel wrote: *Good readers use what they know. Think. Read. Ask "Do I know about this?" Put it together with what I am reading.*

Elissa introduced the *KWL activity* (Ogle, 1986) to her middle school students. Students identify what they already know about a topic (the K), what they want to learn about it (the W), and what they have learned after reading (the L). Mindy wrote the following:

> Good reader behavior: *Think about what I already know, about what I will learn and about what I learned.*
> I did this when I read: *The chapter on the Revolution War.*
> It helped me to: *Know that I knew a lot before I started and it helped me to read fast the things I already knew.*

Mindy's classmate, Rob, wrote:

> Good reader behavior: *Before reading, ask what do I need to know?*
> I did this when I read: *Our science chapter on stars.*
> It helped me to: *Look for the stuff I didn't know like how a star is made.*

Contrast these two log entries with Steve's entry:

> Good reader behavior: *Do K and W and something else.*
> I did this when I read: *In class yesterday.*
> It helped me to: *Read better.*

Good reader response logs, whatever their format, indicate how well students understand the comprehension process and good reader behaviors. They document the students' ability to verbalize this and to assess their own developing proficiency.

Putting It All Together: Fusing Comprehension Instruction and Assessment

As noted throughout this chapter, it is almost impossible to separate comprehension instruction and comprehension assessment. The focus of both is on the good reader behaviors and the processes that readers engage in as they read (Allington, 1994). Because comprehension occurs in the mind, teachers and tutors must instruct by modeling their own thought processes—their own good reader behaviors. Unfortunately, too much comprehension instruction takes the form of telling students what to do without showing them how to do it. Teachers and tutors must describe what is going on in their heads as they read, so that their students can imitate them. Students must also talk about what is in their heads. They must be able to identify the good reader behaviors they are employing. As students talk about good reader behaviors, and as they attempt to imitate a teacher's or tutor's modeling, assessment and instruction merge and become one. All of the assessment activities described in this chapter allow for teacher modeling and for student imitation of that modeling. But how does a teacher or tutor pull all of this together on a daily basis in a very busy classroom?

Some years ago, my teenage son read a book that totally enthralled him. It was *Dune* by Frank Herbert. He immediately suggested that I read it as well. Not being into science fiction, I put him off for some weeks. However, he continued to insist that I would enjoy the book and to ask whether I had started it yet. I finally realized that he wanted me to read *Dune* so that we could talk about it. And so I began reading. I don't think I had finished one chapter before his questions and comments began. What did I think about the book so far? What did I think would happen next? What was my view of this character or that event? His ideas about the book initially provided the framework for our discussion. He eagerly put forth his opinions and perspectives, and listened intently to mine. Later on, as I read more of *Dune*, I set forth discussion agendas for him to respond to. When we disagreed (and we often did), we both enjoyed the friendly argument that ensued. I found that my pleasure in the book was enhanced by a discussion that was driven by diverse perspectives. Mine was the perspective of a middle-aged female who tended to regard science fiction as make-believe. His was the perspective of a young male who saw science fiction as a description of possibilities that might be realized in his own lifetime.

We engaged in practically every activity for comprehension assessment that was mentioned in this chapter. As those of you who have read *Dune* will no doubt remember, Herbert created a lot of new words. Although he thoughtfully provided a glossary, my son and I often discussed the words and the ways they were applied in the text. We often used incidents in our own lives to clarify what one of these new words meant. We asked many questions of each other, but they were seldom literal questions. We assumed that basic understanding was in place. Instead, we focused on convergent, divergent, and evaluative questioning, although we never applied these labels or even differentiated question types. We did not use questioning as a test of retention or basic understanding, but more as a catalyst for discussion. We looked back in the text to locate favorite or key parts. We retold or summarized when it suited our purposes, often as a rationale or explanation for a specific point of view. If I had recorded our conversations, I suspect they would have sounded very much like an ongoing think-aloud. As soon as I finished a chapter, we would go through it, commenting and questioning together as we did so. Obviously, we did not use discussion cards; however, our discussions were very focused, and if one of us initiated a new topic, we were careful to let the other person know. In short, we engaged in a satisfying, often exciting, and never boring discussion about a provocative piece of writing. In doing so, we displayed and applied all of the good reader behaviors.

Allington (2001) refers to what I have described as "thoughtful literacy." He suggests that reading classrooms have placed too much focus on student recitation and remembering. If our students demonstrate basic understanding, we teachers and tutors tend to move on to another selection. We seldom offer students the opportunity to participate in discussions like the one I described. We seldom teach students how to do so. "And if we fail to provide students with models and demonstrations of thoughtful literacy and lessons on how to develop these proficiencies I fear that we will continue to develop students who don't even know that thoughtful literacy is the reason for reading" (Allington, 2001, p. 93).

What does this mean for us as teachers or tutors? We need to show students how to talk about what they have read. Effective assessment and instruction of comprehension do not consist of paper-and-pencil exercises. They are not teacher-directed literal question-and-answer sessions. They consist of a group of readers (of which the teacher is one) sharing their thoughts about a selection, voicing their opinions, listening eagerly to the ideas of others, politely disagreeing with the author or their peers, and going beyond the author's words to make connections with their lives and the world around them. Teachers or tutors do not need a teacher's manual to do this. They just need an exciting and stimulating selection as a starting point—and, in some cases, a simple checklist to keep track of what is going on!

ASSESSING STUDENT PROGRESS IN COMPREHENSION

In order to assess student progress, a teacher or tutor needs to make at least two observations, one at a beginning point and another at an ending point. The teacher or tutor then compares the student's initial performance with his/her later performance. For example, Sandy asked her middle school students to find and write the main ideas in an expository selection. She then modeled and taught a four-step strategy for finding the main idea (Richek, Caldwell, Jennings & Lerner, 2002). After several weeks of practice, she asked them to find the main ideas of a similar expository selection, and noted differences between the two performances.

Noting progress in comprehension is crucial to students' development as good readers. However, it is a rather complex task. Remember that comprehension is affected by a variety of factors, such as prior knowledge and text structure. These can mask student progress if a teacher or tutor is not careful.

As a teacher or tutor, you can compare two performances or multiple performances. More is always better than less; multiple indicators offer a richer tapestry of student progress. However, there are times when you may want to compare two indicators. When doing this, be aware of the possible effect of such factors as prior knowledge and text structure, and follow these guidelines. First, don't mix narrative and expository text. If the student's initial performance was in narrative text, assess later performance in narrative text. Also, never mix familiar and unfamiliar if you can help it. A few simple questions will allow you to determine whether the topic of the selection is familiar or unfamiliar. If you assess initial performance in unfamiliar text, assess later performance in other unfamiliar text. Actually, keeping unfamiliarity constant does not pose much of a problem for expository material, because the content of most expository textbooks is unfamiliar to students

Because of the many factors that can affect a student's performance on any one day, it is better to determine progress from multiple observations or activities. Tying this to the good reader behaviors provides a focus that lets you blend narrative and expository, familiar and unfamiliar. If you have divided your grade book into sections for the different good reader behaviors as suggested in Chapter Two, you can examine the scores and notes recorded under each behavior. If several seem to be out of alignment, you can evaluate these in relation to text structure and/or familiarity.

During a single grading period, Garrett had 16 entries in his grade book under "Good readers determine what is important in the text." These involved reading both narrative and expository text as well as familiar and unfamiliar selections. He coded each activity as E or N for narrative or expository, and F or U for familiar or unfamiliar. The grade book entries represented a variety of selections and activities, including focused discussion, group retelling, written summaries, questions, response journal entries and questions with look-backs. The coding allowed Garrett to note progress and to evaluate lower performance in terms of possible contributing factors.

PUBLISHED TESTS OF COMPREHENSION

Various published formal tests of comprehension are used by diagnostic specialists. Although reading teachers or tutors will seldom have occasion to administer and score such instruments, they should have some idea of their existence and format.

A commonly used group survey test of reading comprehension is the Gates–MacGinitie Reading Tests (MacGinitie & MacGinitie, 1989). The instrument has two subtests, Vocabulary and Comprehension. On the Vocabulary subtest, students identify synonyms in a multiple-choice format. For Comprehension, they read short paragraphs and answer multiple-choice questions.

The Woodcock Reading Mastery Test—Revised (Woodcock, 1987) assesses comprehension in two ways. On the Word Comprehension subtest, students generate antonyms, synonyms, and analogies. For Comprehension, they supply a missing word in a sentence or short paragraph. Like the Woodcock Word Identification and Word Attack subtests, the Word Comprehension and Comprehension subtests are administered individually.

The Gray Oral Reading Test—3 (Wiederholt & Bryant, 1992) is very similar to an informal reading inventory. However, it does provide norm-referenced interpretations of scores on rate, accuracy, and comprehension.

The Test of Reading Comprehension, Third Edition (Brown, Hammel, & Wiederholt, 1995), contains four subtests: Vocabulary, Syntactic Similarity, Paragraph Reading, and Sentence Sequencing.

SUMMARY

- Comprehension is the whole purpose of reading. It is an active process whereby readers use the words of the author to construct a text in their minds.
- Comprehension is affected by background knowledge. If we know something about a topic, we find it easier to comprehend. Teachers and tutors should not assume that comprehension of familiar text represents comprehension of unfamiliar text.
- Comprehension is also affected by the structure of the text. Narrative text has a simpler structure than expository text. The teacher or tutor should not assume that comprehension of narrative text indicates comprehension of expository material.
- There are three purposes of comprehension assessment: to determine levels of comprehension, to determine the presence or absence of good reader behaviors, and to note student progress.
- The IRI process can be used to determine comprehension levels in familiar, unfamiliar, narrative, and expository text.
- The teacher or tutor can assess good reader behaviors by using vocabulary application activities; teacher and student questions; questioning with look-backs; oral or written retellings; think-alouds; focused discussion; and good reader response logs.

• Vocabulary application activities move beyond multiple-choice formats and using the word in a sentence. Meaning sorts, placing words in students' lives, and matching a word with another part of speech can all indicate knowledge of word meaning.

• The teacher or tutor should differentiate memory questions from convergent, divergent, and evaluative thinking questions. The last three can suggest the presence or absence of good reader behaviors. The teacher or tutor should teach students how to generate questions.

• Using questioning with look-backs differentiates between comprehension problems and memory problems. An assessment that does not allow for looking back in the text may underestimate a student's comprehension.

• Oral or written retellings indicate whether a student understands content and can coherently and sequentially tie events or concepts together. The teacher or tutor should construct a checklist to record a student's performance when retelling.

• Think-alouds are readers' verbalizations during the reading process. A simple checklist allows the teacher or tutor to evaluate the kind and quality of student think-alouds. Possible types of think-aloud comments are retelling, inferring, questioning, noting understanding, connecting prior knowledge, and reacting personally.

• Focused discussions are discussions that center on specific good reader behaviors as opposed to emphasizing content. The use of discussion cards is an instructional tool as well as a way of limiting irrelevant comments.

• Good reader response logs allow readers to describe the strategies taught in class and indicate when and how they applied them.

• Thoughtful literacy discussion, the real reason for reading, can employ almost all of the above-described activities.

• It is best to note student progress using multiple indicators. If two indicators are used, the teacher or tutor should be aware of the possible effects of text structure and reader prior knowledge.

ACTIVITIES FOR DEVELOPING UNDERSTANDING

• Compile a list of random words. Use the word-meaning categories to group and regroup them. Note how this activity refines your understanding of word meaning.

• Obtain a series of questions from a teacher's manual. Differentiate the memory questions from the convergent, divergent, and evaluative thinking questions.

• Ask students to answer questions without look-backs and then with look-backs. What differences do you notice?

• Ask students to read and then retell a selection. Construct a retelling guide for assessing the quality of the retelling, and evaluate the students' performance.

• Select two sections of text, an easy one and a difficult one. As you read, think aloud into a tape recorder. Listen to the two tapes. How were your strategies alike and different?

• Read Appendix 7.1 for further practice with thinking aloud.

• Make discussion cards and a checklist for a focused discussion experience. Engage in the discussion and evaluate the experience.

• Complete the self-evaluation form provided at the end of this chapter (following Appendix 7.1).

APPENDIX 7.1

Practice with Thinking Aloud

The following dialogue represents a think-aloud session with four second graders in response to the book *Simon's Surprise* by Ted Staunton (1986). The teacher read the book, approximately two pages at a time, chorally with the students. Then they stopped and thought out loud. What do the comments of the four students tell you about their understanding of the book, as well as their developing awareness of the reading process and what good readers do? How does your analysis of their good reader behaviors differ from mine (presented following the dialogue)?

Text Segment 1

TEACHER: I think I need Simon to wash my car. It's very dirty.

DONNA: I know. I saw it when you drove up.

RICHIE: If Simon's dad doesn't want him to wash the car, he's gonna get in big trouble.

NATHAN: How big does he have to be to wash the car? He looks as big as me, and I can wash a car. Maybe he's like a first grader.

TRISH: My dad takes our car to the car wash, and I stay inside while all the water squirts around. I never washed our car like Simon is going to do, but I bet I could.

RICHIE: I'd rather watch TV than wash a car. He'll get wet and cold. I think he's dumb. He looks like he still has his pajamas on. His mom won't like that!

Text Segment 2

TEACHER: I wonder why his father thought it was raining?

DONNA: That's easy! The hose hit the window.

NATHAN: How can a hose hiss? Snakes hiss, not hoses. Maybe it moves kinda like a snake.

RICHIE: If the windows get wet, that's not good. His dad will yell at him, 'cause they'll get all spotted.

TRISH: It looks like he is having fun. There are more bubbles than at the car wash. I think he must have used a lot of soap.

NATHAN: How can a hose hiss? I want an answer!

TEACHER: Can anyone help Nathan with this?

DONNA: No.

TRISH: Maybe it makes a noise when the water comes out like this (*demonstrates a hissing sound*).

NATHAN: Well, I never heard it.

Text Segment 3

NATHAN: What is he doing? What is on the end of the string?

TEACHER: Can anyone help Nathan?

DONNA: It's a square thing like a dish scrubber.

RICHIE: When his father sees what he did with his fishing rod, he'll be real mad.

TRISH: I think Simon is pretty smart to think of it. How else would he get on top of the car?

RICHIE: He could climb up, but he would probably fall off.

DONNA: I know, it's a sponge!

TEACHER: Simon's mother certainly has a lot of brushes—a lot more than I do.

DONNA: So does my mom. She's got millions of brushes.

NATHAN: Trish, I don't think Simon is smart scrubbing a tire with a toothbrush.

TRISH: Well, it would get into the little holes better than a big brush.

Text Segment 4

TEACHER: Oh, my! Simon is certainly working hard. I think he really wants to do a good job.

DONNA: Well, I would too.

RICHIE: He better do a good job, 'cause he's making a big mess.

NATHAN: It's not easy what he is doing. A car is big, and there's a lot to polish. I wonder why he didn't ask his friends to help.

TEACHER: Maybe he wanted it to be just his surprise.

DONNA: Like a birthday present?

TRISH: I bet he is having a lot of fun. I like to play in water.

Text Segment 5

TEACHER: Well, now the car is finished, and it looks good to me. I guess I need some-one like Simon.

DONNA: Me too.

RICHIE: But there are still a lot of bubbles all around. How will they go away?

NATHAN: That's why his father thinks it snowed.

RICHIE: Now he's going to get it.

TRISH: I think his parents will like what he did. Now they don't have to do it.

Text Segment 6

NATHAN: How can he paint the house? He better not! That would be a real mess! Why does he even want to?

RICHIE: That would be much worse.

TEACHER: I wonder how Simon would go about it.

TRISH: You can get rid of bubbles, but not paint. Like if it spilled. He's not big enough. Maybe for a car but not a house.

TEACHER: Let's imagine how Simon might start.

DONNA: He'd have to find paint.

RICHIE: He better not.

TRISH: I bet his parents lock up the paint. That way he can't get it.

NATHAN: And all the brushes too!

RICHIE: He's kinda like a Dennis the Menace.

DONNA: That was a funny movie.

ANALYSIS OF STUDENTS' GOOD READER BEHAVIORS

- *Donna*: Donna seems the least involved of the four children. She is concerned with reacting to what the teacher says and does not really enter into the plot of the book. She does not really demonstrate any good reader behaviors in relation to the text.
- *Nathan*: Nathan is already demonstrating the good reader behavior of asking questions and finding the answers.
- *Richie*: Richie is clearly a worrier, but his concern about the fate of Simon is

based upon predictions of how the parents will probably react. So Richie is also demonstrating a good reader behavior—making inferences or predictions. One wonders whether Richie's predictions are the result of his own father's behavior.

- *Trish*: Trish immediately relates to story to her own life and evaluates Simon's actions in terms of her own perspective. She is already involved in forming and supporting her opinions—another important good reader behavior.

Teacher or Tutor Self-Evaluation

I tie comprehension assessment to good reader behaviors.

> Regularly   Occasionally   A future goal

I use vocabulary application activities.

> Regularly   Occasionally   A future goal

I differentiate memory questions from convergent, divergent, and evaluative questions.

> Regularly   Occasionally   A future goal

I model and use the look-back process when asking questions.

> Regularly   Occasionally   A future goal

I ask my students to retell what they have read.

> Regularly   Occasionally   A future goal

I use a checklist to assess my students' retellings.

> Regularly   Occasionally   A future goal

I model and engage in the think-aloud process as an alternative to question-and-answer and traditional discussion formats.

> Regularly   Occasionally   A future goal

I use a checklist to assess my students' think-aloud comments.

> Regularly   Occasionally   A future goal

I focus discussion on good reader behaviors.

> Regularly   Occasionally   A future goal

I use discussion cards to focus relevant discussion.

       Regularly   Occasionally   A future goal

I ask my students to use good reader response logs.

       Regularly   Occasionally   A future goal

I foster thoughtful literacy discussions.

       Regularly   Occasionally   A future goal

I note student progress through multiple indicators.

       Regularly   Occasionally   A future goal

I am aware of the possible effect of text structure and prior knowledge upon comprehension performance.

       Regularly   Occasionally   A future goal

EIGHT

Motivation

What Makes Students Want to Read, and How Can We Assess This?

CHAPTER TOPICS

THE ROLE OF MOTIVATION IN THE READING PROCESS

Some years ago, the other members of my family decided that I should take up golf. They offered several reasons why this would be a good idea. It would get me out of the house and into the fresh air and sunshine. It would offer me an opportunity for much-needed exercise. It would provide a challenging activity and an opportunity to learn a new skill. And, most important, I would enjoy it! Frankly, I had no desire to take up golf and I doubted that it would prove enjoyable, so I put my family off as long as I could. However, when they presented me with golf clubs, a golf bag, and golf shoes for Christmas, I gave in. Knowing how much money they had probably spent, I would have felt impossibly guilty if I had not agreed to take lessons and accompany my son on regular excursions to the driving range.

Things did not go well. I never seemed to acquire the basic skills needed to play the game. While my classmates were working on driving the ball in a straight line or gaining more distance, I was still focused on hitting it! Visits to the driving range were a test of endurance both for me and for my long-suffering son. At one point, having watched my abysmal efforts, another golfer whispered to my son, "I'd give it up if I were you, kid!" I breathed a healthy sigh of relief when summer ended and Wisconsin weather prevented any more golf activity. When summer returned, I held my breath hoping that my family members would not renew their efforts. They didn't, and I was very thankful. I hung my golf clubs and bag in the garage, where they remain to this day. I have no doubt that the bag provides a cozy winter home for field mice and an equally cozy summer home for spiders and other insects.

Why begin a chapter on motivation for reading and writing with a story about golf? My sad tale illustrates the important role of motivation in any learning process. The individual involved in learning a skill or a process is basically driven by two questions: "Can I do this?" and "Do I want to do this?" (Wigfield & McCann, 1996–1997). An individual's "self-perceived competence and task value are major determinants of motivation" (Gambrell, Palmer, Codling, & Mazzoni, 1996, p. 518).

In the example just given, my perceived competence was quite negative. I did not think I could learn to play golf, and my experiences tended to validate my belief. Every ball that I didn't hit and every putt that avoided the hole by a wide margin offered additional proof that golf was not for me. In addition, I attached little task value to the game. I did not really want to learn to play golf; I only agreed to please my family, not to please me. In short, I was not motivated to learn golf, and so I did not learn it. My experiences with golf are repeated over and over again in the reading classroom or tutoring session with children who do not think they are good readers and who are not interested in developing their reading skills.

Without motivation, learning does not occur. A motive prompts a person

---

Determinants of Motivation

Perceived competence: "Can I do this?"
Task value: "Do I want to do this?"

to act in a certain way; it provides an incentive for doing and for persisting. In the reading classroom, motivation (or lack of it) is a powerful force. In order to succeed in reading, students need "both the skill and the will" (Gambrell, 1996, p. 15). The role of teachers and tutors is to facilitate acquisition of the skill and to foster development and maintenance of the will. Because motivation is such a crucial element, perhaps the most important job facing a teacher or tutor is to foster a love of reading.

Maintaining motivation for reading activities is not an easy task. Academic motivation naturally tends to decline during elementary school (Pressley, 1998). Whereas kindergartners and first graders are confident that they will learn to read, this positive outlook is seriously diminished by the fifth and sixth grades (McKenna, Ellsworth, & Kear, 1995; Gambrell et al., 1996). Pressley (1998) suggests that this decline in motivation may be due to a growing differentiation between ability and effort. Young children do not discriminate between ability and effort. If they succeed because of effort, they tend to think it is because of their ability. If they fail after putting forth effort, they still see themselves as having high ability because they tried hard. As students become older, they separate the concepts of ability and effort, and come to understand that success can be the result of effort, ability, or a combination of both. Unfortunately, students who experience repeated failure after expending effort tend to adopt a dismal picture of their ability. If they don't believe they have the ability, where is their motivation to continue trying?

A classic piece of research (Butkowsky & Willows, 1988) asked good and poor readers to solve anagram puzzles. Some of the puzzles were solvable and some were not. Good readers persisted longer in their attempts to figure out the unsolvable anagrams. Of even greater interest were their responses when asked two questions: "Why were you able to solve that puzzle?" and "Why were you unable to solve that puzzle?" Good readers took the credit for solving a puzzle and stated that they were good at puzzles. When the good readers failed, they said it was because the puzzle was hard. Poor readers, on the other hand, said that they solved puzzles because the puzzles were easy and failed to solve puzzles because they were not good at puzzles. In other words, good readers, conscious of their own ability as readers, took credit for their success. Poor readers, equally conscious of their lack of reading ability, took credit for their failure!

Motivation is a multidimensional concept. In fact, there are various reasons why a student chooses to read or avoids reading altogether. Most of these reasons can be grouped into one of two categories: *intrinsic* motivation or *extrinsic* motivation. Intrinsic motivation comes from within the individ-

Types of Motivation for Reading

Kinds of intrinsic motivation:	*Kinds of extrinsic motivation*:
Personal involvement.	Compliance.
Interest.	Recognition.
Curiosity.	Grades.
Desire to learn.	Competition.
Challenge.	Avoidance of other tasks.

ual, and is based upon personal interests and previous experience. Extrinsic motivation comes from without; it originates from teachers, parents, family, and society.

There are several kinds of intrinsic motivation for reading (Sweet & Guthrie, 1996). A student may choose to read because of personal involvement: The student is interested in the topic of the selection or the problems of a specific character. Certainly the success of the Harry Potter books is a testament to the power of personal involvement. A student may also read out of curiosity and a desire to learn more about a topic. I remember one struggling reader who read everything he could find about snakes, even books that seemed to be above his instructional reading level. Some readers are challenged by reading certain books. They enjoy mastering complex plots or reading to locate specific information. Some students enjoy the social interaction involved in reading and sharing books. If you have ever enticed a friend to read a book that you particularly enjoyed so you could share reactions and perceptions, you will understand the strong positive effect of social interaction.

Other reasons for reading fall into the category of extrinsic motivation. A student may read a book because the teacher assigned it and the student wants to comply. The student may read for recognition—that is, to amass points or to win prizes. Some students read in order to get good grades. They are motivated by competition and want to be among the best readers in their class. Other students read to avoid other tasks. For example, reading a book may be preferable to studying spelling words.

Intrinsic motivations are the basis of lifelong voluntary reading. Guthrie and Sweet (1996) suggest that they are also needed to learn complex comprehension strategies such as summarizing and inferencing. These strategies are not learned quickly; they require much practice. This makes sense, because children who are intrinsically motivated to read and who therefore read more tend to be better readers. Extrinsic motivations, on the other hand, are short-term. Once the goal is attained, the reading stops. Once the student completes the teacher-assigned task or gains the prize, he or she no longer reads. Extrinsic motivations tend to foster more "shallow processing" and do not "regenerate themselves" (Sweet & Guthrie, 1996, p. 661). Research suggests that extrinsic motivation can actually be detrimental to intrinsic motivation (Cameron & Pierce, 1994).

THE ROLE OF MOTIVATION IN THE READING CLASSROOM OR TUTORING SESSION

What goes on in the reading classroom can positively or negatively affect motivation. The tasks that students engage in can influence their desire to read, their persistence in working through difficult tasks, and their understanding of the goals of the reading process. Think about classroom activities as being of two kinds: *open* activities and *closed* activities (Turner & Paris, 1995). Closed tasks are those that have a single correct answer or one way of proceeding. The teacher or tutor generally prescribes closed tasks, and all students follow the same directions and do the same thing. Some examples of closed tasks are filling out a worksheet or writing answers to questions about a textbook chapter. Open tasks, on the other hand, are more under the students' control. Students set their own goals and choose procedures for meeting them. A teacher or tutor who fosters the use of student-selected literacy

---

Classroom Elements That Foster Motivation to Read

Open rather than closed tasks.

Student choice and control.

Moderate challenge.

Collaboration with peers.

Focus on meaning.

A teacher or tutor who models love of reading.

A classroom filled with books at different levels and on different topics.

Opportunities to interact with others about books.

Self-selection of books.

portfolios is emphasizing an open task. A teacher or tutor who allows students to choose how they will present what they have learned about a topic is offering an open task. Open tasks tend to be more successful in motivating students.

Other classroom elements also foster motivation to read (Turner & Paris, 1995). Choice is a factor. Students who can choose the books they read, the topics they write about, and the tasks they pursue tend to be more motivated. Challenge also plays a part. Students prefer a moderate challenge. If a task is too easy, they become bored; if it is too difficult, they become frustrated. Student control is another factor. Students are more motivated if they are allowed to choose partners for group work and to pursue their own interests in reading. Collaboration with peers likewise increases motivation. Anyone who has ever acquired a fresh perspective or a new idea from sharing with peers can appreciate the power of collaboration. A focus on meaning is also a key factor in motivation. If students find an activity meaningless, they will be less motivated to pursue it. The fact that a teacher or tutor finds it meaningful does not make it so for the student. Students need to know why they are engaging in a specific activity and what it will mean to them. Here is where those good reader behaviors come into play! Consequences can also play a role; gaining stars or stickers can motivate students. However, self-evaluation and a realization that one is becoming a better reader will have a more lasting impact than any external reward.

Gambrell (1996) describes the classroom culture that fosters a love of reading as incorporating several components. The teacher or tutor is a model who values reading and shares his or her own literacy experiences with the students. The classroom environment is full of books on a variety of topics and representative of various genres and difficulty levels. There are many opportunities to interact with others about books. Students are allowed to self-select books and choose ways to share them.

Establishing a climate for motivation involves more than choosing certain activities and avoiding others. Pressley (1998) suggests that classrooms should convey clear messages to students that can affect their motivation to engage in literacy activities: "Every teacher and parent can send the message that people get smarter by trying hard, that part of getting smart is bouncing back from failures, and that school is about becoming better, not becoming the best" (p. 236). In other words, ability is not fixed. Students need to realize that it can and does grow with effort. It is natural to fail, but if students can learn from their mistakes, failure then becomes a powerful tool for learning. Progress is what matters. If a student interprets success as being the "best," what are his or her chances of attaining that goal? There can be only one "best" in a classroom. However, every student can demonstrate progress! Clearly documenting that progress is a key motivational tool in the reading classroom.

PURPOSES OF MOTIVATION ASSESSMENT

What should a teacher or tutor attempt to learn about motivation? There are three important questions that any teacher or tutor should ask about his or her students: (1) "What are the interests of my students?" (2) "How do my students feel about themselves as readers?" (3) "What value do my students place upon reading?"

Why should a teacher or tutor know about students' interests? Students who are interested in a topic will value reading about that topic. "Strong interest can frequently cause the reader to transcend not only his independent but also his so-called instructional level. Such is the power of self-motivation" (Hunt, 1996–1997, p. 280). A teacher or tutor needs to know students' interests in order to select books for the classroom library, choose selections for instruction, and suggest books for individual reading.

Why should a teacher or tutor know how students feel about themselves as readers? Self-perceived competence is a key element in motivation. People who think they are good at something are more motivated to engage in that activity than people who think they are incompetent. Students "who are positively motivated to read have a strong sense of their reading competence or efficacy" (Wigfield & McCann, 1996–1997, p. 360). They believe that they can master a reading skill, and they are more likely to persist in doing so. Negative self-perceptions can be changed, but in order to do this, the teacher or tutor needs to know how students feel about themselves as readers.

Why should a teacher or tutor know the extent to which students value reading? If all students in a class enjoy reading and see it as a worthwhile activity, the teacher or tutor is fortunate indeed. He or she only needs to build on that positive base. However, when reading is not valued, many teachers or tutors rely upon extrinsic motivation to involve students in literacy. Wouldn't it be better to know early in the school year that students lack intrinsic motivation, and set goals to increase that motivation?

Motivation assessment measures fall into two categories; the first is observation, and the second consists of interviews and surveys. The teacher or tutor can learn a lot about a student's motivation from just watching the student's behavior. Motivation for reading can also be assessed by interviewing the student about his or her interests or feelings about reading. The teacher or tutor can construct a survey or use a published one.

USING OBSERVATION TO ASSESS MOTIVATION

What should a teacher or tutor look for in order to use observation as an assessment tool? Consider the following scenario. It is time for self-selected silent reading. Most of the students locate their books and settle down to read quietly. Richard, on the other hand, cannot seem to find the book he was reading yesterday. After fruitlessly searching in his desk and book bag, he informs the teacher that he has nothing to read. The teacher suggests that he select a new book. Richard slowly wanders over to the library shelf. He aimlessly pulls out several books and then carefully replaces them. A sound from outside draws his attention, and he spends several minutes staring out the window. The teacher comes over and asks Richard whether he has found a book. She selects several for Richard to peruse. Finally, he selects one at random and returns slowly to his seat. While the other students are engrossed in their books, Richard aimlessly turns a few pages, closes the book, and puts his head down on his desk. Toward the end of the silent reading period, a clearly bored Richard leans over and snatches a book from Clorinda, whispering loudly, "Let me see what you are reading!" Of course, Clorinda does not respond positively, and the teacher has to intervene. Richard's behavior during self-selected reading certainly paints a picture of an unmotivated reader. Ideally, his teacher will have recorded his behavior in some way (perhaps in the form of an anecdotal record) and will attempt to find out why Richard has behaved as he did. Is it because there are no books in the classroom library that Richard is interested in reading? Is Richard avoiding reading because he has experienced so much failure that he finds it more comfortable to shun reading altogether? Perhaps there are no books that he can read with ease.

What observable classroom behaviors suggest motivation to read or lack of it? Students who do not actively participate in self-selected reading may place little value on reading. Students who display reluctance to visit the school library may be similarly unmotivated. Another possible signal is inability to find a book to read. When students share their reading orally or in reading logs, students who do not like to read have little to say. Teachers or tutors should note these behaviors on a class checklist or as anecdotal records.

A teacher or tutor is always looking for patterns of behavior, not isolated incidents. Any student can have a bad day because of difficulties at home or problems with peers, and as a consequence may act like Richard. It is important for the teacher or tutor to have some system for recording observed behavior, or it can easily be forgotten. It is not easy to facilitate classroom activities, provide firm classroom management, and keep track of what the students are doing or not doing. Forgetting can take place very easily!

USING INTERVIEWS AND SURVEYS TO ASSESS MOTIVATION

The questions asked during an interview and the questions asked on a survey probably do not differ. What can be discovered in an individual interview can probably also be learned through a survey. Perhaps the most direct way to determine whether a student likes to read or thinks he or she is a good reader is to ask. Unfortunately, individual interviews take time, and the teacher or tutor has to make certain that the rest of the class is suitably involved while the interview takes place. Interviews have another drawback: Sometimes students tell teachers and tutors what they think the teacher or tutor wants to hear. Some students find it difficult to state baldly that they dislike reading or feel that they are poor readers. A survey may be less threatening, and it has the added advantage of being administered to the entire class at one sitting.

Surveys also have some drawbacks but the teacher or tutor can adjust for these. One drawback is that students may understand the survey directions differently. Some surveys offer the respondent four choices. For example, a survey entry might be as follows:

I read for fun every day.
Always   Usually   Sometimes   Never

Before administering a survey of this sort, the teacher or tutor should discuss the answer choices with the students. What does "Always" mean? What is the difference between "Usually" and "Sometimes"? This ensures that the students will have a uniform interpretation of the answer choices.

Another drawback is that the teacher or tutor cannot assume all students will be able to read the survey independently. It is a good idea to read the survey to them, pausing after each question to allow time for marking the answers. If the survey contains open-ended questions, assure the students that you are more interested in their answers than in correct spelling and punctuation. Otherwise, some students will write very little in order to avoid words they cannot spell. Others may pay more attention to spelling and punctuation than to the quality of the answer.

Constructing a Survey

An interest survey is simple to construct. You do so by asking your students to tell you their reading interests. Some students are very aware of the role that reading plays in their lives; these students will immediately describe their interests. Other students, however, are less conscious of what interests them. One way to involve all students in the brainstorming process is to ask them to name favorite books and tell what they are mainly about. You can also have the students page through their reading textbook and suggest topics and genres of interest to them. Record all of these on the chalkboard or on chart paper. Then ask everyone to take out a sheet of paper and write the three or four topics or genres that would be at the top of their list of reading preferences. Or you can transcribe the entire list and ask students to underline or check those that appeal to them. Because you are using interests generated from the students, you avoid the trap of constructing a survey that does not include some key items of interest to your students.

Published Surveys

Several surveys have been published in reading journals, and the teacher or tutor should consider using these to assess motivation. First, it is always easier to use a survey that is already constructed than to design one. Second, published surveys have generally been carefully constructed and pilot-tested with well-thought-out scoring guidelines.

The Elementary Reading Attitude Survey (McKenna & Kear, 1999) addresses the task value of reading. The survey combines questions with pictorial answers. The comic strip character Garfield is presented in poses that depict four reactions to each question: "Very happy," "A little happy," "A little upset," and "Very upset." The survey includes 20 questions equally divided between a focus on recreational reading and a focus on academic reading. The questions begin with "How do you feel . . . ?" Recreational questions relate to the perceived importance of reading for fun in school, at home, and during vacation; the perceived importance of receiving books as presents; and the perceived importance of going to the library. Academic questions ask the students how they feel about worksheets, reading schoolbooks, reading class, reading tests, and reading out loud in class. The authors present detailed instructions for scoring the survey and converting raw scores to percentile ranks.

Henk and Melnick (1999) devised the Reader Self-Perception Scale (RSPS) to measure how intermediate students feel about themselves as readers. The RSPS is based upon the existence of a direct link between reader self-perceptions and reading behavior. "Children who believe they are good readers probably enjoy a rich history of reader engagement and exhibit a strong likelihood of continued positive interactions with text. By contrast, children who perceive themselves as poor readers probably have not experienced much in the way of reading success. They almost surely will not look toward reading as a source of gratification" (p. 235). The survey employs 33 questions that ask the student to respond in one of five ways: "Strongly agree", "Agree", "Undecided", "Disagree," and "Strongly disagree". The questions are structured around four categories. The first is "Progress," which identifies a student's perception of present reading skill compared to past efforts. The second category is "Observational Comparison," in which the student compares his/her performance to the performance of peers. "Social Feedback", the third category, focuses on the kind of input given to the students from teachers, peers, and family. The last category is "Physiological States," which centers on internal feelings experienced during reading. Students receive separate scores for all four areas. The RSPS is appropriate for intermediate grades. The authors explain that the self-perceptions of students below fourth grade are not clearly formed or very accurate.

Gambrell et al. (1996) developed the Motivation to Read Profile. The profile has two parts: a survey that can be administered to a group, and an interview that is administered individually. The survey assesses reader self-concept by asking students about perceptions of their competence as readers and their performance as compared to peers. The survey assesses reading task value by asking students about the value they place upon different reading tasks and activities, such as reading books, receiving books as presents, talking about books, and going to the library. The survey is composed of 20 cued-response items such as the following:

I think libraries are
    a great place to spend time
    an interesting place to spend time
    an OK place to spend time
    a boring place to spend time (p. 218)

The interview focuses on individual preferences for books, stories, and authors, and on how reading material is located. It is divided into three categories of open-ended questions: narrative text, informational text, and general reading. A sample interview question is as follows: "Tell me about the most interesting story or book you have read this week (or even last week). . . . How did you know or find out about this story?" (p. 221).

Gambrell et al. (1996) emphasize that results of the Motivation to Read Profile should be used "to create more meaningful, motivational contexts for reading instruction" (p. 229). For example, a low score on the portion of the survey assessing reader self-concept might indicate a need for activities to enhance feelings of success while reading. A low score on the portion assessing reading task value might suggest the need for more meaningful reading experiences.

SUMMARY

- Without motivation, learning does not occur. Motivation can be categorized as intrinsic or extrinsic.
- Intrinsic motivation comes from within the individual. Intrinsic reasons for reading and writing include personal involvement, curiosity, challenge, and social interaction. Intrinsic motivation is the basis of lifelong reading and fosters the development of complex comprehension strategies.
- Extrinsic motivation come from without. Extrinsic reasons for reading include compliance, recognition, competition, and avoidance of other tasks.
- A variety of activities can create a motivating classroom environment: open activities as opposed to closed tasks, student choice, moderate challenge, student control, and collaboration.
- The teacher or tutor who values reading and writing and shares this with students can also be a positive motivating force.
- Classrooms should embody the messages that effort increases ability; that failure is a natural part of learning; and that the purpose of learning is to progress, not to be the best.
- Purposes for assessing motivation are to determine students interests, to determine students' self-perceptions as readers, and to determine the value students place upon reading.
- Motivation can be assessed through observation and through surveys. The teacher or tutor can construct a survey or can use surveys published in reading journals.

ACTIVITIES FOR DEVELOPING UNDERSTANDING

- Identify something that you did not learn, and analyze this from the perspective of motivation.
- Construct an interest survey for a specific age group.
- Choose one of the published surveys, and administer it to an individual or group. Score the survey, and state what you have learned about the individual's or group's motivation for reading.
- Complete the self-evaluation form provided on the next page.

Teacher or Tutor Self-Evaluation

I use open classroom tasks to increase motivation.

        Regularly   Occasionally   A future goal

I employ student choice to increase motivation.

        Regularly   Occasionally   A future goal

I foster collaboration to increase motivation.

        Regularly   Occasionally   A future goal

I maintain a focus on meaning to increase motivation.

        Regularly   Occasionally   A future goal

My classroom contains a wide variety of reading and writing materials.

        Regularly   Occasionally   A future goal

I establish a climate for motivation by stressing student progress.

        Regularly   Occasionally   A future goal

I assess the interests of my students.

        Regularly   Occasionally   A future goal

I use observational techniques to assess student motivation for reading.

        Regularly   Occasionally   A future goal

I use interviews and/or surveys to assess student motivation for reading.

        Regularly   Occasionally   A future goal

NINE

Standardized Tests

What Do They Tell Us about Reading Performance?

CHAPTER TOPICS

Description of Standardized Tests
Standardized Test Validity and Reliability
Standardized Test Scores
Interpretation of Standardized Test Scores
Uses and Misuses of Standardized Tests
Summary
Activities for Developing Understanding

DESCRIPTION OF STANDARDIZED TESTS

Standardized tests are measures of student achievement in which a student's score is compared to a standard of performance (Trice, 2000). A student's score is not reported as the number correct or the number wrong. It is not recorded as a percent or a letter grade. When standardized tests are developed, they are field-tested on a large sample of students. This sample is called a *norm group*. Scores of the norm group provide the standards for interpreting the scores of all other students who take the test.

Let's say that fourth graders were field-tested across the country in October. They had an average score of 52 correct in reading. Since these fourth graders were in their second month of fourth grade, the score of 52 was set as 4.2 (fourth grade, second month). When your student Sallie got 52 correct, she was also assigned a score of 4.2.

When a student's score is interpreted in comparison to the scores of students in the norm group, we call the test a *norm-referenced* measure. When a student's score is compared to a cutoff score set by the test authors and usually influenced by norm group scores, we call the test a *criterion-referenced* measure. To return to our example, a norm-referenced test would change when the test publishers again field-tested and sampled fourth graders across the country. The average score for these fourth graders might be 53 correct or 49 correct. Therefore, a higher or lower score for the number of correct items might result in the same designation of 4.2. A norm-referenced test fluctuates each time the test is normed. On the other hand, a criterion-referenced test may stay the same. In our example, the test makers might choose to retain the original 52 correct as the level of performance. Standardized tests are usually nationally normed; that is, the norm group represents students from regions throughout the nation. Some standardized tests are locally normed as well.

There are different kinds of standardized tests. Standardized *achievement tests* measure what students have learned. *Aptitude tests* measure a student's potential for achievement. Intelligence tests such as the widely used Wechsler Intelligence Scale for Children are measures of aptitude.

Standardized tests take various forms. Some are multiple-choice measures, where the student chooses one of four or five possible answers and records this on a score sheet by filling in little circles. Some combine multiple-choice sections with writing samples. In these, the multiple-choice sections are scored by a computer, and the writing samples are scored by groups of trained teachers. Some standardized tests involve an oral question-and-answer format; the examiner asks questions and records the student's answers. Others require the student to perform such tasks as reading a list of words, putting together a puzzle, or sequencing a series of pictures. The examiner records the student's performance in terms of accuracy, and sometimes in terms of the amount of time it takes the student to complete each task. Some standardized tests can be administered to large groups. Others can only be administered to one individual at a time.

STANDARDIZED TEST VALIDITY AND RELIABILITY

Designers of standardized tests are concerned that their measures exhibit validity and reliability. *Validity* simply means that the test measures what it claims to measure. For example, if a standardized test of reading comprehension is valid, it would be appropriate to interpret student scores as indicating acceptable or unacceptable comprehension ability. *Reliability* means that the test exhibits consistency. It "refers to the likelihood that students will receive similar scores with successive administrations and scorings of the assessment" (Kapinus, 1994, p. 580). If a student takes a standardized reading test in March and again in June, the results should not be contradictory. If two examiners score a student's performance, directions for scoring and interpreting should also be reliable. That is, both examiners' efforts should yield similar results.

Standardized test developers attempt to establish validity in several ways. *Content validity* "refers to the adequacy with which the instrument measures a representative sample of behaviors and content domain about which inferences are to be made" (Ravid, 2000, p. 264). In other words, do the test items adequately reflect the skills, behaviors, or content to be measured? With regard to achievement tests, it is important to compare the content of these tests to the district or school curriculum. Do they match? If so, the test has content validity. If not, the test does not possess content validity and should not be used.

Another form of validity is *criterion validity*. To what extent is performance on one test related to performance on other measures (the criterion)? There are two types of criterion validity: *concurrent validity* and *predictive validity*. "Concurrent validity refers to how well the test we wish to validate correlates with another well-established instrument which measures the same thing" (Ravid, 2000, p. 265). Test makers use a statistic called *correlation* to do this. Correlation establishes a relationship between two or more sets of scores. If two standardized vocabulary tests are highly correlated, this indicates that they are measuring the same thing and thus have concurrent validity. Does the test predict future student performance? If so, it possesses predictive validity. Many measures of phonemic awareness predict later reading performance. Students who possess phonemic awareness as preschoolers are better readers in first and second grades. This is an example of predictive validity.

Standardized tests address reliability or consistency in several ways. *Test–retest reliability* means that a test is administered twice to the same group of people. Scores from one administration are compared and correlated to the second administration. If the test is consistent, the two sets of scores will be related. For standardized tests that have two alternate forms, *alternate-form validity* must be established. If both forms are to be considered equivalent, scores on one form must be consistent with scores on the other. Students are administered both forms, and scores from one form are correlated with scores from the other. *Split-half reliability* means correlating or comparing test questions to determine whether the difficulty level is relatively consistent across the test. For example, scores on even-numbered items are usually compared with scores on odd-numbered items.

STANDARDIZED TEST SCORES

Teachers and tutors are rarely concerned with standardized test construction, the acceptability of the norm group, and issues of validity and reliability. Although they should have some understanding of these issues, the truth is that states and school districts choose standardized measures; teachers and tutors have little input into the decision. The role of a teacher or tutor is to understand a student's score and interpret it for parents. Standardized scores come in various forms: *grade equivalents*, *percentiles*, *stanines*, and *standard scores*. Each one tells the teacher or tutor the same thing in a slightly different way.

Grade Equivalents

On the surface, grade equivalents seem very easy to interpret, but unfortunately they are very often misinterpreted. Teachers and tutors tend to interpret a grade equivalent score of 3.6 (meaning the sixth month of third grade) as indicating that students who achieve this score can read or do math at a middle third-grade level. Nothing could be farther from the truth! In order to understand grade equivalents, a teacher or tutor needs to consider where they come from. Remember that student performance on a standardized test is always compared to the scores of the norm group. Suppose that a large number of third graders in the norm group were tested in the sixth month of third grade (which would be February). Their average raw score (total number correct on the test) was 43 correct items. That score would be assigned a grade equivalent of 3.6, and any student who attained the same score would also receive a grade equivalent score of 3.6. Different individuals in a norm group are generally tested at different times during a school year to arrive at average scores that represent different months, such as 3.3 and 3.9. What happens if no norm samples are tested during some months? Test makers employ a variety of complex statistical manipulations to arrive at a full span of scores for any one grade level, ranging from 3.0 to 3.9 in the case of third grade.

What is the problem with grade equivalents? Grade equivalents are based on the notion that learning is constant throughout the year—in other words, that it occurs in regular monthly increments. Any teacher or tutor can recognize the fallacy of this premise! In addition, teachers, tutors, and parents tend to think of grade equivalent scores as similar to school grade levels, but they are actually very different. Grade equivalent scores simply indicate that a student's score is similar to the norm group's score at that grade level and on that test level. As such, it only represents a general estimate of achievement. Consider the following scenario. A second grader takes a test containing content appropriate for second grade. The student's performance is well above average and is therefore assigned a grade equivalent of 4.5. Will this student be able to read and comprehend material that is appropriate for fourth grade? Grade equivalent scores are often erroneously interpreted to say this. However, all the score tells us is that the student has obtained the same score that fourth graders achieved on second-grade content. Perhaps the student can read at a fourth-grade level and perhaps he or she can't. A lot will depend on the curriculum of the student's school or district and the match of that curriculum to the content of the test. But it is wrong to infer that high performance on a second-grade standardized test level means equally high performance in a fourth-grade classroom level. Grade equivalents are best interpreted as rough estimates of achievement, not as absolute indicators of classroom performance.

Percentile Scores

"A percentile score indicates the percentage of students you did better than" (Trice, 2000, p. 108). Percentile scores can range from 0 to 100. If a student scores at the 35th percentile, this means that the student did better than 35% of the students in the norm group. Similarly, a student who scores at the 75th percentile did better than 75% of the norm group sample. Percentile scores are often confused with percent scores. A percent score of 50 usually means poor performance and a nonpassing grade. A percentile score of 50 indicates average performance; the student did better than 50% of the norm group. Sixty-eight percent of a norm group's scores tend to fall between the percentile scores of 15 and 84; these scores are considered to indicate average performance. However, it is somewhat difficult to explain to a parent that a percentile score of 35 is not necessarily an indication of poor performance! In addition, the teacher or tutor needs to realize that the difference between raw scores that convert to a percentile of 65 and a percentile of 75 may be very small. It is best to think of percentiles, like grade equivalents, as broad indicators.

Stanine Scores

Stanine scores range from 1 to 9, with scores from 4 to 6 indicating average performance. Stanine scores tend to annoy people because they seem less precise than percentiles or grade equivalents. Some manuals caution that two scores should not be considered significantly different if they are in the same stanine or adjacent stanines (Cangelos, 2000). If we accept this, raw scores that convert to stanine scores of 5 and 6 would not be considered very different. Neither would raw scores that convert to stanine scores of 4 and 3. Like grade equivalents and percentiles, stanines tell us where a student has scored in relation to the norm group.

Standard Scores

It may be easiest to understand standard scores in relation to IQ. A student takes an intelligence test and achieves a raw score (a certain number of correct items). This raw score is converted to a standard score that has an average of 100, with a give or take of 15 points. (Statisticians call this give and take a *standard deviation*, but we do not need to go into that.) This means that any converted score that falls between 85 and 115 represents an average IQ. A score above 115 is considered above average, and a score below 85 is considered below average. All standardized tests convert raw scores to standard scores but the average and the give and take may be different. A standard score of 100 on an achievement test may not be the same as a score of 100 on an intelligence test. The Scholastic Aptitude Test (SAT) college entrance examination has an average verbal or mathematical score of 500, with a give and take of 100. Colleges or universities who will not accept any student with an SAT verbal or math score lower than 400 are saying that, at the very least, they want average performers. The teacher or tutor needs to determine what numbers represent the average and the give and take on a standardized test, in order to interpret the scores correctly.

INTERPRETATION OF STANDARDIZED TEST SCORES

A student scored well on a standardized reading test. What does this score tell us about the student? It probably tells us several things:

> The student understood the directions.
> The student followed the directions.
> The student was motivated to do his or her best.

The student was not unduly distracted during the test administration.

The student was not troubled with health problems, such as a stomach-ache, a headache, or a sore knee.

The student was not troubled by psychological problems, such as undue test anxiety, family difficulties, or being excluded from games at recess.

The student was relatively well rested.

The student did not lose his or her place and mark answers in the wrong circles.

The student paced him- or herself appropriately.

The student possessed test-taking skills appropriate to the test format.

The student could read the words.

The student could comprehend the content.

Any standardized test score is probably due to any one of these factors or to a combination of them. As a result, a low score may not indicate poor reading ability; it may simply indicate that the testing day was a bad day for that student.

The same thing happens in the classroom. Teachers and tutors can offer many examples of good students who perform poorly on some measure of assessment. However, in the classroom, a teacher or tutor can easily reevaluate a student's performance at another time. This is not an option for standardized tests. The student gets one chance and only one chance. Any interpretation of test results should take this into account.

As a teacher or tutor, how should you interpret scores for yourself and for parents? The most important thing to remember is that all standardized scores represent comparisons to the scores of a norm group. It is important to use norm group terminology with parents. For example, suppose you are telling parents that their daughter attained a percentile score of 65. Instead of saying "Ellen did better than 65% of those who took the test," say, "Ellen's score was higher than 65% of the norm group—a national sample of students on whom the test was tried." Parents as well as teachers and tutors must interpret scores in relation to the norm group, not in relation to students in their school or district (Cangelos, 2000).

Avoid characterizing students as average, above average, or below average; always relate performance to the norm sample. Why is this important? Suppose that a student scores above average in relation to the norm group. This student may not be above average with regard to his or her school or district. Using the term *above average* by itself, without reference to the norm group, can lead to erroneous assumptions on the part of parents.

Don't feel that you have to interpret every type of score: standard score, grade equivalent, percentile, and stanine. They all basically indicate the same thing—a comparison of the student's score to the scores of the norm group. Choose the one that you understand the best and feel the most comfortable with, and explain that.

Emphasize that a score on any standardized test is only one test sampling; it represents one day's performance. Always interpret the results of a standardized test in relation to classroom performance. Your assessment of a student's performance is more meaningful and more accurate than any standardized test can be. Pull out the grade book that you have divided into good reader behaviors, and describe the student's performance in terms of these. Lay out the student's portfolio, and show the parents how the student has improved over time. Explain what the student still needs to work on, and describe how you intend to design instruction to accomplish this. You will find that this makes much more sense to parents, and that as a result, the standardized test scores tend to diminish in importance. The "most valuable and valid information about student learning comes not from an isolated and decontextualized 'snapshot' of student performance, but from those who work closely with students on a daily basis" (Wolf, 1993, p. 519).

USES AND MISUSES OF STANDARDIZED TESTS

"Good assessment should look like good instruction by providing contexts for activities, allowing for social interaction, providing time for reflection, and engaging students' interests and motivation" (Kapinus, 1994, p. 579). If you accept this statement—and it is difficult to quarrel with it—standardized tests are easy to criticize. They bear little resemblance to classroom assessment measures or to the real reading process. Many are made up of short reading passages taken out of context, along with questions that focus on literal comprehension and on trivial details. Many incorporate multiple-choice questions that deny students the opportunity to offer their own interpretations and personal reactions to the text.

On the other hand, standardized tests can "provide quick, reliable data on student performance" (International Reading Association [IRA], 1999, p. 258) by painting a broad picture of achievement on certain specific tasks. They are useful for comparing scores to national norms. They are appropriate for "comparisons for purposes of reporting to the public; screening for further evaluation, and monitoring general effects of curricula" (Lewandowski & Martens, 1990, p. 384). If one acknowledges that standardized tests are only one means of measuring student performance, they can effectively supplement more authentic classroom assessment. Unfortunately, there is a widespread perception on the part of the public that students are not achieving as they should and that teachers are not teaching effectively (Farr, 1992). The public tends to view standardized, norm-referenced assessment as a way to force school reform and to keep track of the quality of U.S. schools. If one interprets a standardized score as a rough estimate of student achievement and as only one type of estimate, this is not necessarily a bad thing. However, standardized assessment, like anything else, can be wisely used or abysmally misused.

It is not difficult to cite the misuses of individual and group standardized tests. They are misused when standardized scores are considered more accurate, more representative, and more important than classroom assessment measures. They are misused when they become the only index of a school's effectiveness. They are misused when they are regarded as the only method of measuring a teacher's or tutor's competence. They are misused when they become the primary or only qualification for grade promotion, graduation, and acceptance into special educational services. The board of directors of the IRA has expressed a strong concern about the misuse of standardized testing: "Our concern is that testing has become a means of controlling instruction as opposed to a way of gathering information to help students become better readers" (IRA, 1999, p. 257).

Individual and group standardized tests are used wisely when they are regarded as only one means of measuring individual achievement or school effectiveness. They are used wisely when scores are considered as estimates of individual or school achievement, not as absolute indicators. They are used wisely when teachers and tutors teach test-taking skills to acquaint the students with standardized formats, but refrain from teaching test content. They are used wisely when teachers and tutors pay most attention to covering their school or district curriculum, to fostering good reader behaviors, and to meeting their students' needs as opposed to teaching the content of the test. They are used wisely when it is recognized that they provide only a sample of reading behavior and probably do not reflect the curriculum of the school or district.

Standardized tests probably will not go away—and, unfortunately, they will continue to be misused. The teacher or tutor must understand the possible contributions of standardized measures and place them in perspective. "It should also be remembered that the long-standing primary purpose of large-scale testing has been to provide a general assessment as to how groups of students are progressing in a school district. Such information, if it does not become the focus of instruction, can be one piece of information used to contribute to a broad base of information for planning, supporting, and evaluating school- and system-wide curricula and instruction" (Farr, 1992, p. 34).

The teacher or tutor is responsible for conducting authentic and meaningful assessment in the classroom or tutoring session. This assessment takes place continually and over time. This assessment focuses upon good reader behaviors and provides a chronicle of student progress. The teacher or tutor must realize that this is a awesome responsibility—one that no standardized measure can ever duplicate. The teacher or tutor should not apologize for classroom assessment measures or consider them less worthy or less sensitive than standardized test scores. Well-thought-out and well-designed classroom assessment tells a teacher or tutor much more about a student's reading and writing than any standardized measure can, no matter how valid and reliable it may be.

SUMMARY

- Standardized tests are tests in which students' scores are compared to a standard—the scores of the norm group.
- Standardized tests can be measures of achievement or aptitude. They can be group or individual. They can involve a variety of formats.
- Standardized tests should be valid; that is, they should measure what they claim to measure. Test makers are careful to establish content, concurrent, and predictive validity.
- Standardized tests should be reliable. If a student takes the same test twice, the scores on both measures should be consistent and noncontradictory. Test makers establish test–retest validity, alternate-form validity, and split-half reliability.
- Standardized tests yield different kinds of scores: grade equivalent scores, percentile scores, stanine scores, and standard scores.
- All standardized test scores compare the student's score to the scores of the norm group.
- A grade equivalent score means that the student received the same raw score as the average student in the norm sample for that grade, month, and test level. A grade equivalent score cannot be equated with a classroom grade level.
- Percentile scores range from 1 to 100 and indicate how many students in the norm sample scored above the student. They are not the same as percent scores. A percentile score of 50 represents average performance. A score of 50% usually represents a nonpassing grade.

- Stanine scores range from 1 to 9 with scores of 4 to 6 representing average performance.
- Standard scores are based upon an average and the give and take of that average across students. In order to interpret average performance in relation to the norm group, a teacher or tutor must know the average and the give and take of the standardized measure.
- Scores on a standardized test are affected by a variety of factors besides reading ability (anxiety, presence or absence of distractions, ability to understand and follow directions, good health, appropriate pacing, etc.).
- Scores on a standardized test only represent one sampling of a student's ability. They must always be interpreted in relation to classroom performance.
- Teachers and tutors should always use norm group terminology when interpreting standardized scores for parents. Otherwise, parents may interpret a student's performance in relation to a single school or district.
- Standardized tests can be misused if more importance is placed upon standardized scores than upon classroom performance, or if they are used as the only index of school, teacher, and student competence.
- Standardized test scores can be used wisely if they are regarded as only one means of measuring effectiveness and as rough estimates of achievement, not as absolute indicators.

ACTIVITIES FOR DEVELOPING UNDERSTANDING

- Pretend you are planning for a conference with parents. Choose one type of score (grade equivalent, percentile, stanine, or standard score) and plan what you will say to the parents about a high score and a low score.
- Locate the manuals of several group and individual standardized tests. What are the average and the give and take of their standard scores?
- Interview several teachers regarding their perceptions of standardized tests. To what degree do they feel the tests accurately reflect the performance of their students?
- Interview several individuals who are not in the education profession. What are their perceptions of standardized tests?
- Interview several students regarding their perceptions of standardized test. How do they feel about taking them?

General Summary
Assessing the Good Reader Behaviors

Good readers pronounce unfamiliar words accurately.

- Listen to students read orally.
  - —Graded passages
  - —Graded word lists
  - —Nonsense words
- Observe students sort words on the basis of letters and sounds.
- Administer the Names Test.
- Analyze miscues.
- Ask students how they identify words.

Good readers recognize words automatically.

Good readers read fluently—that is, accurately, quickly, and expressively.

- Listen to students read orally.
  - —Graded passages
  - —Graded word lists, timed
- Determine reading rate.
- Use a checklist to assess intonation.

Good readers learn new words and refine the meanings of known ones.

- Observe students sorting words on the basis of meaning.
- Ask students to put a word in their lives.
- Ask students to match a word with a noun, verb, adjective, or adverb.

Good readers connect what they know with the information in the text.

- Ask students questions that focus directly on this behavior: "How can you connect this to your life, to another text, to the world at large?"
- Ask students to look back in the text to make connections with their lives, other texts, or the world at large.
- Focus on connecting with prior knowledge during think-alouds.
- Use cards on making connections during focused discussions.
- Include making connections as a heading on a checklist or rubric.
- Focus on making connections in good reader response logs.
- Focus on a student's ability to make connections when you are reading student journals or holding student conferences.

Good readers determine what is important in the text.

- Ask students questions that focus directly on this behavior: "What was the most important part of this selection and why? Was this part important and why?"
- Ask students to look back in the text to determine important elements.
- Ask students to retell or summarize; focus on determining importance when assessing this.
- Use cards that direct student attention to important parts during focused discussions.
- Include determining importance as a heading on a checklist or rubric.
- Focus on determining importance in good reader response logs.
- Focus on a student's ability to make connections when you are reading student journals or holding student conferences.

Good readers recognize the structure of the text.

- Ask students questions that focus directly on this behavior: "What are the parts of narratives? What pattern is the author using?"
- Ask students to look back in the text to locate narrative parts or to identify expository patterns.

- Ask students to retell or summarize; focus on text structure when you are assessing this.
- Use cards on text structure during focused discussions.
- Include text structure as a heading on a checklist or rubric.
- Focus on text structure in good reader response logs.

Good readers summarize and reorganize ideas in the text.

- Ask students to retell or summarize.
- Focus on retelling during think-alouds.
- Focus on retelling/summary in good reader response logs.

Good readers make inferences and predictions.

- Ask students questions that focus directly on this behavior: "What do you predict will happen next? Why do you think this happened? What might happen if . . . ?"
- Ask questions that assess convergent, divergent, and evaluative thinking.
- Ask students to look back in the text to make inferences or to locate clues for inferences.
- Focus on inferring during think-alouds.
- Use cards on inferring during focused discussions.
- Include inferring as a heading on a checklist or rubric.
- Focus on inferring in good reader response logs.
- Focus on a student's ability to infer while you are reading journals or holding student conferences.

Good readers construct visual images.

- Ask students that focus directly on this behavior: "What picture do you have in your mind?"
- Ask students to look back in the text to locate sections that call up imagery.
- Use cards on imagery during focused discussions.
- Include imagery on a checklist or rubric.
- Focus on a student's use of imagery in writing.
- Focus on imagery in good reader response logs.
- Focus on a student's ability to construct imagery when you are holding student conferences.

Good readers ask questions of themselves and the author, and read to find answers.

- Ask students to construct questions.
- Focus on questioning during think-alouds.
- Use cards on questions during focused discussion.

Good readers synthesize information from different sources.

- Ask questions that focus directly on this behavior: "How is this like or unlike . . . ?"
- Ask questions that assess convergent, divergent, or evaluative thinking.
- Include synthesis on a checklist or rubric.
- Focus on synthesizing in good reader response logs.
- Focus on a student's ability to synthesize while you are reading journals or holding student conferences.

Good readers form and support opinions on ideas in the text.

- Ask students questions that focus directly on this behavior: "What is your opinion about . . . ? Why do you think so?"
- Ask questions that assess convergent, divergent, or evaluative thinking.
- Focus on reacting personally during think-alouds.
- Use cards that focus on forming opinions during focused discussion.
- Include forming and supporting opinions on a checklist or rubric.
- Focus on forming and supporting opinions in good reader response logs.
- Focus on a student's ability to form and support opinions when you are reading student journals and holding student conferences.

Good readers recognize the author's purpose/point of view/style.

- Ask questions that focus directly on this behavior: "What was the author's purpose in writing this? What does the author believe about . . . ? Why did the author choose this style?"
- Ask questions that assess convergent, divergent, or evaluative thinking.
- Ask students to look back in the text to determine purpose or point of view.
- Use cards that focus on the author during focused discussions.
- Focus on author purpose/point of view/style while you are reading journals or holding student conferences.

Monitor comprehension and repair comprehension breakdowns.

- Ask questions that focus directly on this behavior: "What don't you understand? How can you find the answer?"
- Ask students to look back in the text to clear up misunderstandings.
- Focus on noting understanding or lack of understanding during think-alouds.
- Focus on monitoring comprehension in good reader response logs.

Choose to read for enjoyment and enrichment.

- Ask questions that focus directly on the behavior: "Do you like to read? What do you like to read about?"
- Administer motivation surveys.
- Observe student during free-reading periods.

References

Adams, M. J. (1990). *Beginning to read: Thinking and learning about print. A summary.* Urbana–Champaign: University of Illinois, Center for the Study of Reading.

Adams, M. J., Foorman, B. R., Lundberg, I., & Beeler, T. (1998). *Phonemic awareness in young children.* Baltimore: Brookes.

Afflerbach, P. (1993). Report cards and reading. *The Reading Teacher, 46,* 458–465.

Allen, M. N. (1989). One, two, three—Ah-choo! In D. Alvermann, C. A. Bridge, B. A. Schmidt, L. W. Searfoss, & P. Winograd (Eds.), *Come back here, crocodile* (pp. 92–100). Lexington, MA: Heath.

Allington, R. L. (1977). If they don't read much, how they ever gonna get good? *Journal of Reading, 21,* 57–61.

Allington, R. L. (1983). Fluency: The neglected reading goal. *The Reading Teacher, 36,* 556–561.

Allington, R. L. (1994). The schools we have. The schools we need. *The Reading Teacher, 48,* 14–29.

Allington, R. L. (2001). *What really matters for struggling readers.* New York: Addison Wesley Longman.

Armbruster, B. B., Mitsakas, C. L., & Rogers, V. R. (1986). *America's history.* Lexington, MA: Ginn.

Ball, E. W., & Blachman, B. A. (1991). Does phoneme awareness training in kindergarten make a difference in early word recognition and spelling? *Reading Research Quarterly, 26,* 49–66.

Baumann, J. F., Jones, L. A., & Siefert-Kessell, N. (1993). Using think alouds to enhance children's comprehension monitoring abilities. *The Reading Teacher, 47,* 187–193.

Bear, D. R., Invernizzi, M., Templeton, S., & Johnston, F. (2000). *Words their way: Word study for phonics, vocabulary, and spelling instruction.* Upper Saddle River, NJ: Prentice-Hall.

Benson, J. T., Fortier, J. D., Grady, S. M., Karbon, I. C., & Last, E. L. (1998). *Wisconsin's model standards for English language arts.* Madison: Wisconsin Department of Public Instruction.

Bergeron, B. S., Wermuth, S., & Hammer, R. C. (1997). Initiating portfolios through shared learning: Three perspectives. *The Reading Teacher, 50,* 552–562.

Bradley, L., & Bryant, P. (1983). Categorizing sounds and learning to read: A causal connection. *Nature, 30,* 419–421.

Brigance, A. H. (1976). *Brigance Diagnostic Inventories.* North Billerica, MA: Curriculum Associates.

Brown, C. S., & Lytle, S. L. (1988). Merging assessment and instruction: Protocols in the classroom. In S. M. Glazer, L. W. Searfoss, & L. M. Gentile (Eds.), *Reexamining reading diagnosis: New trends and practices.* Newark, DE: International Reading Association.

Brown, V. I., Hammel, D. D., & Wiederholt, J. L. (1995). *Test of Reading Comprehension* (3rd ed.). Austin, TX: Pro-Ed.

Butkowsky, I. S., & Willows, D. M. (1980). Cognitive–motivational characteristics of children varying in reading ability: Evidence for learned helplessness in poor readers. *Journal of Educational Psychology, 72,* 408–422.

Byrne, B., & Fielding-Barnsley, R. (1991). Evaluation of a program to teach phonemic awareness to young children. *Journal of Educational Psychology, 83,* 451–455.

Caldwell, J., Fromm, M., & O'Connor, V. (1997–1998). Designing an intervention for poor readers: Incorporating the best of all worlds. *Wisconsin State Reading Association Journal, 41,* 7–14.

Cameron, J., & Pierce, W. D. (1994). Reinforcement, reward, and intrinsic motivation: A meta-analysis. *Review of Educational Research, 64,* 363–423.

Cangelos, J. S. (2000). *Assessment strategies for monitoring student learning.* New York: Addison Wesley Longman.

Carroll, J. B., Davies, P., & Richman, B. (1971). *Word frequency book.* Boston, MA: Houghton Mifflin.

Carver, R. B. (1990). *Reading rate: A review of research and theory.* San Diego, CA: Academic Press.

Ciardiello, A. V. (1998). Did you ask a good question today?: Alternative cognitive and metacognitive strategies. *Journal of Adolescent and Adult Literacy, 42,* 210–219.

Clay, M. M. (1972). *Sand—The Concepts about Print Test.* Portsmouth, NH: Heinemann.

Clay, M. M. (1979). *Stones—The Concepts about Print Test.* Portsmouth, NH: Heinemann.

Clay, M. M. (1993). *An observation survey of early literacy achievement.* Portsmouth, NH: Heinemann.

Cowley, J. (1999). *Mrs. WishyWashy.* New York: Philomel.

Creech, S. (1994). *Walk two moons.* New York: Harper Trophy.

Cunningham, P. G. (1990). The Names Test: A quick assessment of decoding ability. *The Reading Teacher, 44,* 124–129.

Cunningham, P. M. (1992, October). Presentation given at West Bend, WI, School District.

Cunningham, P. M., & Allington, R. L. (1999). *Classrooms that work.* New York: Addison Wesley Longman.

DeLain, M. T. (1995). Equity and performance based assessment: An insider's view. *The Reading Teacher, 48,* 440–442.

Dowhower, S. L. (1991). Speaking of prosody: Fluency's unattended bedfellow. *Theory Into Practice, 30,* 165–173.

Duffelmeyer, F. A., Kruse, A. E., Merkeley, D. J., & Fyfe, S. A. (1999). Further validation and enhancement of the Names Test. In S. J. Barrentine (Ed.), *Reading assessment: Principles and practices for elementary teachers* (pp. 177–188). Newark, DE: International Reading Association.

Ehri, L. C. (1991). Development of the ability to read words. In R. Barr, M. L. Kamil, P. Mosenthal, & P. D. Pearson (Eds.), *Handbook of reading research* (Vol. 2, pp. 383–417). White Plains, NY: Longman.

Ehri, L. C. (1997). *The development of children's ability to read words.* Paper presented at the convention of the International Reading Association, Atlanta, GA.

Emerson, F. (1977). Nobody comes to dinner. In D. Alvermann, C. A. Bridge, B. A. Schmidt, L. W. Searfoss, & P. Winograd (Eds.), *Come back here, crocodile* (pp. 248–256). Lexington, MA: Heath.

Englert, C. S., & Hiebert, E. H. (1984). Children's developing awareness of text structures in expository material. *Journal of Educational Psychology, 76,* 65–74.

Farr, R. (1992). Putting it all together: Solving the reading assessment puzzle. *The Reading Teacher, 46,* 26–37.

Gambrell, L. B. (1996). Creating classroom cultures that foster reading motivation. *The Reading Teacher, 50,* 14–23.

Gambrell, L. B., Palmer, B. M., Codling, R. M., & Mazzoni, S. A. (1996). Assessing motivation to read. *The Reading Teacher, 49,* 518–533.

Gates, A. I., McKillop, A. S., & Horowitz, E. C. (1981). *Gates–McKillop–Horowitz Reading Diagnostic Tests.* New York: Teachers College Press.

Glass, S. (1989). *The effect of prior knowledge on reading miscues and comprehension of narrative text.* Unpublished master's thesis, Marquette University.

Goodman, K. S. (1969). Analysis of reading miscues: Applied psycholinguistics. *Reading Research Quarterly, 5,* 9–30.

Goodrich, H. (1996–1997). Understanding rubrics. *Educational Leadership, 54,* 14–17.

Gough, P. B., & Juel, C. (1991). The first stages of word recognition. In L. Rieben & C. A. Perfetti (Eds.), *Learning to read: Basic research and its implications* (pp. 47–56). Hillsdale, NJ: Erlbaum.

Harris, A. J., & Sipay, E. R. (1990). *How to increase reading ability* (8th ed.). New York: Addison Wesley Longman.

Harvey, S., & Goudvis, A. (2000). *Strategies that work*. York, ME: Stenhouse.

Henk, W. A., & Melnick, S. A. (1999). The Reader Self-Perception Scale (RSPS): A new tool for measuring how children feel about themselves as readers. In S. J. Barrentine (Ed.), *Reading assessment: Principles and practices for elementary teachers* (pp. 233–246). Newark, DE: International Reading Association.

Hill, B. C., Ruptic, C., & Norwick, L. (1998). *Classroom based assessment*. Norwood, MA: Christopher Gordon.

Hoffman, J. V., & Isaacs, M. E. (1991). Developing fluency through restructuring the task of guided oral reading. *Theory into Practice, 30,* 185–194.

Horowitz, R. (1985). Text patterns: Part I. *Journal of Reading Research, 28,* 448–454.

Huey, E. B. (1968). *The psychology and pedagogy of reading*. Cambridge, MA: MIT Press. (Original work published 1908)

Hunt, L. C. (1996–1997). The effects of self-selection, interest, and motivation upon independent, instructional, and frustration levels. *The Reading Teacher, 50,* 278–282.

International Reading Association (IRA). (1999). High-stakes assessment in reading: A position statement of the IRA. *The Reading Teacher, 53,* 257–263.

Johnson, D. D. (1971). The Dolch list reexamined. *The Reading Teacher, 24,* 449–457.

Johnson, M. J., Kress, R. A., & Pikulski, P. L. (1987). *Informal reading inventories* (2nd ed.). Newark, DE: International Reading Association.

Johnston, P. (1992a). Nontechnical assessment. *The Reading Teacher, 46,* 60–62.

Johnston, P. (1992b). Snow White and the seven warnings: Threats to authentic evaluation. *The Reading Teacher, 46,* 250–252.

Johnston, P. (1997). *Knowing literacy: Constructive literacy assessment*. York, ME: Stenhouse.

Juel, C. (1988). Learning to read and write: A longitudinal study of 54 children from first through fourth grades. *Journal of Educational Psychology, 80,* 437–447.

Kapinus, B. (1993). The balancing act. *The Reading Teacher, 47,* 62–64.

Kapinus, B. (1994). Looking at the ideal and the real in large-scale reading assessment: The view from two sides of the river. *The Reading Teacher, 47,* 578–580.

Koskinen, P. A., & Blum, I. H. (1984). Paired repeated reading: A classroom strategy for developing fluent reading. *The Reading Teacher, 40,* 70–75.

Leslie, L., & Allen, L. (1999). Factors that predict success in an early intervention project. *Reading Research Quarterly, 34,* 404–424,

Leslie, L., & Caldwell, J. (2001). *The Qualitative Reading Inventory 3*. New York: Addison Wesley Longman.

Lewandowski, L. J., & Martens, B. K. (1990). Selecting and evaluating standardized reading tests. *Journal of Reading, 33,* 384–388.

Lundberg, I., Frost, J., & Peterson, O. (1988). Effects of an extensive program for stimulating phonological awareness in preschool children. *Reading Research Quarterly, 23,* 263–284.

Maccinati, J. L. (1985). Using prosodic cues to teach oral reading fluency. *The Reading Teacher*, *39*, 206–211.

MacGinitie, W. H., & MacGinitie, R. K. (1989). *Gates–MacGinitie Reading Tests* (3rd ed.). Chicago: Riverside.

McKenna, M. C. (1983). Informal reading inventories: A review of the issues. *The Reading Teacher*, *36*, 670–679.

McKenna, M. C., Ellsworth, R. A., & Lear, D. J. (1995). Children's attitudes toward reading: A national survey. *Reading Research Quarterly*, *30*, 934–956.

McKenna, M. C., & Kear, D. J. (1999). Measuring attitude toward reading: A new tool for teachers. In S. J. Barrentine (Ed.), *Reading assessment: Principles and practices for elementary teachers* (pp. 199–214). Newark, DE: International Reading Association.

Meyer, B. S. F., & Freedle, R. O. (1984). Effectiveness of discourse type on recall. *American Educational Research Journal*, *21*, 121–143.

Nathan, R. G., & Stanovich, K. E. (1991). The causes and consequences of differences in reading fluency. *Theory into Practice*, *30*, 176–184.

Ogle, D. (1986). KWL: A teaching model that develops active reading of expository text. *The Reading Teacher*, *39*, 564–570.

O'Neill, J. (1994). Making assessment meaningful: "Rubrics" clarify expectations, yield better feedback. *Association for Supervision and Curriculum Development Update*, *36*, 1–5.

Paradis, E. E., Chatton, B., Boswell, A., Smith, M., & Yovich, S. (1991). Accountability: Assessing comprehension during literature discussions. *The Reading Teacher*, *45*, 8–17.

Perfetti, C. A. (1985). *Reading ability*. New York: Oxford University Press.

Perfetti, C. A. (1988). Verbal efficiency in reading ability. In M. Daneman, G. E. MacKinnon, & T. G. Waller (Eds.), *Reading research: Advances in theory and practice* (Vol. 6, pp. 109–143). New York: Academic Press.

Pflaum, S. W., Walberg, H. J., Karegianes, M. L., & Rassher, S. W. (1980). Reading instruction: A quantitative analysis. *Educational Researcher*, *9*, 12–18.

Pressley, M. (1998). *Reading instruction that works: The case for balanced teaching*. New York: Guilford Press.

Pressley, M., & Afflerbach, P. (1995). *Verbal protocols in reading: The nature of constructively responsive reading*. Hillsdale, NJ: Erlbaum.

Rasinski, T. V. (1986). Repeated reading—naturally. *The Reading Teacher*, *39*, 244–245.

Rasinski, T. V. (1988). Making repeated reading a functional part of classroom reading instruction. *Reading Horizons*, *39*, 250–254.

Ravid, R. (2000). *Practical statistics for educators*. Lanham, MD: University Press of America.

Regner, M. (1992). *Predicting growth in reading in regular and special education*. Unpublished doctoral dissertation, Marquette University.

Rhodes, L. K., & Nathenson-Mejia, S. (1992). Anecdotal records: A powerful tool for ongoing literacy assessment. *The Reading Teacher*, *45*, 502–509.

Richards, M. (2000). Be a good detective: Solve the case of oral reading fluency. *The Reading Teacher, 53,* 534–539.

Richek, M. A., Caldwell, J. S., Jennings, J. H., & Lerner, J. (2002). *Reading problems: Assessment and teaching strategies.* New York: Addison Wesley Longman.

Sakiey, E., & Fry, E. (1979). *3000 instant words.* Highland Park, NJ: Dreier Educational Systems.

Samuels, S. J. (1979). The method of repeated readings. *The Reading Teacher, 32,* 403–408.

Samuels, S. J. (1988). Decoding and automaticity: Helping poor readers become automatic at word recognition. *The Reading Teacher, 41,* 756–761.

Sawyer, D. (1987). *The Test of Awareness of Language Segments* (TALS). Rockville, MD: Aspen.

Spache, G. D. (1981). *Diagnosing and correcting reading difficulties.* Boston: Allyn & Bacon.

Spear-Swerling, L., & Sternberg, R. J. (1996). *Off track: When poor readers become "learning disabled."* Boulder, CO: Westview Press.

Stahl, S. A., Heubach, K., & Cramond, B. (1997). Fluency-oriented reading instruction. In *Changing reading instruction in second grade: A fluency-oriented approach.* Athens: National Reading Research Center, University of Georgia.

Stanovich, K. E. (1980). Toward an interactive-compensatory model of individual differences in the development of reading fluency. *Reading Research Quarterly, 16,* 32–71.

Stanovich, K. E. (1986). Matthew effects in reading: Some consequences of individual differences in the acquisition of literacy. *Reading Research Quarterly, 21,* 360–407.

Stanovich, K. E. (1988). *Children's reading and the development of phonological awareness.* Detroit: Wayne State University Press.

Stanovich, K. E. (1991). Word recognition: Changing perspectives. In R. Barr, M. L. Kamil, P. Mosenthal, & P. D. Pearson (Eds.), *Handbook of reading research* (Vol. 2, pp. 418–452). New York: Longman.

Stanovich, K. E. (1993–1994). Romance and reality. *The Reading Teacher, 47,* 280–291.

Stanovich, K. E. (2000). *Progress in understanding reading.* New York: Guilford Press.

Staunton, T. (1986). *Simon's surprise.* Toronto: Kids Can Press.

Stein, N. L. (1979). How children understand stories: A developmental analysis. In L. Katz (Ed.), *Current topics in early childhood education* (Vol. 2, pp. 261–290). Norwood, NJ: Ablex.

Stein, N. L., & Glenn, C. (1979). An analysis of story comprehension in elementary school children. In R. O. Freedle (Ed.), *Advances in discourse processes: Vol. 2. New directions in discourse processes* (pp. 53–120). Norwood, NJ: Ablex.

Sweet, A. P., & Guthrie, J. T. (1996). How children's motivations relate to literacy development and instruction. *The Reading Teacher, 49,* 660–662.

Taylor, B. M. (1992). Text structure, comprehension, and recall. In S. J. Samuels & A.

E. Farstrup (Eds.), *What research has to say about reading comprehension* (pp. 220–235). Newark, DE: International Reading Association.

Tierney, R. J. (1998). Literacy assessment refined: Shifting beliefs, principled possibilities, and emerging practices. *The Reading Teacher, 51*, 374–390.

Tierney, R. J., Carter, M., & Desai, L. (Eds.). (1991). *Portfolio assessment in the reading and writing classroom.* Norwood, MA: Christopher Gordon.

Trice, A. D. (2000). *A handbook of classroom assessment.* New York: Addison Wesley Longman.

Turner, J., & Paris, S. G. (1995). How literacy tasks influence children's motivation for literacy. *The Reading Teacher, 48*, 662–673.

Valencia, S. E. (1990a). Alternative assessment: Separating the wheat from the chaff. *The Reading Teacher, 44*, 60–61.

Valencia, S. E. (1990b). A portfolio approach to classroom reading assessment: The whys, whats, and hows. *The Reading Teacher, 43*, 338–340.

van Dijk, T. A., & Kintsch, W. (1983). *Strategies of discourse comprehension.* New York: Academic Press.

Vukelich, C. (1997). Assessing young children's literacy: Documenting growth and informing practice. *The Reading Teacher, 50*, 430–434.

Wade, S. (1990). Using think-alouds to assess comprehension. *The Reading Teacher, 43*, 442–451.

Wide Range Achievement Test 3 (1993). Wilmington, DE: Wide Range, Inc.

Wiederholt, J. L., & Bryant, B. R. (1992). *Gray Oral Reading Test—3.* Austin, TX: Pro-Ed.

Wigfield, A., & McCann, A. D. (1996–1997). Children's motivation for reading. *The Reading Teacher, 50*, 360–362.

Wilson, P. T. (1988). *Let's think about reading and reading instruction: A primer for tutors and teachers.* Dubuque, IA: Kendall/Hunt.

Winograd, P. (1994). Developing alternative assessments: Six problems worth solving. *The Reading Teacher, 47*, 420–423.

Wolf, K. P. (1993). From formal to informal assessment: Recognizing the role of the classroom teacher. *Journal of Reading, 36*, 518–523.

Woodcock, R. W. (1987). *Woodcock Reading Mastery Test—Revised.* Circle Pines, MN: American Guidance Service.

Yopp, H. K. (1999). A test for assessing phonemic awareness in young children. In S. J. Barrentine (Ed.), *Reading assessment: Principles and practices for elementary teachers* (pp. 166–176). Newark, DE: International Reading Association. (Original work published 1995)

Zakaluk, B. L., & Samuels, S. J. (1988). *Readability: Its past, present, and future.* Newark, DE: International Reading Association.

Zutell, J., & Rasinski, T. V. (1991). Training teachers to attend to their students' oral reading fluency. *Theory into Practice, 30*, 211–217.

Index